Graphis Design Annual 2001

Graphis Design Annual 2001

The International Annual of Design and Illustration
Das internationale Jahrbuch über Design und Illustration
Le répertoire internationale du design et de l'illustration

Publisher and Creative Director: B. Martin Pedersen

Editors: Vance Lin, Heinke Jenssen
Art Director: Lauren Slutsky

Assistant Editor: Michael Porciello
Design & Production Assistant: Joseph Liotta

Published by Graphis Inc.

Dedicated to:
Tibor Kalman (1949-1999)
P. Scott Makela (1960-1999)
Ross Littell (1924-2000)

A. Nadafkay

(opposite) Illustration: Guy Billout

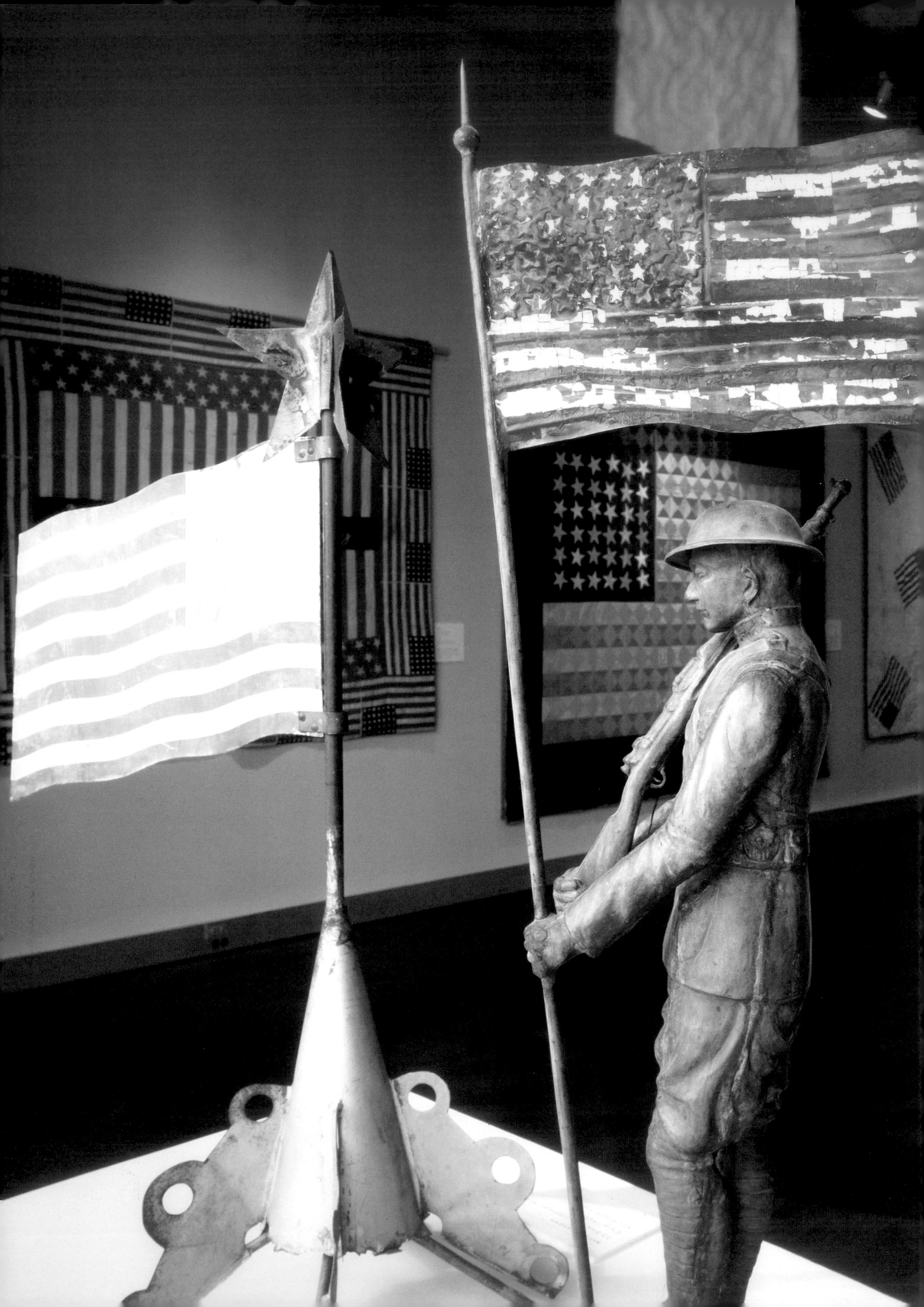

Contents Inhalt Sommaire

Commentary by David Carson ... 6

Annual Reports, Jahresberichte, Rapports annuels ... 12
Books, Bücher, Livres ... 20
Brochures, Broschüren, Brochures ... 34
Calendars, Kalender, Calendriers ... 54
Catalogues, Kataloge, Catalogues ... 56
Corporate Identity ... 66
Editorial, Redaktionell, Rédactionnel ... 78
Environmental, Öffentlicher Raum, Design environnemental ... 98
Exhibits, Ausstellungen, Expositions ... 110
Games, Spiele, Jeux ... 119
Illustration, Illustrationen, Illustrations ... 120
Letterhead, Briefschaften, Papiers à lettres ... 130
Logos ... 138
Menus, Speisekarten, Cartes menus ... 146
Music, Musik, Musique ... 147
New Media, Neue Medien, Nouveaux médias ... 152
Packaging, Packungen, Packaging ... 160
Paper Companies, Papierhersteller, Fabricaints de papier ... 182
Posters, Plakate, Affiches ... 190
Products, Produkte, Produits ... 212
Promotion ... 216
Shopping Bags, Tragtaschen, Sacs ... 234
Stamps, Briefmarken, Timbres ... 238
T-Shirts ... 242

Index, Verzeichnisse, Index ... 246

Remarks: We extend our heartfelt thanks to contributors throughout the world who have made it possible to publish a wide and international spectrum of the best work in this field. Entry instructions for all Graphis Books may be requested from: **Graphis Inc.**, 307 Fifth Avenue, Tenth Floor, New York, NY 10016 or visit our Web site, www.graphis.com

(opposite) From the AIGA exhibit Stars and Stripes: A Graphic History of an American Icon *by Kit Hinrichs*

Anmerkungen: Unser Dank gilt den Einsendern aus aller Welt, die es uns durch ihre Beiträge ermøglicht haben, ein breites, internationales Specktrum der besten Arbeiten zu veröffentlichen. Teilnahmebedingungen für die Graphis-Bücher sind erhältlich bei: **Graphis Inc.**, 307 Fifth Avenue, Tenth Floor, New York, NY 10016. Besuchen Sie uns im World Wide Web, www.graphis.com

(gegenüber) Aus der AIGA-Ausstellung Stars and Stripes: A Graphic History of an American Icon *von Kit Hinrichs*

Remerciements: Toute notre reconnaissance va aux designers du monde entier dont les envois nous ont permis de constituer un vaste panorama international des meilleures création. Les modalités d'inscription peuvent être obtenues auprès de: **Graphis Inc.**, 307 Fifth Avenue, Tenth Floor, New York, NY 10016. Rendez-nous visite sur notre site web: www.graphis.com

(ci-contre) Tiré de l'exposition Stars and Stripes: A Graphic History of an American Icon *par Kit Hinrichs, patronnée par l'AIGA*

ISBN: 1-888001-88-7 Printed by DNP.

http://www.package-land.com
Recycled

(opposite) Self promotion for Package Land Co., Ltd. by Yasuo Tanaka

"As we enter a new decade, a n
crop of passionate, talented, in
itive designers will emerge to re
claim their profession (tempora
hijacked by a misguided few in
nineties)."

David Carson Statement from the Graphis Design Annual 2000

«In dieser neuen Dekade wird eine neue Generation von talentierten, intuitiven, leidenschaftlichen Designern auftauchen und ihre Ansprüche auf ihr Gewerbe geltend machen (nachdem es sich in den Neunzigerjahren vorübergehend in den Händen einiger weniger Fehlgeleiter befunden hat).»

David Carson Statement aus Graphis Design Annual 200

«Dans la décennie à venir, une nouvelle génération de designers talentueux, intuitifs et passionnés verra le jour et redonnera sa vitalité à une profession qui, dans les années 90, avait été en quelque sorte prise en otage par une petite clique de mauvais maîtres à penser.»

David Carson Citation de l'ouvrage Design Annual 200

Design Annual 2001

Design Firm: Herman Miller, Inc. Art & Creative Director: Stephen Frykholm Designer: Yang Kim Copywriter: Clark Malcolm Client: Herman Miller, Inc.

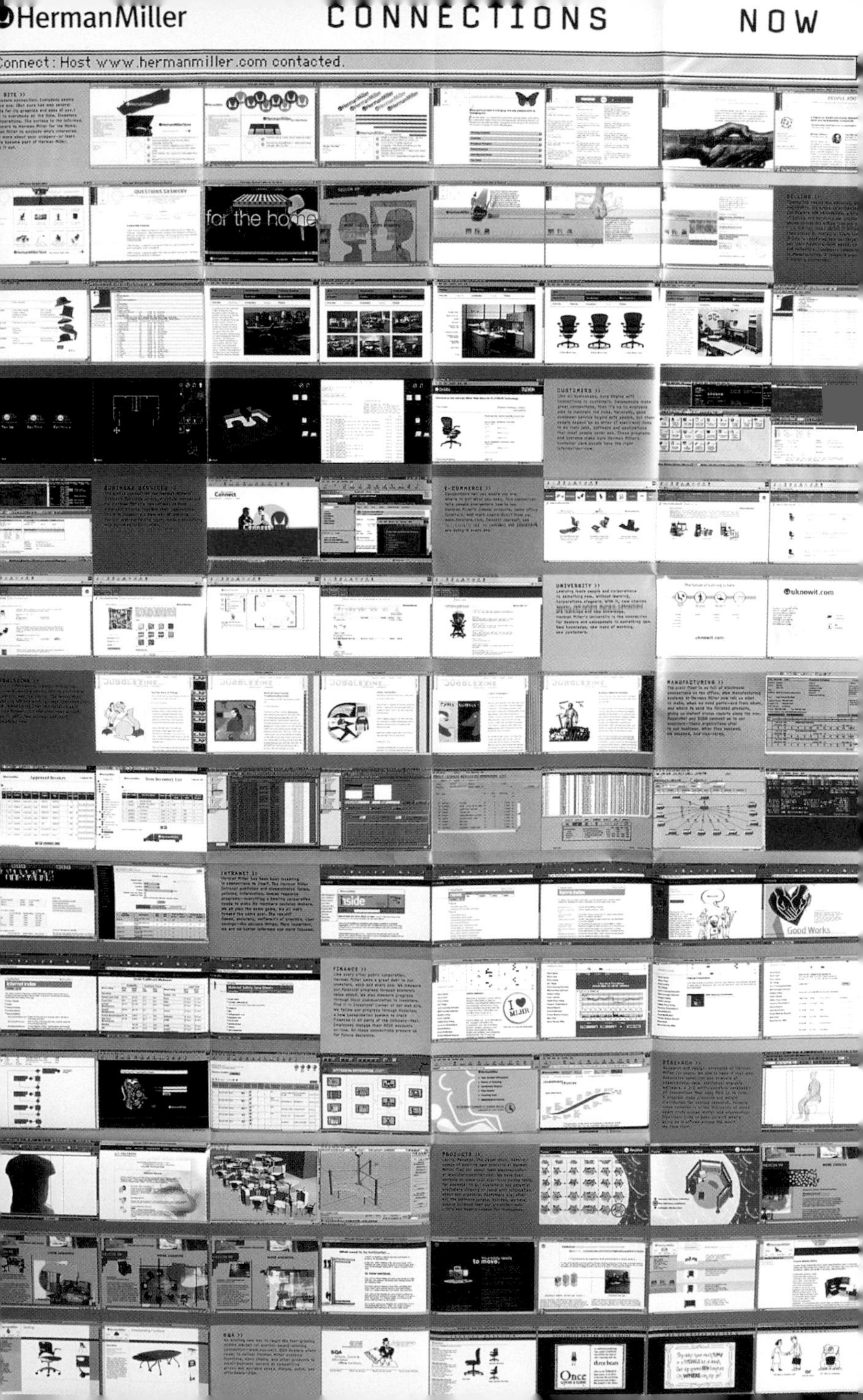
HermanMiller
CONNECTIONS
NOW
Connect: Host www.hermanmiller.com contacted.
for the home
Connect
uknowit.com
JUGGLEZINE
Inside
Good Works

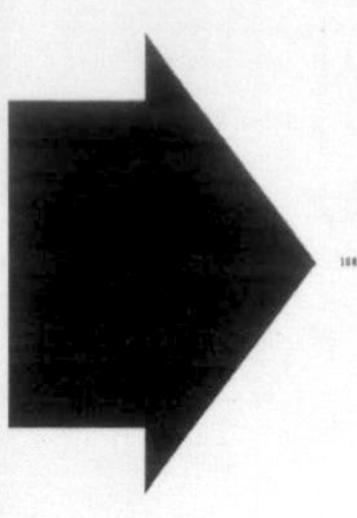

Design Firm: Cahan and Associates Art & Creative Director: Bill Cahan Designer: Michael Braley Copywriter: Joanna di Paolo Client: Identix

I SEE TREMENDOUS GROWTH POTENTIAL AHEAD, THANKS TO A BUSINESS MODEL THAT
LEVERAGES OUR BRAND ACROSS PRODUCT CATEGORIES AND GEOGRAPHIC REGIONS.

Design Firm: E.A.I. Creative Director: Matt Rollins Designers: David Cannon, Nicole Riekki Copywriter: Lindsay Beaman Client: Polo Ralph Lauren

NEWS

on ERP software within the year.

NEWS

NEWS

Chairman, pg. 2; President, pg. 5; Good News, pg. 9; Financials, pg. 20

1998 Financial Highlights
DA Consulting Group, Inc.*

Years ended December 31,

(Consolidated amounts in thousands, except per share amounts and number of employees)	1996	1997	1998
Operating Data:			
Revenue	$26,202	$44,204	**$80,132**
Operating income*	2,212	2,756	**7,090**
EBITDA* (Earnings Before Interest, Taxes, Depreciation and Amortization)	2,465	2,990	**7,948**
Net income*	1,441	1,606	**4,299**
Number of employees	353	568	**863**
Balance Sheet Data:			
Cash and cash equivalents	$ 2,199	$ 3,664	**$ 9,971**
Working capital	1,629	4,101	**25,585**
Total assets	8,549	20,135	**48,903**
Total debt	731	3,970	–
Shareholders' equity	3,071	7,943	**34,944**
Per Share Data (Diluted):			
Net income*	$ 0.32	$ 0.32	**$ 0.69**
Net income	$ 0.01	$ 0.28	**$ 0.69**
Weighted average shares outstanding	4,462	5,053	**6,233**

*Before employee stock-related charges

1998 At A Glance

February	DACG acronym adopted for worldwide marketing use, replacing DA Consulting Group, Inc.
April	**Became a public company on April 24.**
June	Mexico City office opened to service clients in Mexico. Caracas office opened to meet demands in Venezuela and other Latin American countries. **At mid-year, revenue nearly doubled to $19.7 million from $9.9 million in 1997.**
August	Board of Directors elected Nicholas Marriner to Chairman and Patrick Newton to President.
September	Launched "e-learning" for business systems training. New training tool, DA FIT/Fast Implementation Toolkit™, introduced to support demand for faster SAP™ implementations.
October	SAP software selected to manage DACG's internal business information systems.
November	Became SAP AG Global Consulting Partner. Licensed SAP's training tool "InfoDB" and incorporated into DACG training solutions. The Hague sales office opened to serve Belgium, The Netherlands and Luxembourg.
December	Became PeopleSoft Global Education Services Alliance Partner. Dilip Keshu joined DACG as EVP of Asia Pacific Division. **Record year-end revenues of $80.1 million, reflecting an 80% increase over 1997.**

1

GOOD

Fortune 500 companies all over the world will spend 3.8 billion dollars

BAD N

Most of them won't know how to use it.

GOOD

We're there to teach them. DACG 1998 Annual Report

MORE

Mobile Then Global, page 10; Fortune 500, page 12;

GOOD

Between Our Ears, page 14; We Hear You, page 16;

NEWS

Staying Ahead, page 18.

9

Design Firm: Pentagram Design Art Director: Lowell Williams Designers: Julie Hoyt, Wendy Carnegie Illustrator: Wendy Carnegie Client: DA Consulting Group

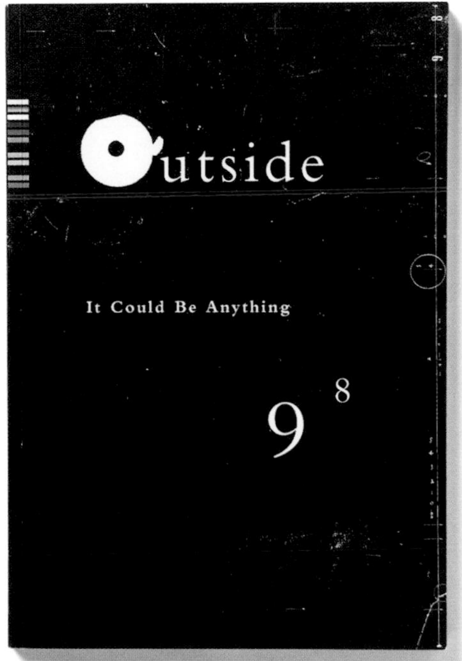

Design Firm: Jennifer Sterling Design Art & Creative Director, Designer: Jennifer Sterling Photographer: Marko Laurisha Copywriter: Eric LaBrecque Client: DSP Communications

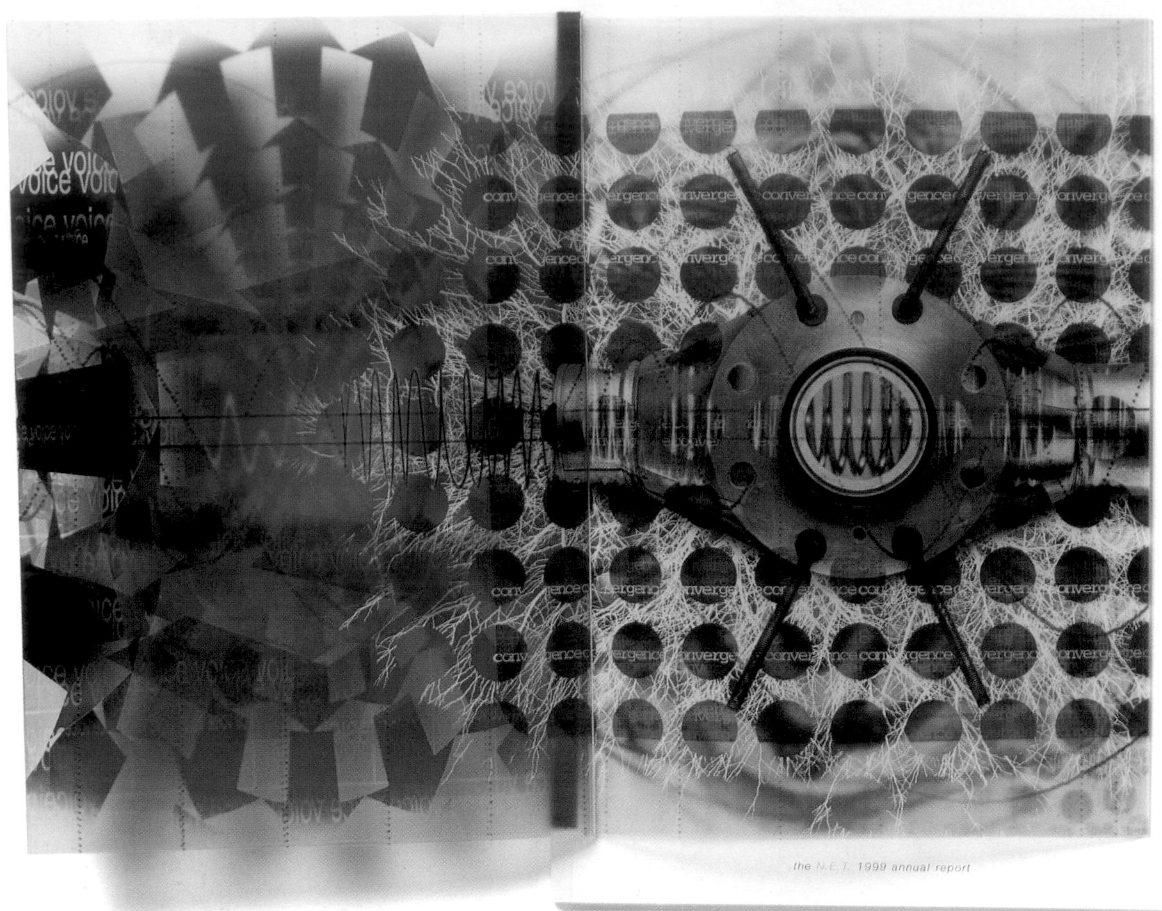

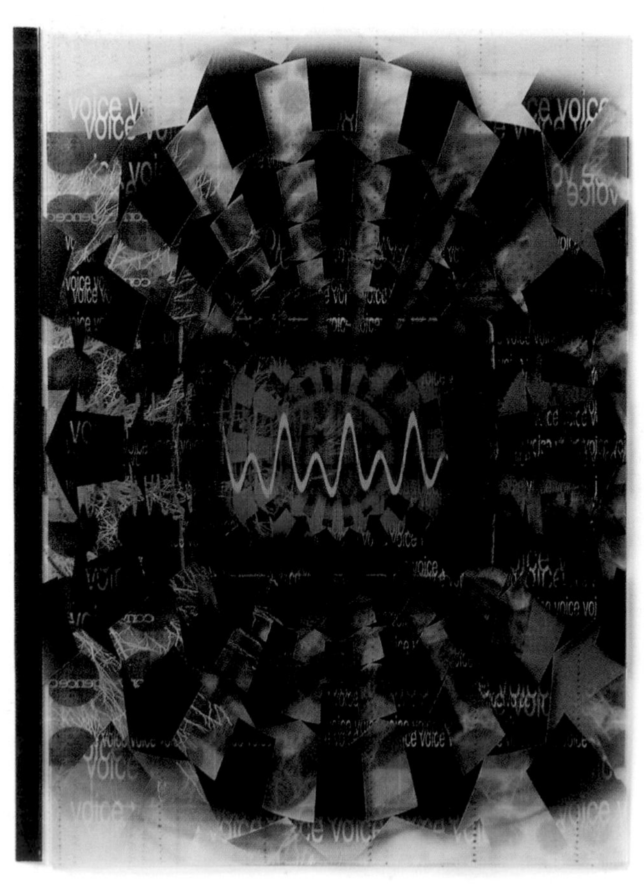

Design Firm: Schulte Design Art Director: Paul Schulte Designer: Paul Ziller Photographer & Illustrator: Glen Gyssler Client: N.E.T.

American Photography 15

Design Firm: Sagmeister Inc. Art & Creative Director: Stefan Sagmeister Designers: Hjalti Karlsson, Stefan Sagmeister Client: American Photography

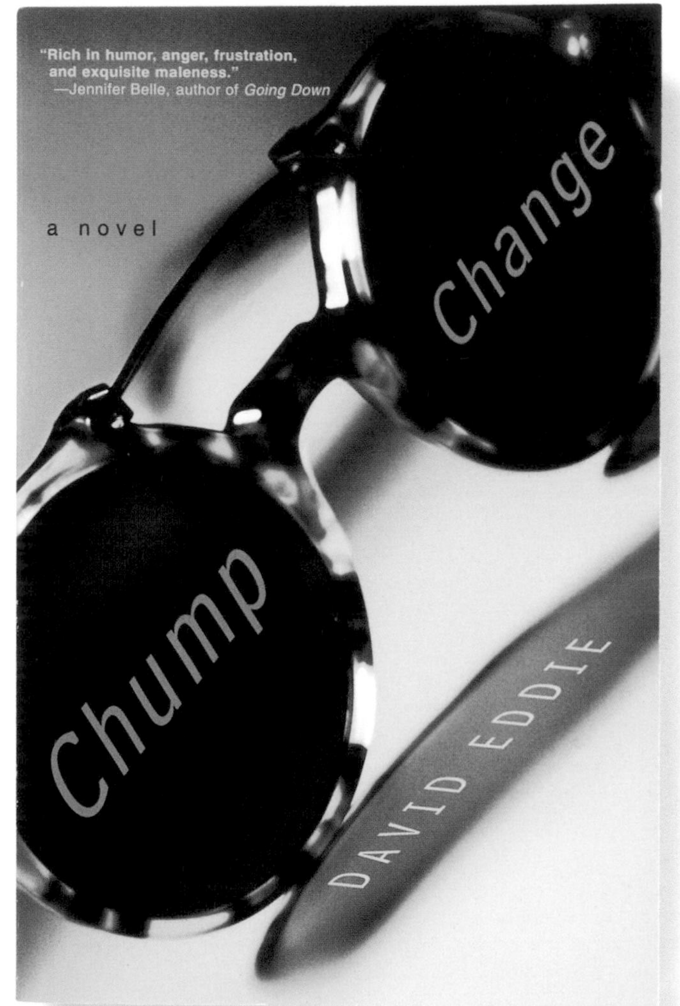

(left) Designer: J.K. Lambert Client: Random House (right) Designer: Archie Fergusen Client: Riverhead Books/Penguin Putnam, Inc.

(left) Designer: Brenden Hitt Client: Delta Fiction/Random House (right) Designer: Todd Radom Client: Total/Sports Illustrated

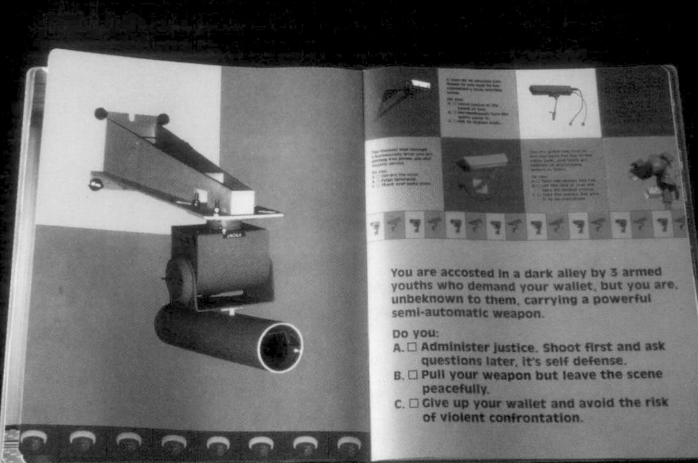
You are accosted in a dark alley by 3 armed youths who demand your wallet, but you are, unbeknown to them, carrying a powerful semi-automatic weapon.
Do you:
A. ☐ Administer justice. Shoot first and ask questions later, it's self defense.
B. ☐ Pull your weapon but leave the scene peacefully.
C. ☐ Give up your wallet and avoid the risk of violent confrontation.

YOUR
DAVID BYRNE

RHÔNE-POULENC
CIIT
CHEMICAL INSTITUTE OF
UAI TECHNOLOGY
PHOENIX-HECHT
HARRIS
SEMICONDUCTOR
Sumitomo Electric
US EPA
ENVIRONMENTAL
RESEARCH
CENTER
CIBA-GEIGY
Data General
LITESPEC
Sumitomo Electric
IBM

esign Firm: Sagmeister Inc. Art & Creative Directors: Stefan Sagmeister, David Byrne Designers & Illustrators: Hjalti Karlsson, Stefan Sagmeister Photographer & Copywriter: David Byrne Client: Edimar

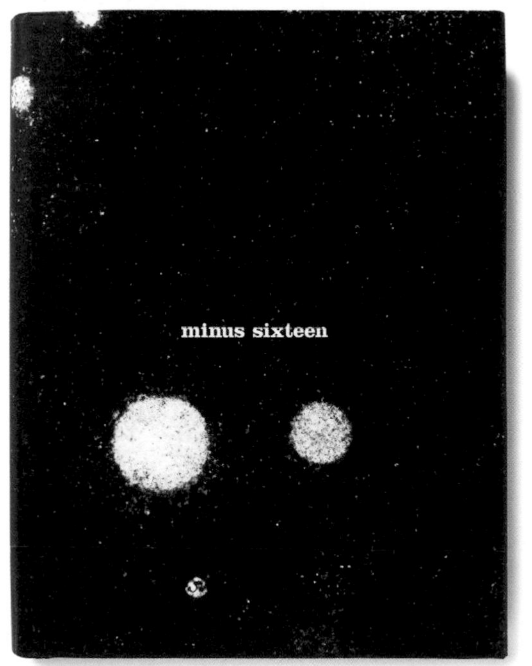

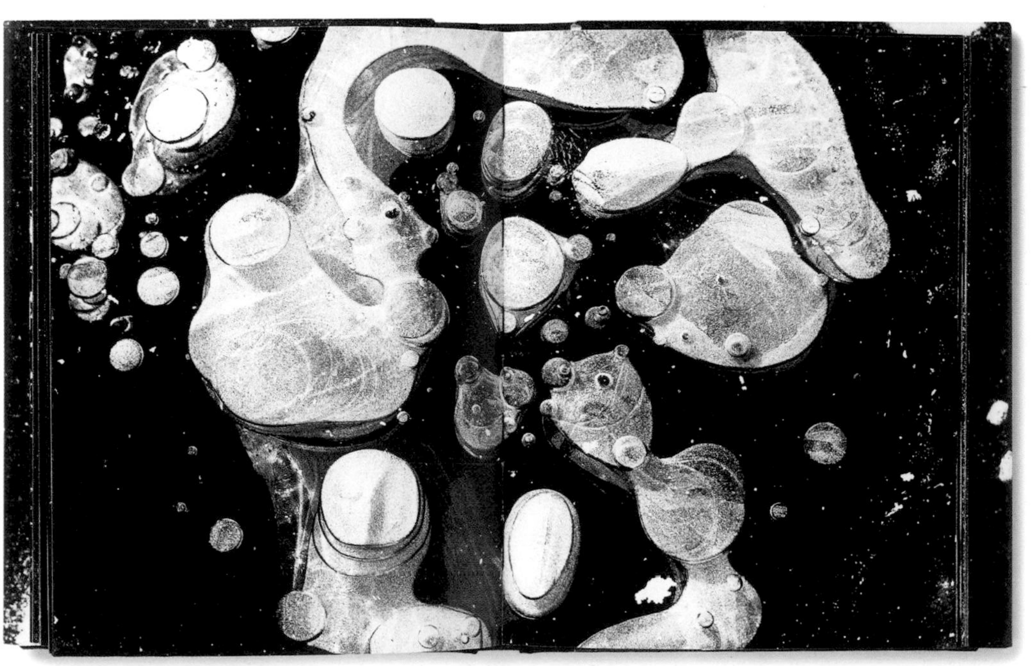

Design Firm: Browns/London Art Director & Photographer: Robin Broadbent Creative Director & Designer: Michael Turner Client: Robin Broadbent

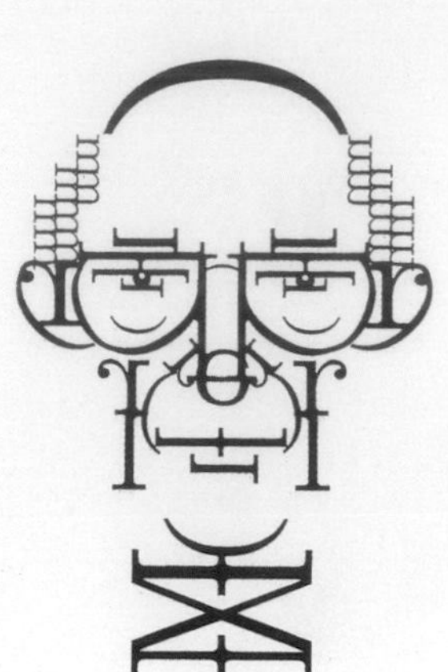

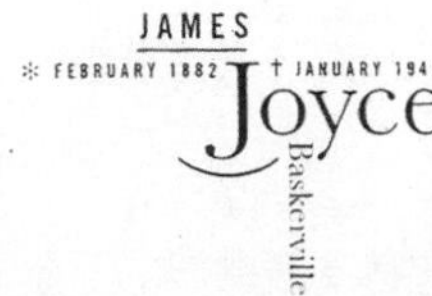

Creative Director & Designer: Roberto De Vicq De Cumptich

Design Firm: Drive Communications Art Director: Michael Graziolo Client: Collectors Press, Inc.

Design Firm: Sagmeister Inc. Art & Creative Director: Stefan Sagmeister Designers: Hjalti Karisson, Stefan Sagmeister Photographer & Copywriter: Lou Reed Illustrators: Stefan Sagmeister, Jan Wilker Client: Hyperion Press

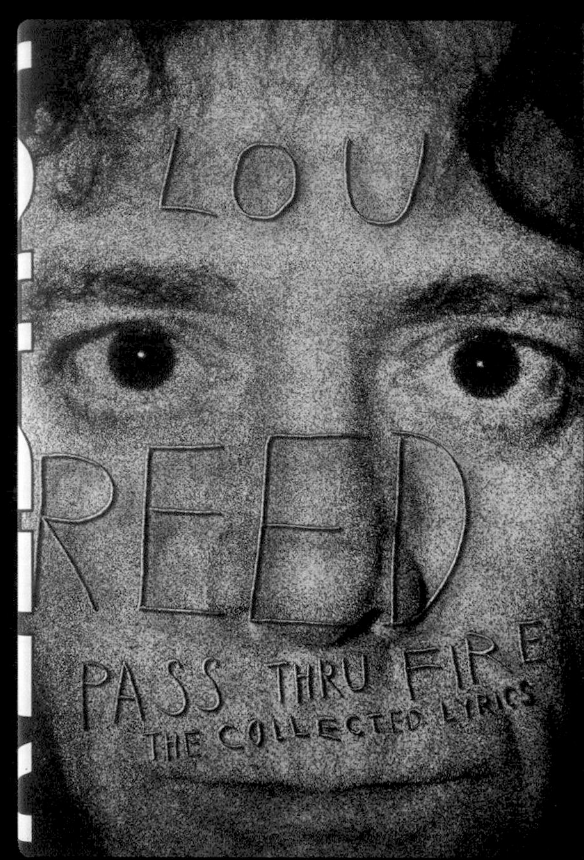

Lou Reed
Pass Thru Fire
The Collected Lyrics
Caroline Says II
The Kids
Oh, Jim
The Bed
Sad Song
Lou Reed

Design Firm: Charles S. Anderson Design Art Director: Charles S. Anderson Designers: Charles S. Anderson, Todd Piper-Hauswirth, Jason Schulte Photographers: Aaron Dimel, Eric Emmings, Jim Castle Illustrators: Charles S. Anderson, Todd Piper-Hauswirth, Jason Schulte, Erik Johnson, Kyle Hames, Zak Custer Copywriter: Stephen Fenichell Client: CSA Images

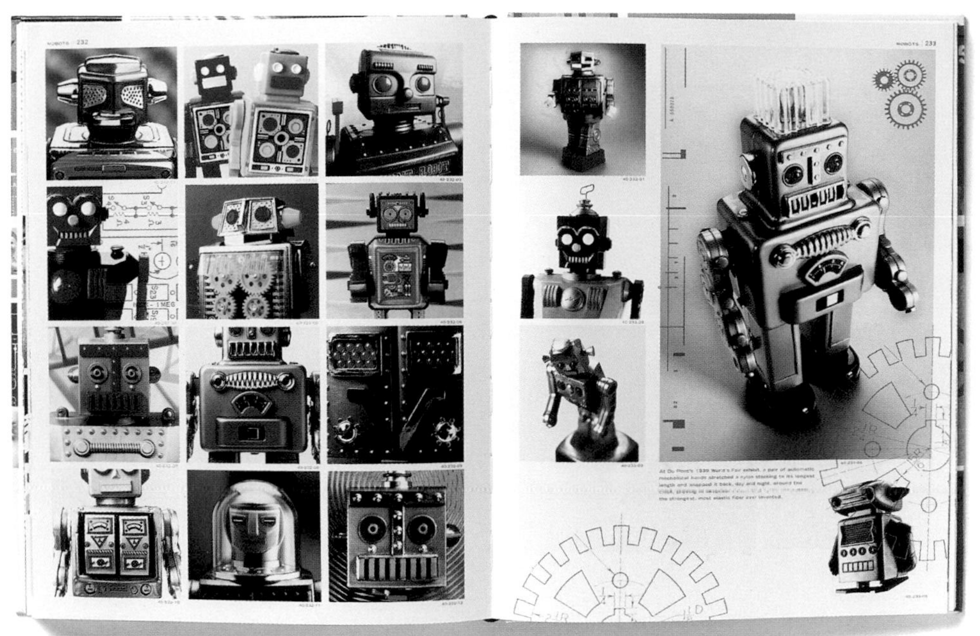

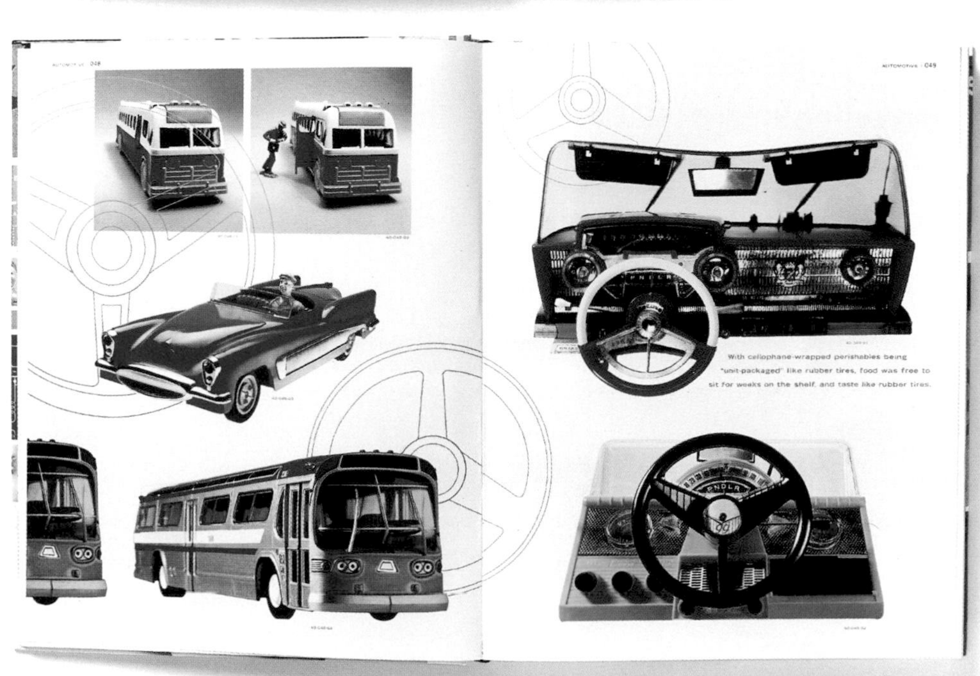

With cellophane-wrapped perishables being
"unit-packaged" like rubber tires, food was free to
sit for weeks on the shelf, and taste like rubber tires.

(top) Design Firm: Tangram Strategic Design Art & Creative Director, Designer: Enrico Sempi Client: UTET Unione Tipografico-Editrice Torinese (bottom) Design Firm: Factor Design Art & Creative Director: Johannes Erner Designer: Marius Fahrner, Photographers: Heribert Schindler, Ulrich Hoppe Copywriter: Jan Weiles Client: Romsturm Ferristpapiere

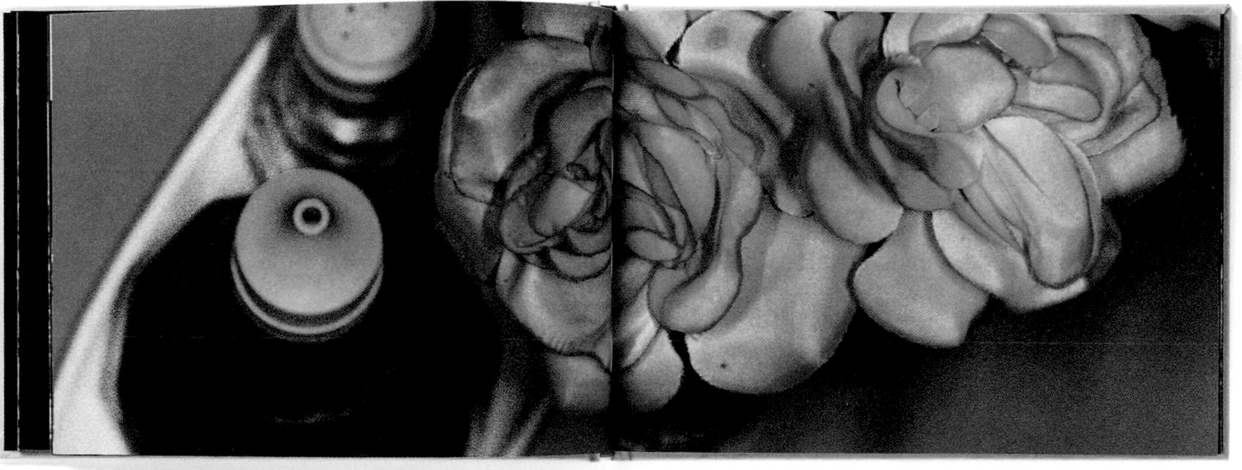

Design Firm: Browns/London Creative Director: Jonathan Ellery Designers: Jonathan Ellery, Lee Liversedge Photographers: Martin Parr, Magnum Client: Munkedals Ab

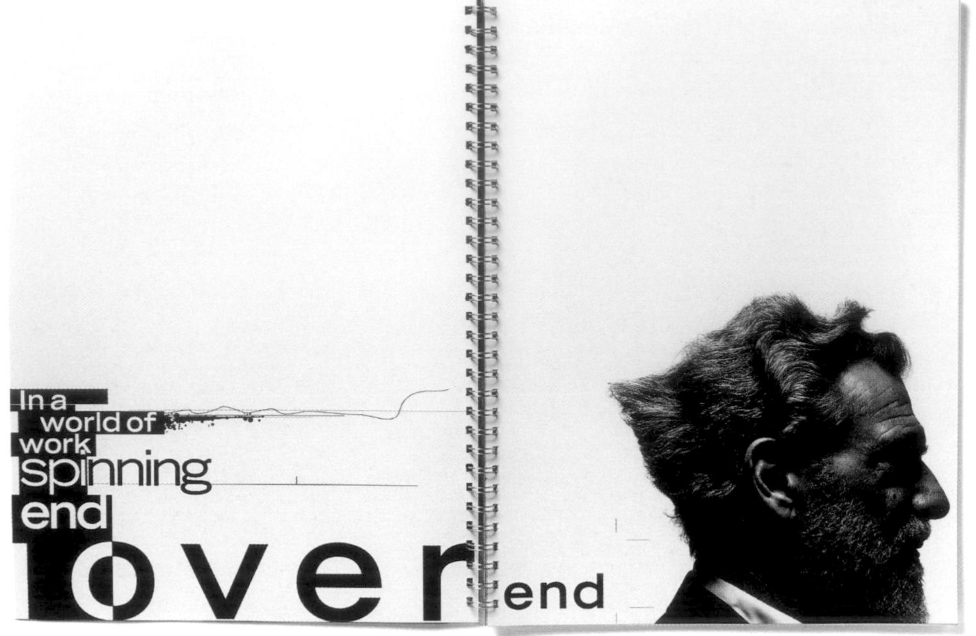
In a
world of
work
spinning
end
over
end

Work.
version
2.0.

We live and work in extraordinary times. The entire concept of the company is being challenged and transformed. The old rules of how companies work, how work gets done, and who does the work are out the window. At the same time, talented people by the millions have gone out on their own. They are creating a completely new kind of work force—independent, uniquely skilled, intensely motivated. It is a time of tumultuous change. And for those willing to seize the moment, it is a time of phenomenal opportunity.

Design Firm: Digitas Art Director: Toshi Ide Creative Directors: Toshi Ide, David Haskell Designers: Toshi Ide, Nancy Glazer, Susan Pearson, Segal Orit Photographer: John Midgley Copywriter: David Haskell Client: Aquent

Introducing Aquent. We've turned the whole idea of staffing on its ear. We're not here just to fill positions. We're here to help the working world work better. That starts with providing talented people everything they need to work the way they want to work—from training to marketing to health benefits. Not surprisingly, this attracts an astonishing array of great talent. The kind of talent you need to move your entire orga

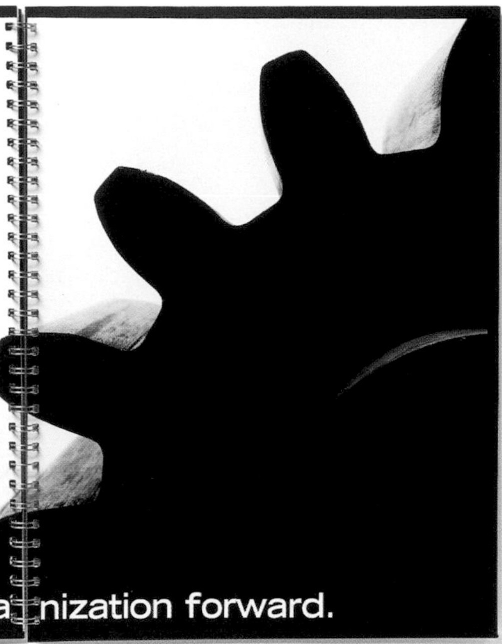

When it comes to helping your organization win in the new working world, no piece of technology can match the power of a single great individual. Knowing this, we have dedicated Aquent to bringing you together with individuals who possess unique abilities, brilliance, and internal fire. And we continually provide them with new skills, new training, new sources of motivation—so they can constantly produce extraordinary business results for you.

over

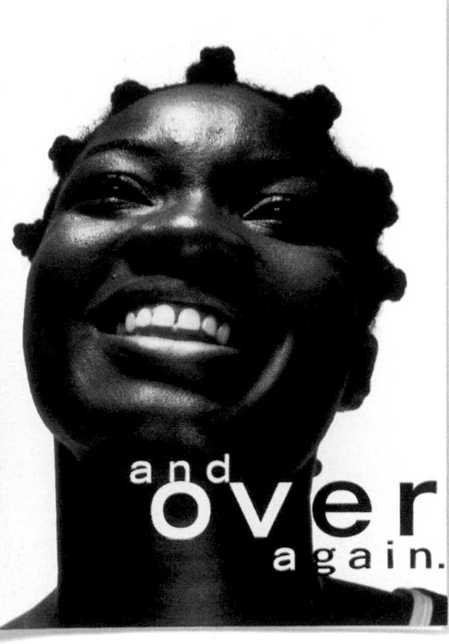

Design Firm: RBMM Designer: Tanya Freach Photographer: Joe Patronite Client: Joe Patronite

Brochures 36,37

XL 1200C SPORTSTER 1200 CUSTOM
In the opinion of many, the original 1200 Custom put together an unbeatable combination of Sportster® performance and Harley-Davidson® good looks. Just the chromed-out 1200 engine was enough to have riders drooling on their boots. For 1999 we've dialed it up to the next notch. The foot controls are forward, pushing the styling even further. The front suspension is taller. There are classic new drag bars on the Custom's unique chrome riser. It's a dazzling look, from the 21" laced front wheel to the slotted disc in the rear. We could only top it with a cloisonné emblem on the tank.

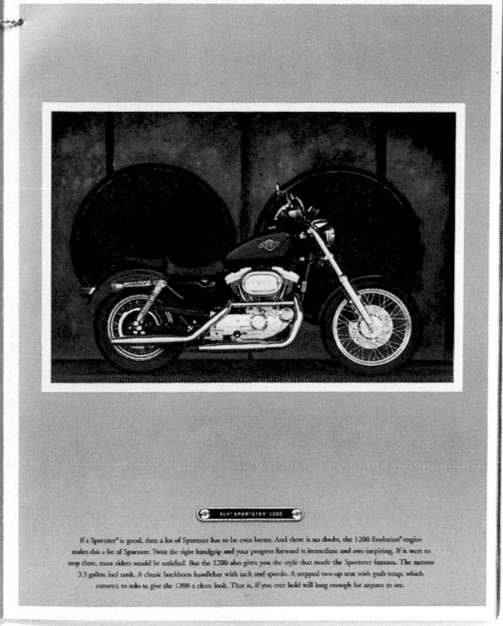

XLH SPORTSTER 1200
If a Sportster® is good, then a lot of Sportster has to be even better. And there is no doubt, the 1200 Evolution® engine makes this a lot of Sportster. Twist the right handgrip and your progress forward is immediate and awe-inspiring. If it were to stop there, most riders would be satisfied. But the 1200 also gives you the style that made the Sportster famous. The narrow 3.3 gallon fuel tank. A classic buckhorn handlebar with tach and speedo. A stepped two-up seat with grab strap, which converts to solo to give the 1200 a clean look. That is, if you ever hold still long enough for anyone to see.

Harley-Davidson
Ask most people to conjure up the best image of motorcycling from their youth, and this is it. The big, strong lines. The broad windshield. The massive chrome headlamp and nacelle. The Road King® brings it all back.
Under all the brilliant chrome and lustrous paint lies our latest touring performance. At the center is eighty-eight cubic inches of Twin Cam 88,® isolation mounted in our touring frame.
The combination is ready for any kind of road trip you have in mind. And at day's end, the windshield and passenger pillion detach. You can have a custom look that beats anything on the strip, minutes after blowing into town.

Design Firm: Carmichael Lynch Art Director, Designer & Illustrator: Peter Winecke Creative Director: Jim Nelson Photographer: Todd Johnson Copywriter: Sheldon Clay Client: Harley Davidson

Design Firm: Frost Design Ltd. Art & Creative Director: Vince Frost Designers: Vince Frost, Melanie Mues Client: Photonica

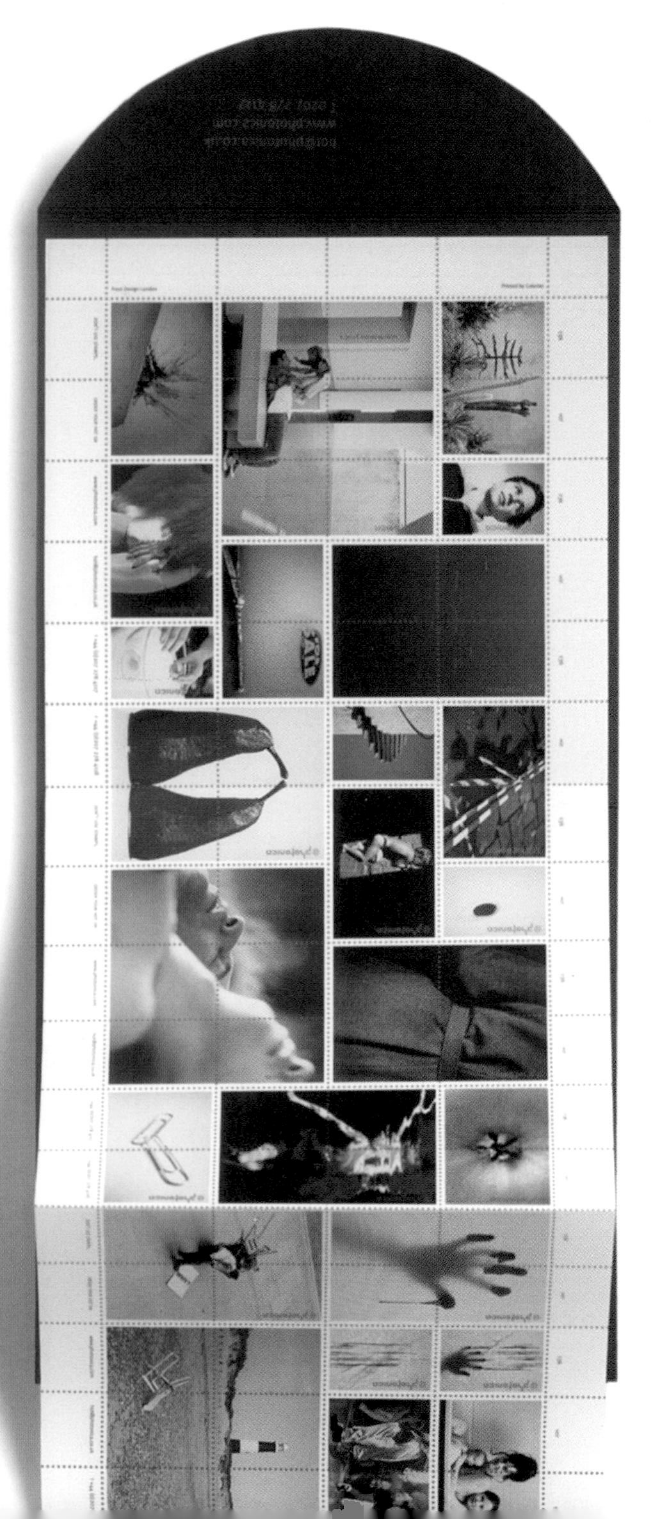

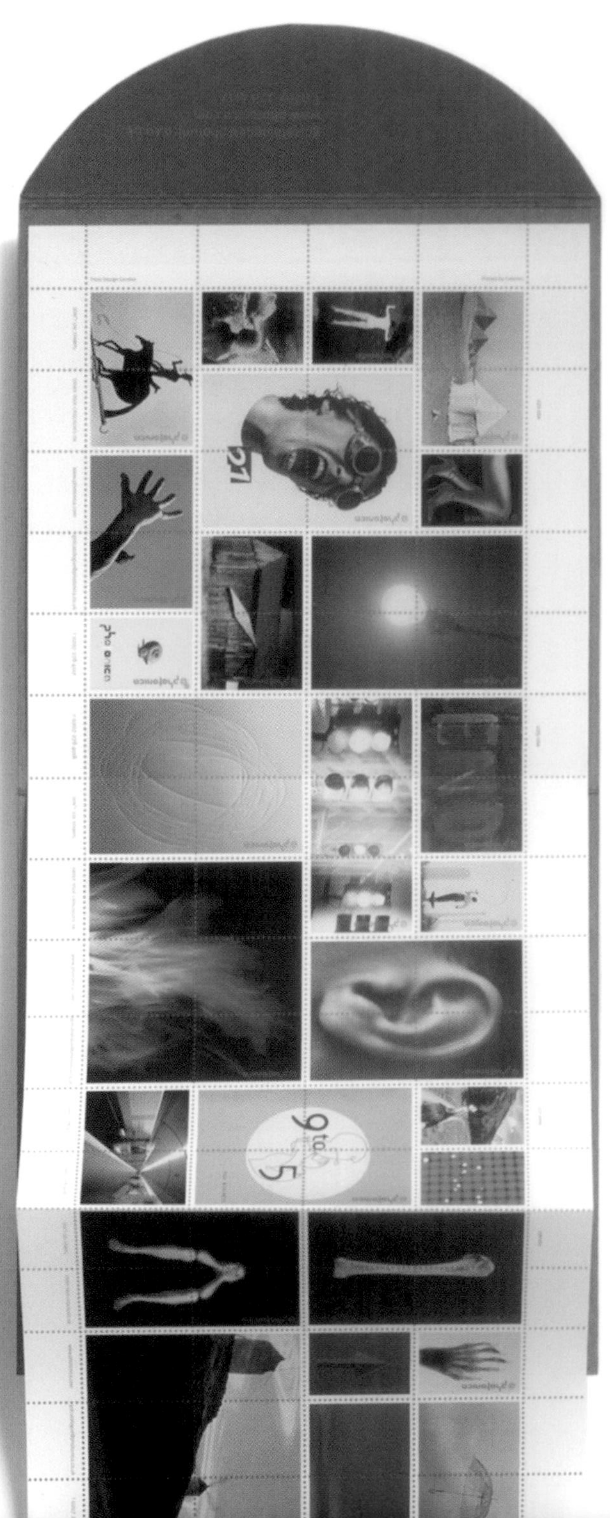

EUROPA

Design Firm: Oliver Kuhlmann Design Art Director & Photographer: Mark Katzman Designer: Michael Thede Illustrator: Matthew Katzman Copywriters: Betty Manlin, Mark Katzman, Greg Ward Client: Ferguson & Katzman

Design Firm: E.A.I. Creative Director: Phil Hamlett Designers: Lee Nichols, David Cannon Photographer: Greg Slater Copywriter: Robert Roth Client: Dickson's/Wiliamson

1. What is the difference between a dog and a flea?

Riddle
Dogs.

ENTER THE RIDDLE DOGS CONTEST!
See Inside Back Cover For Details

DESIGNED BY
The Pushpin Group
NEW YORK

PRINTED BY
Berman Printing Co.
CINCINNATI

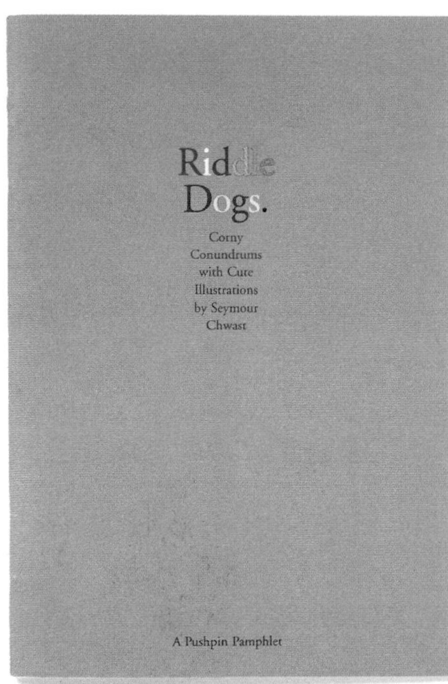

9. What is the difference
between a greyhound
and a locomotive?

Design Firm: The Pushpin Group, Inc. Designer & Illustrator: Seymour Chwast Client: The Pushpin Group, Inc.

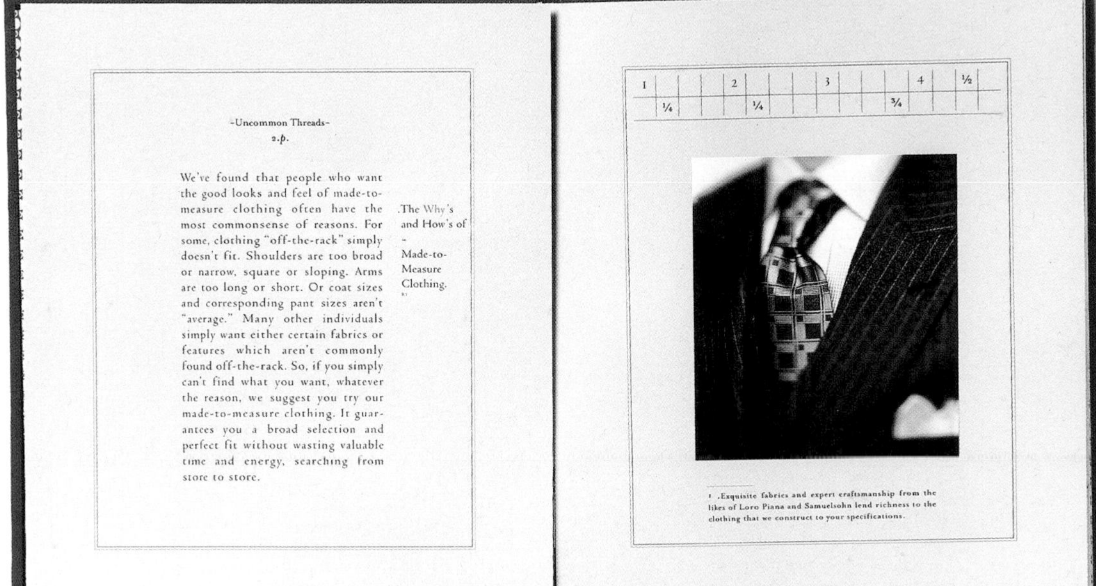

-Uncommon Threads-
2.p.
We've found that people who want the good looks and feel of made-to-measure clothing often have the most commonsense of reasons. For some, clothing "off-the-rack" simply doesn't fit. Shoulders are too broad or narrow, square or sloping. Arms are too long or short. Or coat sizes and corresponding pant sizes aren't "average." Many other individuals simply want either certain fabrics or features which aren't commonly found off-the-rack. So, if you simply can't find what you want, whatever the reason, we suggest you try our made-to-measure clothing. It guarantees you a broad selection and perfect fit without wasting valuable time and energy, searching from store to store.
.The Why's and How's of
-
Made-to-Measure Clothing.
1
2
3
4
½
¼
¼
¾
1 .Exquisite fabrics and expert craftsmanship from the likes of Loro Piana and Samuelsohn lend richness to the clothing that we construct to your specifications.

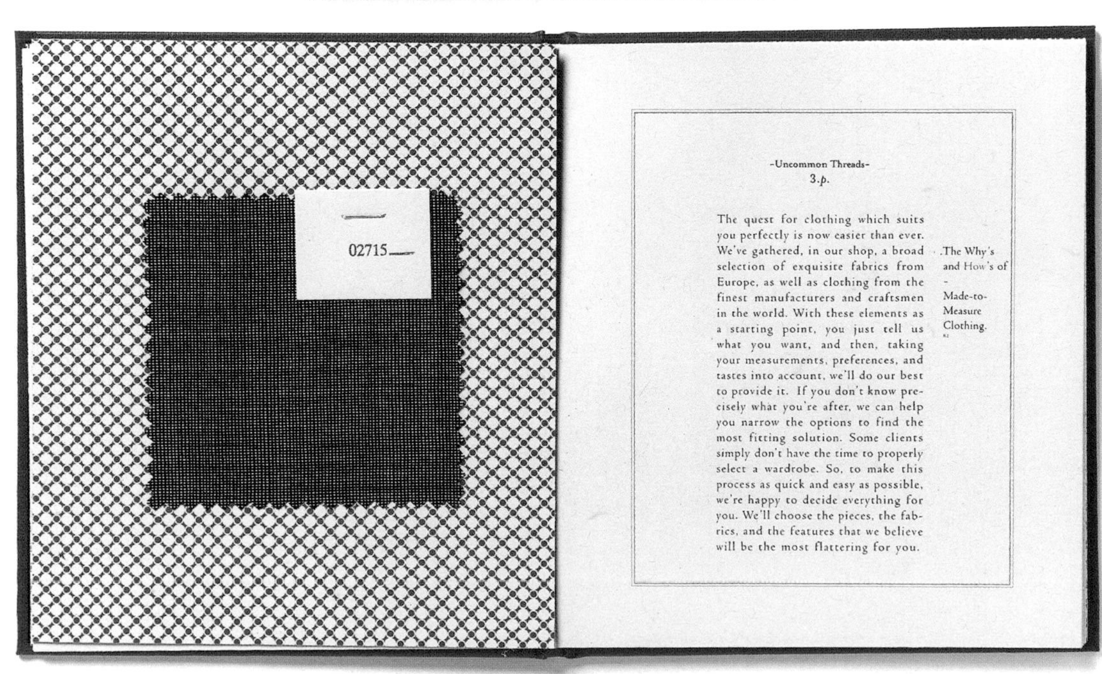

02715
-Uncommon Threads-
3.p.
The quest for clothing which suits you perfectly is now easier than ever. We've gathered, in our shop, a broad selection of exquisite fabrics from Europe, as well as clothing from the finest manufacturers and craftsmen in the world. With these elements as a starting point, you just tell us what you want, and then, taking your measurements, preferences, and tastes into account, we'll do our best to provide it. If you don't know precisely what you're after, we can help you narrow the options to find the most fitting solution. Some clients simply don't have the time to properly select a wardrobe. So, to make this process as quick and easy as possible, we're happy to decide everything for you. We'll choose the pieces, the fabrics, and the features that we believe will be the most flattering for you.
.The Why's and How's of
-
Made-to-Measure Clothing.

Design Firm: Slaughter Hanson **Art Director & Designer:** Marion English **Photographer:** Don Harbor **Illustrator:** David Webb **Copywriter:** Kathy Oldham **Client:** Plains Clothes

celebrated ccac alumni and faculty include erik adigard, opal pamer adisa, lynn kirby kit hinrichs, robert arneson, patrick coyne john mc cracken, sydney carson, robert bechtle, richard mc lean, barry katz, leslie becker, gigi biederman, steven skov holt linda fleming, kathai brown, john mattos aaron betsky, squeal carnwath, tomie de paola, michael cronai, dennis crowe, david karam, stephanie seyer coyne, judith foosaner, lucille tenazas, marilyn da silva jeanne finley, ralphgoings, gary hutton

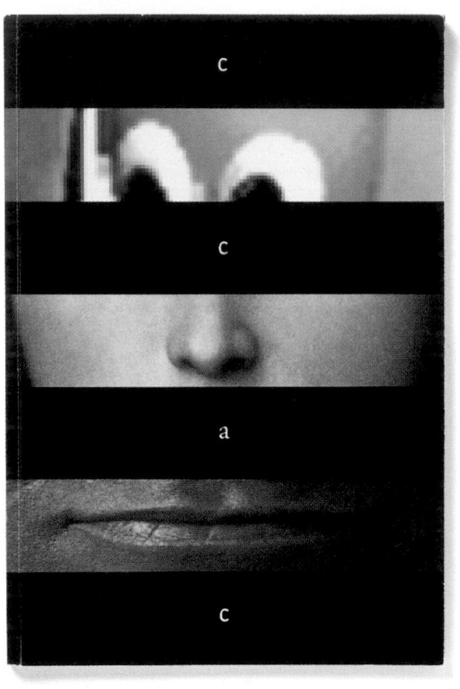
c
c
a
c

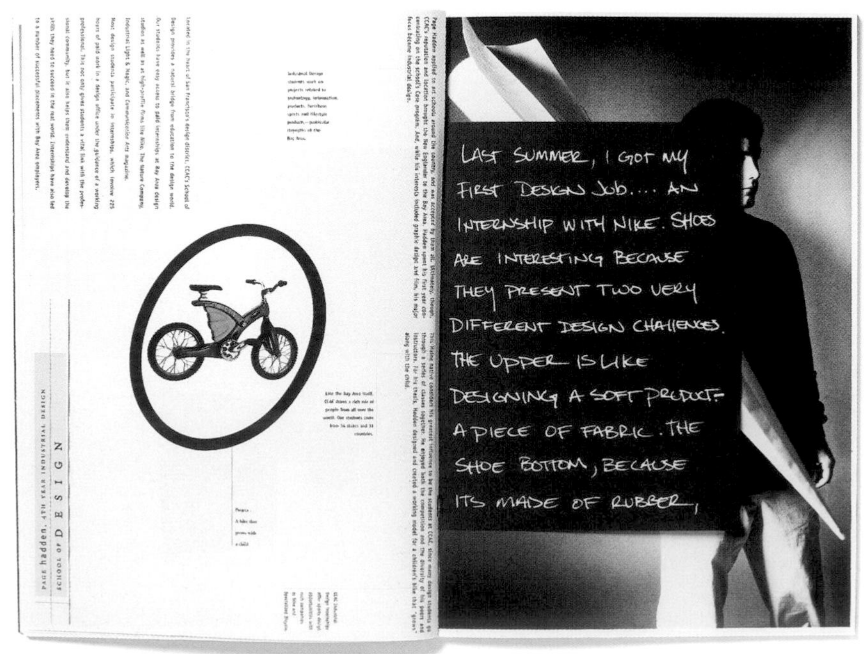
LAST SUMMER, I GOT MY FIRST DESIGN JOB.... AN INTERNSHIP WITH NIKE. SHOES ARE INTERESTING BECAUSE THEY PRESENT TWO VERY DIFFERENT DESIGN CHALLENGES. THE UPPER IS LIKE DESIGNING A SOFT PRODUCT- A PIECE OF FABRIC. THE SHOE BOTTOM, BECAUSE ITS MADE OF RUBBER,
SCHOOL OF DESIGN

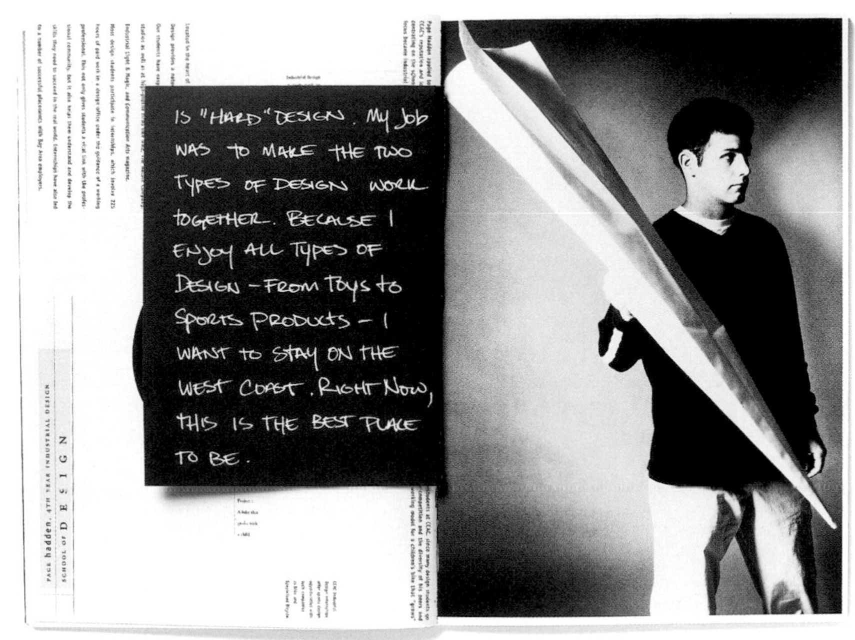

IS "HARD" DESIGN. MY JOB WAS TO MAKE THE TWO TYPES OF DESIGN WORK TOGETHER. BECAUSE I ENJOY ALL TYPES OF DESIGN - FROM TOYS TO SPORTS PRODUCTS - I WANT TO STAY ON THE WEST COAST. RIGHT NOW, THIS IS THE BEST PLACE TO BE.
PAGE hadden, 4TH YEAR INDUSTRIAL DESIGN
SCHOOL OF DESIGN

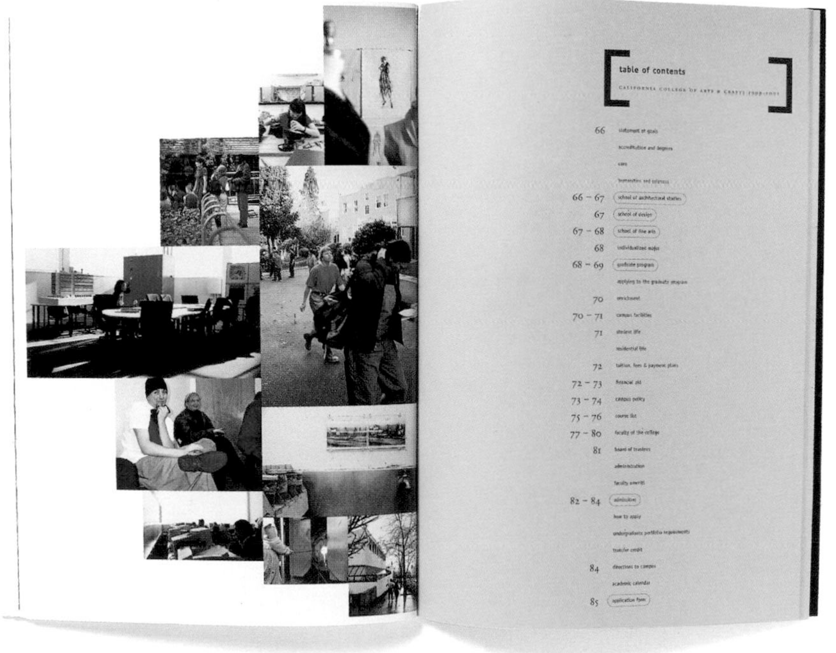

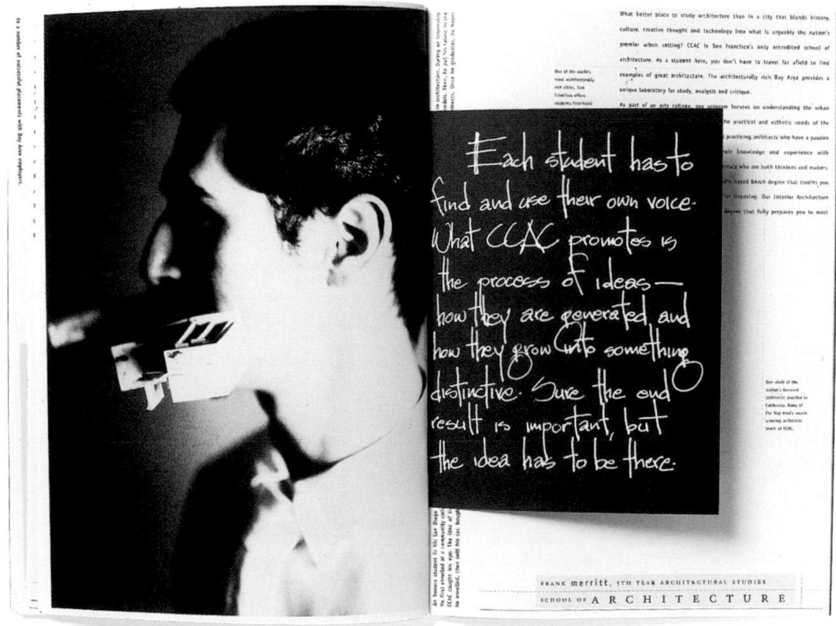

Each student has to find and use their own voice. What CCAC promotes is the process of ideas— how they are generated and how they grow into something distinctive. Sure the end result is important, but the idea has to be there.
FRANK merritt, 5TH YEAR ARCHITECTURAL STUDIES
SCHOOL OF ARCHITECTURE

Design Firm: Vanderbyl Design Art & Creative Director, Designer: Michael Vanderbyl Photographers: Todd Hido, David Peterson Client: California College of Arts & Crafts

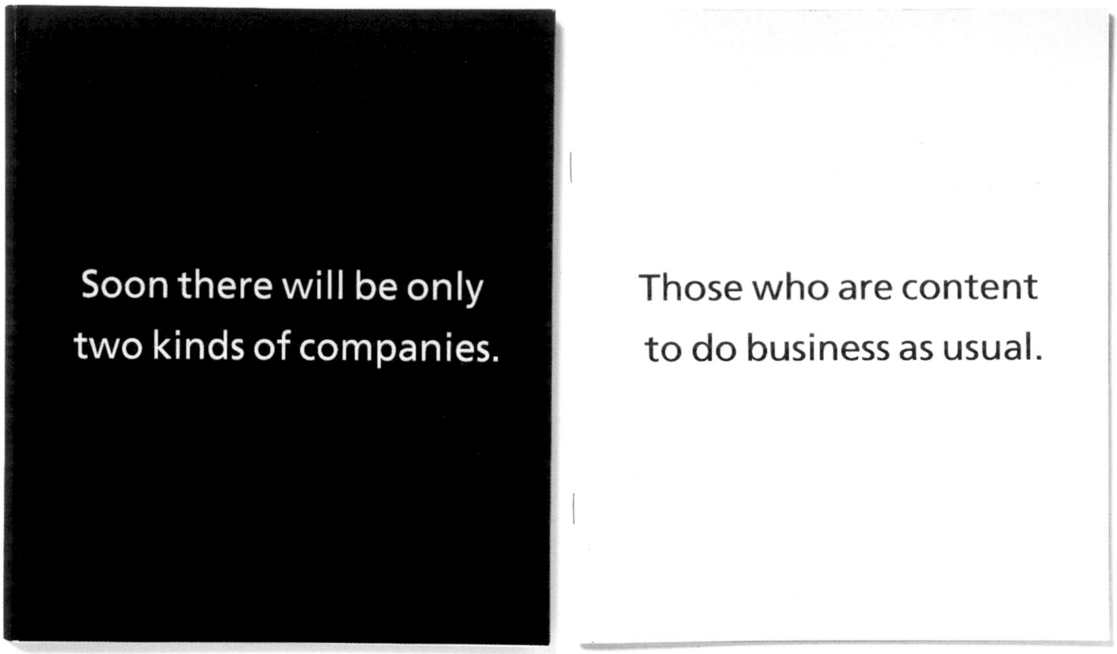

as usual. Business as usual. Business as usual. Business as usual. Business as usual. Business as usual.
Business as usual. Business as usual. Business as usual. Business as usual. Business as usual. Business
as usual. Business as usual. Business as usual. Business as usual. Business as usual. Business as usual.
Business as usual. Business as usual. Business as usual. Business as usual. Business as usual. Business
as usual. Business as usual. Business as usual. Business as usual. Business as usual. Business as usual.
Business as usual. Business as usual. Business as usual. Business as usual. Business as usual. Business
as usual. Business as usual. Business as usual. Business as usual. Business as usual. Business as usual.
Business as usual. Business as usual. Business as usual. Business as usual. Business as usual. Business
as usual. Business as usual. Business as usual. Business as usual. Business as usual. Business as usual.
Business as usual. Business as usual. Business as usual. Business as usual. Business as usual. Business
as usual. Business as usual. Business as usual. Business as usual. Business as usual. Business as usual.
Business as usual. Business as usual. Business as usual. Business as usual. Business as usual. Business
as usual. Business as usual. Business as usual. Business as usual. Business as usual. Business as usual.
Business as usual. Business as usual. Business as usual. Business as usual. Business as usual. Business
as usual. Business as usual. Business as usual. Business as usual. Business as usual. Business as usual.
Business as usual. Business as usual. Business as usual. Business as usual. Business as usual. Business
as usual. Business as usual. Business as usual. Business as usual. Business as usual. Business as usual.
Business as usual. Business as usual. Business as usual. Business as usual. Business as usual. Business
as usual. Business as usual. Business as usual. Business as usual. Business as usual. Business as usual.
Business as usual. Business as usual. Business as usual. Business as usual. Business as usual. Business
as usual. Business as usual. Business as usual. Business as usual. Business as usual. Business as usual.
Business as usual. Business as usual. Business as usual. Business as usual. Business as usual. Business
as usual. Business as usual. Business as usual. Business as usual. Business as usual. Business as usual.
Business as usual. Business as usual. Business as usual. Business as usual. Business as usual. Business
as usual. Business as usual. Business as usual. Business as usual. Business as usual. Business as usual.
Business as usual. Business as usual. Business as usual. Business as usual. Business as usual. Business
as usual. Business as usual. Business as usual. Business as usual. Business as usual. Business as usual.
Business as usual. Business as usual. Business as usual. Business as usual. Business as usual. Business
as usual. Business as usual. Business as usual. Business as usual. Business as usual. Business as usual.
Business as usual. Business as usual. Business as usual. Business as usual. Business as usual. Business
as usual. Business as usual. Business as usual. Business as usual. Business as usual. Business as usual.
Business as usual. Business as usual. Business as usual. Business as usual. Business as usual. Business
as usual. Business as usual. Business as usual. Business as usual. Business as usual. Business as usual.

Business as usual. Business as usual. Business as usual. Business as usual. Business as usual. Business
as usual. Business as usual. Business as usual. Business as usual. Business as usual. Business as usual.
Business as usual. Business as usual. Business as usual. Business as usual. Business as usual. Business
as usual. Business as usual. Business as usual. Business as usual. Business as usual. Business as usual.
Business as usual. Business as usual. Business as usual. Business as usual. Business as usual. Business
as usual. Business as usual. Business as usual. Business as usual. Business as usual. Business as usual.
Business as usual. Business as usual. Business as usual. Business as usual. Business as usual. Business
as usual. Business as usual. Business as usual. Business as usual. Business as usual. Business as usual.
Business as usual. Business as usual. Business as usual. Business as usual. Business as usual. Business
as usual. Business as usual. Business as usual. Business as usual. Business as usual. Business as usual.
Business as usual. Business as usual. Business as usual. Business as usual. Business as usual. Business
as usual. Business as usual. Business as usual. Business as usual. Business as usual. Business as usual.
Business as usual. Business as usual. Business as usual. Business as usual. Business as usual. Business
as usual. Business as usual. Business as usual. Business as usual. Business as usual. Business as usual.
Business as usual. Business as usual. Business as usual. Business as usual. Business as usual. Business
as usual. Business as usual. Business as usual. Business as usual. Business as usual. Business as usual.
Business as usual. Business as usual. Business as usual. Business as usual. Business as usual. Business
as usual. Business as usual. Business as usual. Business as usual. Business as usual. Business as usual.
Business as usual. Business as usual. Business as usual. Business as usual. Business as usual. Business
as usual. Business as usual. Business as usual. Business as usual. Business as usual. Business as usual.
Business as usual. Business as usual. Business as usual. Business as usual. Business as usual. Business
as usual. Business as usual. Business as usual. Business as usual. Business as usual. Business as usual.
Business as usual. Business as usual. Business as usual. Business as usual. Business as usual. Business
as usual. Business as usual. Business as usual. Business as usual. Business as usual. Business as usual.
Business as usual. Business as usual. Business as usual. Business as usual. Business as usual. Business
as usual. Business as usual. Business as usual. Business as usual. Business as usual. Business as usual.
Business as usual. Business as usual. Business as usual. Business as usual. Business as usual. Business
as usual. Business as usual. Business as usual. Business as usual. Business as usual. Business as usual.
Business as usual. Business as usual. Business as usual. Business as usual. Business as usual. Business
as usual. Business as usual. Business as usual. Business as usual. Business as usual. Business as usual.
Business as usual. Business as usual. Business as usual. Business as usual. Business as usual. Business
as usual. Business as usual. Business as usual. Business as usual. Business as usual. Business as usual.
Business as usual. Business as usual. Business as usual. Business as usual. Business as usual. Business
as usual. Business as usual. Business as usual. Business as usual. Business as usual. Business as usual.

Soon there will be only two kinds of companies.

Those who are content to do business as usual.

as usual. Business as usual. Business as usual. Business as usual. Business as usual. Business as usual.
Business as usual. Business as usual. Business as usual. Business as usual. Business as usual. Business
as usual. Business as usual. Business as usual. Business as usual. Business as usual. Business as usual.
Business as usual. Business as usual. Business as usual. Business as usual. Business as usual. Business
as usual. Business as usual. Business as usual. Business as usual. Business as usual. Business as usual.
Business as usual. Business as usual. Business as usual. Business as usual. Business as usual. Business
as usual. Business as usual. Business as usual. Business as usual. Business as usual. Business as usual.
Business as usual. Business as usual. Business as usual. Business as usual. Business as usual. Business
as usual. Business as usual. Business as usual. Business as usual. Business as usual. Business as usual.
Business as usual. Business as usual. Business as usual. Business as usual. Business as usual. Business
as usual. Business as usual. Business as usual. Business as usual. Business as usual. Business as usual.
Business as usual. Business as usual. Business as usual. Business as usual. Business as usual. Business
as usual. Business as usual. Business as usual. Business as usual. Business as usual. Business as usual.
Business as usual. Business as usual. Business as usual. Business as usual. Business as usual. Business
as usual. Business as usual. Business as usual. Business as usual. Business as usual. Business as usual.
Business as usual. Business as usual. Business as usual. Business as usual. Business as usual. Business
as usual. Business as usual. Business as usual. Business as usual. Business as usual. Business as usual.
Business as usual. Business as usual. Business as usual. Business as usual. Business as usual. Business
as usual. Business as usual. Business as usual. Business as usual. Business as usual. Business as usual.
Business as usual. Business as usual. Business as usual. Business as usual. Business as usual. Business
as usual. Business as usual. Business as usual. Business as usual. Business as usual. Business as usual.
Business as usual. Business as usual. Business as usual. Business as usual. Business as usual. Business
as usual. Business as usual. Business as usual. Business as usual. Business as usual. Business as usual.
Business as usual. Business as usual. Business as usual. Business as usual. Business as usual. Business
as usual. Business as usual. Business as usual. Business as usual. Business as usual. Business as usual.
Business as usual. Business as usual. Business as usual. Business as usual. Business as usual. Business
as usual. Business as usual. Business as usual. Business as usual. Business as usual. Business as usual.
Business as usual. Business as usual. Business as usual. Business as usual. Business as usual. Business
as usual. Business as usual. Business as usual. Business as usual. Business as usual. Business as usual.
Business as usual. Business as usual. Business as usual. Business as usual. Business as usual. Business
as usual. Business as usual. Business as usual. Business as usual. Business as usual. Business as usual.
Business as usual. Business as usual. Business as usual. Business as usual. Business as usual. Business
as usual. Business as usual. Business as usual. Business as usual. Business as usual. Business as usual.

Business as usual. Business as usual. Business as usual. Business as usual. Business as usual. Business
as usual. Business as usual. Business as usual. Business as usual. Business as usual. Business as usual.
Business as usual. Business as usual. Business as usual. Business as usual. Business as usual. Business
as usual. Business as usual. Business as usual. Business as usual. Business as usual. Business as usual.
Business as usual. Business as usual. Business as usual. Business as usual. Business as usual. Business
as usual. Business as usual. Business as usual. Business as usual. Business as usual. Business as usual.
Business as usual. Business as usual. Business as usual. Business as usual. Business as usual. Business
as usual. Business as usual. Business as usual. Business as usual. Business as usual. Business as usual.
Business as usual. Business as usual. Business as usual. Business as usual. Business as usual. Business
as usual. Business as usual. Business as usual. Business as usual. Business as usual. Business as usual.
Business as usual. Business as usual. Business as usual. Business as usual. Business as usual. Business
as usual. Business as usual. Business as usual. Business as usual. Business as usual. Business as usual.
Business as usual. Business as usual. Business as usual. Business as usual. Business as usual. Business
as usual. Business as usual. Business as usual. Business as usual. Business as usual. Business as usual.
Business as usual. Business as usual. Business as usual. Business as usual. Business as usual. Business
as usual. Business as usual. Business as usual. Business as usual. Business as usual. Business as usual.
Business as usual. Business as usual. Business as usual. Business as usual. Business as usual. Business
as usual. Business as usual. Business as usual. Business as usual. Business as usual. Business as usual.
Business as usual. Business as usual. Business as usual. Business as usual. Business as usual. Business
as usual. Business as usual. Business as usual. Business as usual. Business as usual. Business as usual.
Business as usual. Business as usual. Business as usual. Business as usual. Business as usual. Business
as usual. Business as usual. Business as usual. Business as usual. Business as usual. Business as usual.
Business as usual. Business as usual. Business as usual. Business as usual. Business as usual. Business
as usual. Business as usual. Business as usual. Business as usual. Business as usual. Business as usual.
Business as usual. Business as usual. Business as usual. Business as usual. Business as usual. Business
as usual. Business as usual. Business as usual. Business as usual. Business as usual. Business as usual.
Business as usual. Business as usual. Business as usual. Business as usual. Business as usual. Business
as usual. Business as usual. Business as usual. Business as usual. Business as usual. Business as usual.
Business as usual. Business as usual. Business as usual. Business as usual. Business as usual. Business
as usual. Business as usual. Business as usual. Business as usual. Business as usual. Business as usual.
Business as usual. Business as usual. Business as usual. Business as usual. Business as usual. Business
as usual. Business as usual. Business as usual. Business as usual. Business as usual. Business as usual.
Business as usual. Business as usual. Business as usual. Business as usual. Business as usual. Business
as usual. Business as usual. Business as usual. Business as usual. Business as usual. Business as usual.

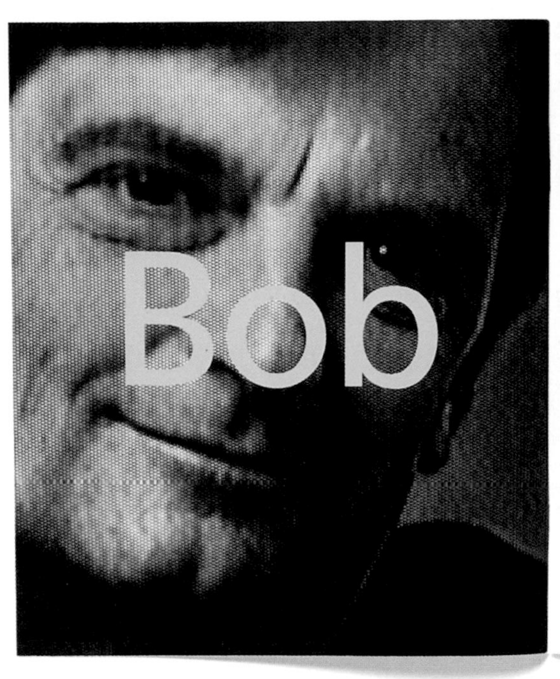

This is Bob.
He built and ran billion-dollar
businesses at IBM.

Those who will exploit
the technology revolution.

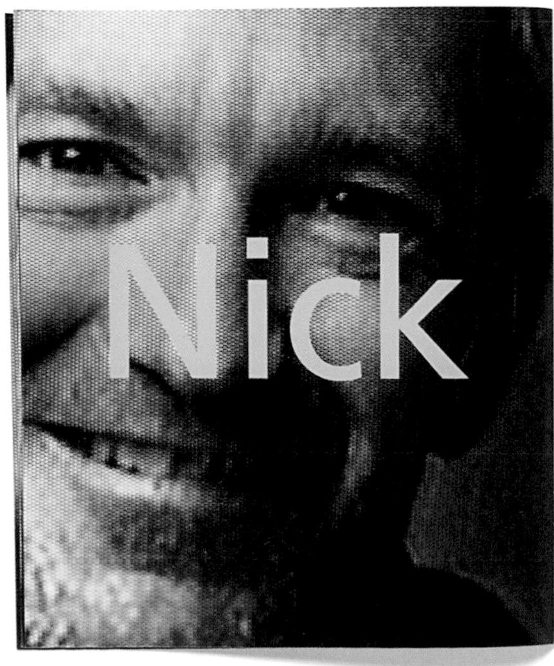

This is Nick.
He founded three technology
companies, and created the standard for
secure Internet commerce.

Design Firm: Bielenberg Design Art Director: John Bielenberg Designer: Erik Cox Photographer: Barry Robinson Copywriter: Rich Binell Client: Scient

TODAY, DESIGNERS ARE ACCUSTOMED TO DIGITALLY ALTERING PHOTOGRAPHS TO ENHANCE THEIR APPEARANCE, TO FIX SMALL BLEMISHES OR TO MARRY VARIOUS IMAGES TOGETHER TO HELP TELL A BETTER STORY. AT THE TURN OF THE CENTURY, PEOPLE WERE ENTERTAINED BY VIEWING HAND-PAINTED GLASS SLIDES PROJECTED ON A WALL OR SCREEN BY A SO-CALLED MAGIC LANTERN. THE PHOTOGRAPHERS USED BLACK AND WHITE NEGATIVES TO MAKE THE GLASS SLIDES, THEN PAINTED THEM WITH WATERCOLORS TO CREATE LIFELIKE SCENES.

Design Firm: Herring Design Designer & Copywriter: Jerry Herring Photographer: Frederick Monsen Client: Herring Design Quarterly

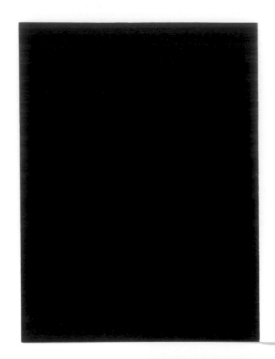

Design Firm: Design Guys Art Director & Copywriter: Steven Sikora Designer: Dawn Selg Target Stores

Design Firm: Sackett Design Associates Art Director: Mark Sackett Designers: James Sakamoto, Wendy Wood, George White Photographers: Michal Venera, Catherine Buchanan Client: San Francisco International Airport

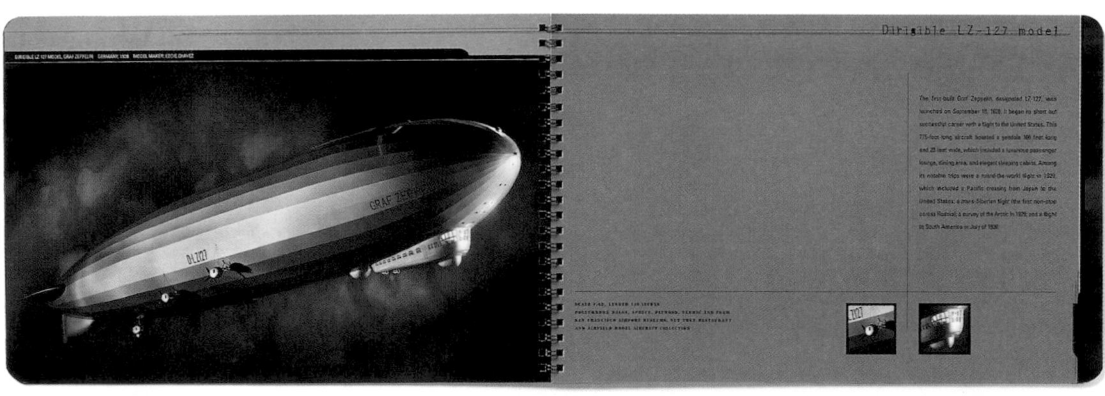

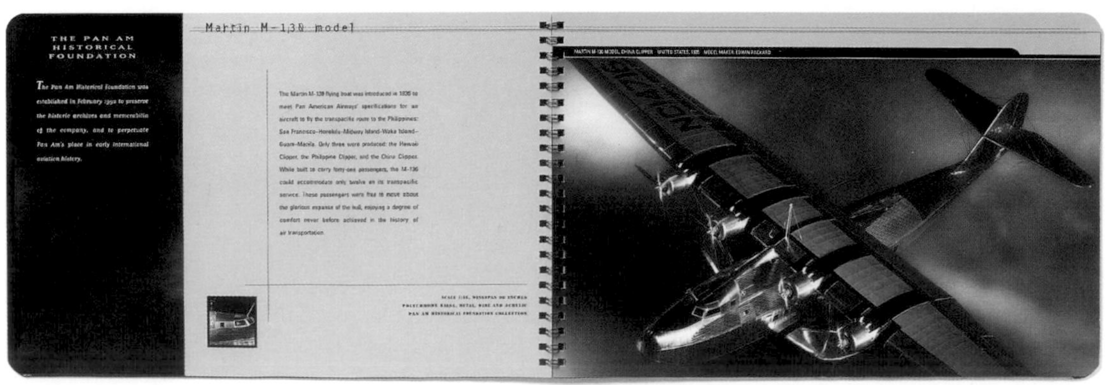

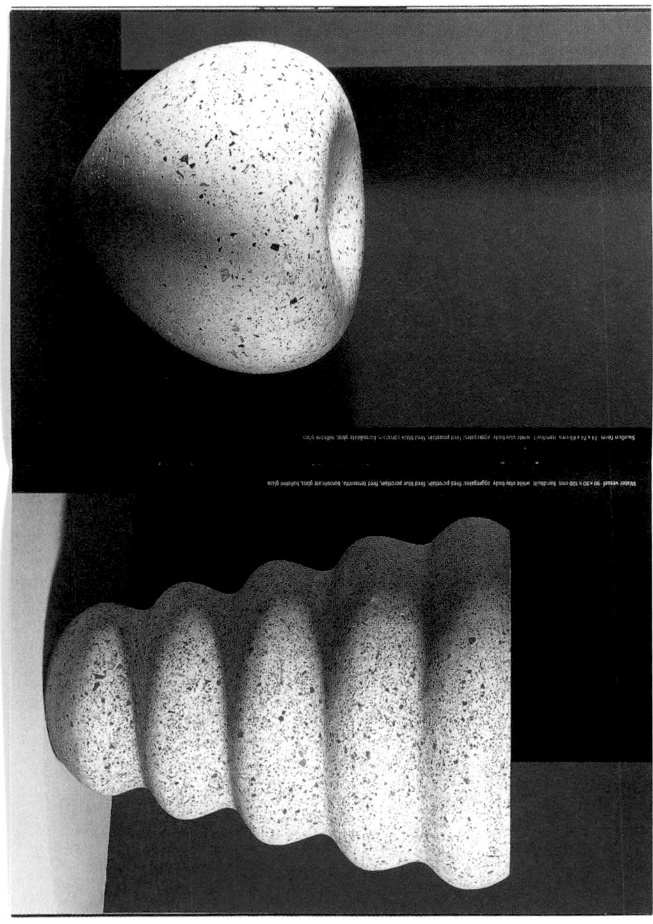

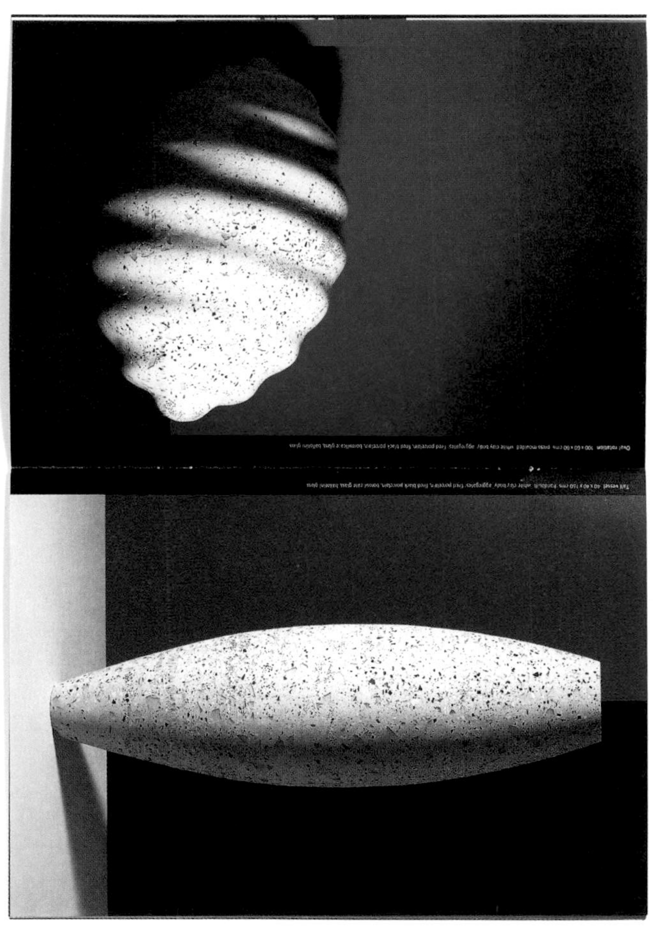

Design Firm: Mytton Williams Art Director: Bob Mytton Designer: Danielle Way Photographer: Sebastian Mylius Client: Felicity Aylieff

Saks Fifth Avenue
CBS, Inc.

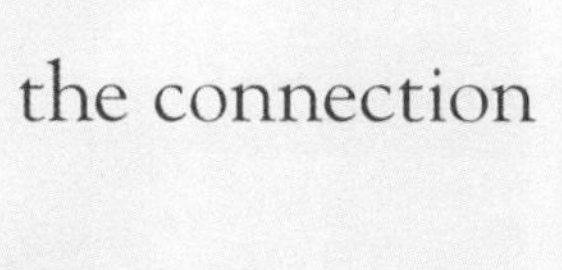
the connection

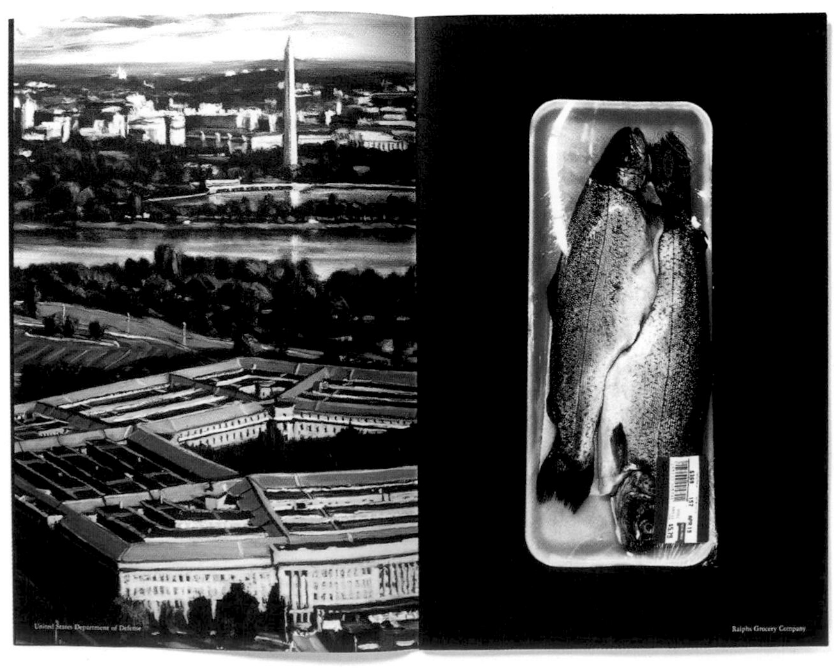
United States Department of Defense
Ralphs Grocery Company

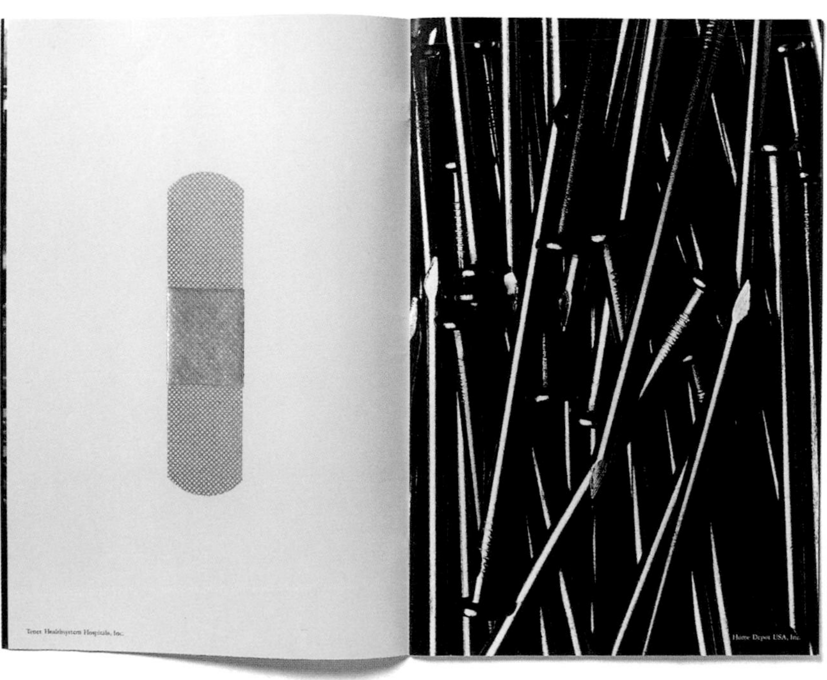

Design Firm: Cahan & Associates Art & Creative Director: Bill Cahan Designer: Michael Braley Photographers: Robert Schlatter, William Mercer Illustrator: Nanette Biers Copywriter: Maria Peevey Client: New Energy

Design Firm: Shinnoske Inc. Art Directors: Shinnoske Sugisaki, Katsuhiko Nakamura Designers: Shinnoske Sugisaki, Chiaki Okuno Photographer: Luke H. Ozawa Client: All Nippon Airways

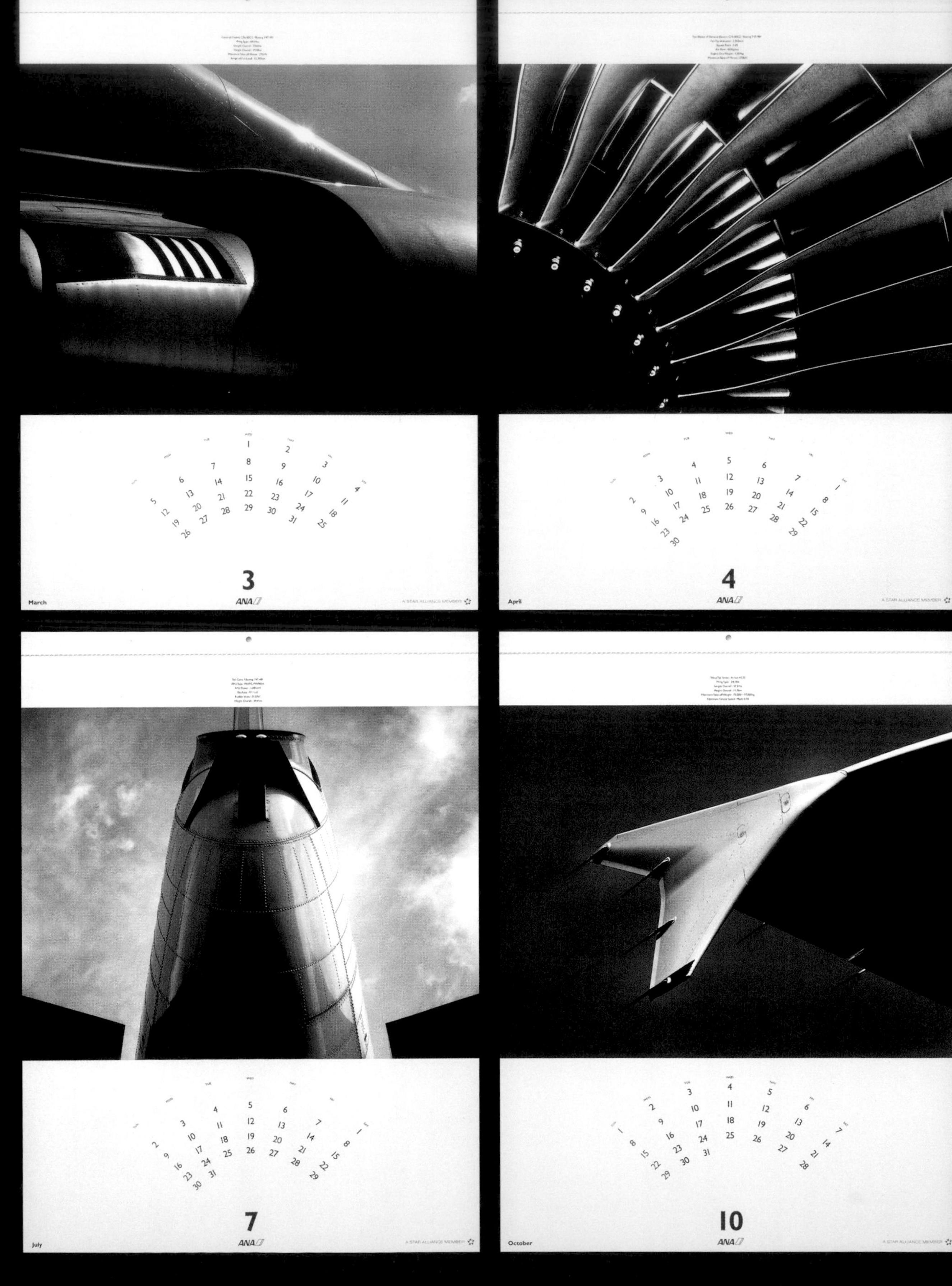

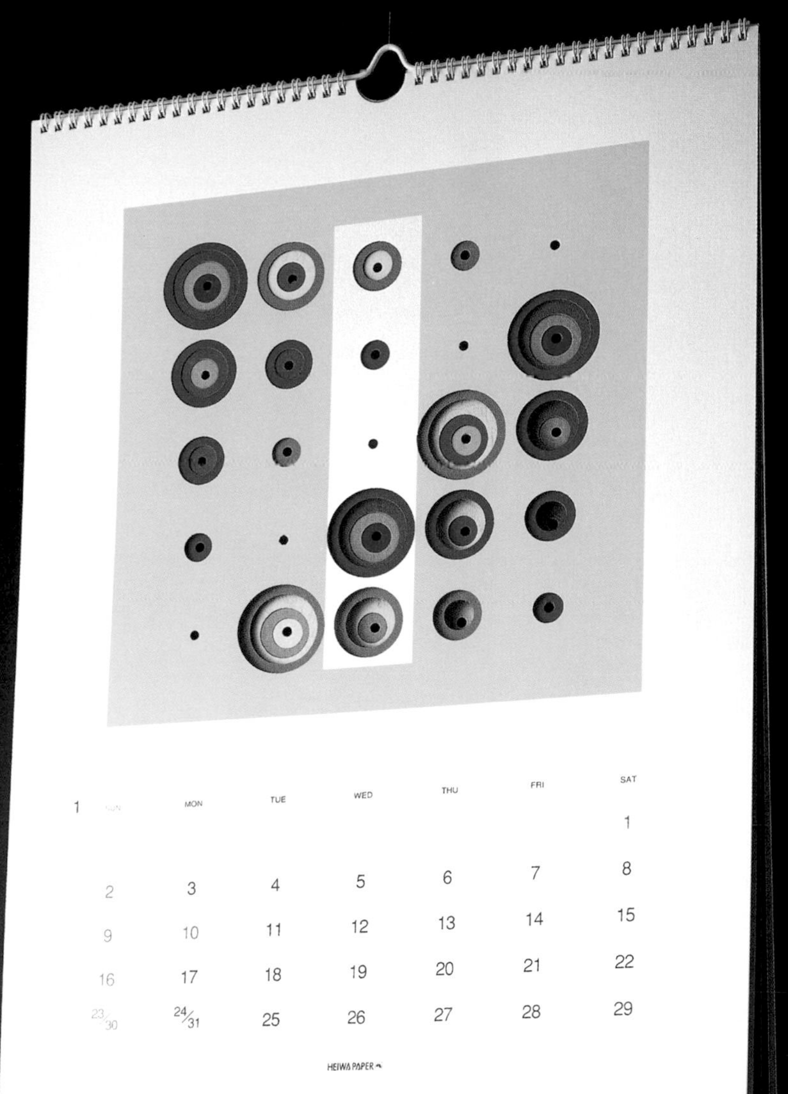

Design Firm: Packaging Create Inc. Art Director: Akio Okumura Designer: Takako Okemoto Client: Heiwa Paper

Firm: Elixir Design, Inc. Art Director: Jennifer Jerde Designers: Nathan Durrant, Eric Heiman, Jennifer Tolo, Holly Holmquist, Merel Kennedy, Leslie Charles Photographer: Michael McRae Copywriter: Karryll Nason Clients: Elixir Design, McRae Studios, Artisan Color

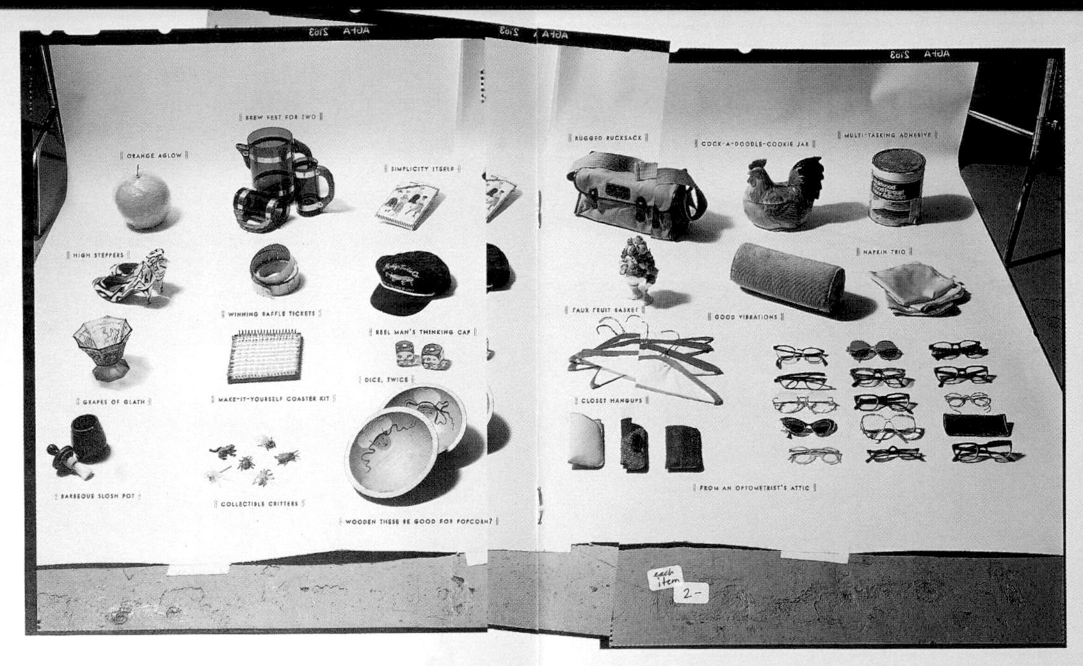

OXFORD SUMMER 1999 2000

Design Firm: Fabio Ongarato Design Art & Creative Director: Fabio Ongarato Designers: Fabio Ongarato, Simone Elder Photographer: Derek Henderson Client: Oxford Menswear

Palakona Split Bamboo Rods

MARVEL

Known as President Eisenhower's favorite rod, the Marvel reigned as the most prized Hardy Palakona from 1925 to 1970. With its traditional slow action and built-in reserve power, the Marvel can punch through the most frustrating headwinds and precisely present the smallest dries. It's the lightest practical rod to trick highly selective trout on spooky spring creeks. And the fluid feel is enough to make any bamboo enthusiast grin with delight.

C.C. de FRANCE

In the early part of the century, if you were a serious fly caster, you attended the European casting tournaments held by the Casting Club of France. It was here in 1911 that John James Hardy cast a world record 81' with his 7' Palakona. The rod revolutionized bamboo design with its unique taper and smooth line turnover. After the tournament Mr. Hardy's rod was christened the C. C. de France and its production spanned 50 years until 1961. Wrapped with deep ruby thread, the C.C. de France is an exquisite masterpiece.

PHANTOM

During the middle 60's the Phantom was the rod to own. Designed by Jim Hardy, the Phantom's firm butt section matched with a slightly stiffer tip was all the rage. It gave anglers the ability to roll cast long distances and drop dry flies with pinpoint accuracy. The Phantom balances well in the hand and becomes a true extension of the anglers' forearm. Wrapped in black tyings, the Phantom is a welcomed addition to any serious collection.

LIGHTWEIGHTS

In 1997 Hardy introduced three Lightweight Palakonas exclusively for the American market. The Lightweight tapers are medium fast with a sweet progressive action. Lightweights turnover tight loops with a lower-middle to tip flexing profile. The Blue Ridge, Catskill and Yellowstone are excellent choices for your first Palakona.

Model	Length	Sections	Tips	Weight	Rod / Blank
Marvel	7'	3	2	2 7/8 oz	$1800 / 1260
Marvel	7'6"	3	2	3 1/8 oz	$1850 / 1295
C.C. de France	7'	2	2	3 3/8 oz	$1575 / 1102
Phantom	6'10"	2	2	3 1/8 oz	$1545 / 1082
Blue Ridge	6'	2	2	2 3/4 oz	$1465 / 1025
Catskill	6'8"	2	2	3 1/8 oz	$1475 / 1032
Yellowstone	7'2"	2	2	3 3/8 oz	$1495 / 1046

All Palakonas are supplied with original polished aluminum hardware, two tips, hand-fitted rosewood ferrule plugs, deluxe rod bag and the best English bridle leather case.

L to R: 7' Marvel, 6'8" Catskill, 7'6" Marvel and 7' C.C. de France

-5-

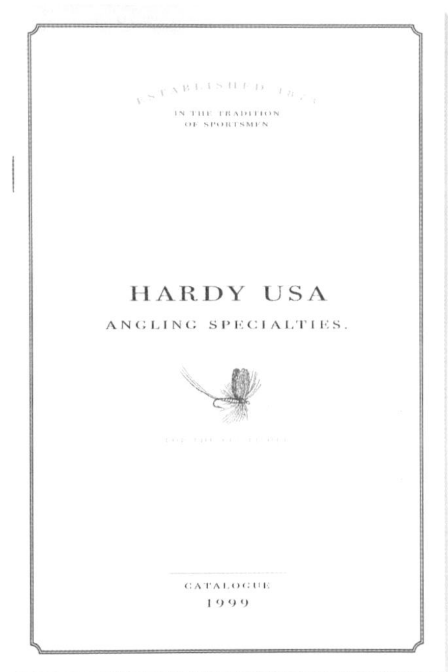

IN THE TRADITION
OF SPORTSMEN
HARDY USA
ANGLING SPECIALTIES.
CATALOGUE
1999

Fly Lines

ULTRALITE FLOATING Designed for the Ultralite and Ultralite Plus range of rods, these lines maximize casting efficiency in fast action rods. A specialized coating makes the super soft, straight and buoyant Ultralite our best selling line. Chartreuse Green and Hi-Vis White in 83' WF3 to WF9 and DT3 to DT6. $48

ULTRALITE SALMON Performing flawlessly when matched to our Salmon/Spey rods, the Ultralite Salmon's unique taper gives excellent loop control, line turnover and wind penetration. Low specific gravity allows better floatation and less surface disturbance. Chartreuse Green and Hi-Vis White in 90' DT9 and DT10. $60

DRY FLY FLOATING The economically priced Dry Fly Floating line has been a part of our range for more than 15 years. Its blue coating has proven to be the most durable coating on the market. The line has excellent shooting properties and floatability. Great for our Featherlite, Smuggler and Perfection Glass rods. Ice Blue in 83' WF4 to WF6. $38

CLEAR SINKING Designed for stillwater, deep nymphing and saltwater anglers, our Clear Sinking line is virtually undetectable under water. Its has a uniform sink rate of 1.5 to 2.0 inches per second. Clear in 81' WF5 to WF9. $52

LEATHER FLY WALLETS Made by our leather rod tube craftsman, these wallets make the perfect gifts for die-hard fly tyers. Ideal for nymphs, streamers and steelhead patterns. Smooth Leather $62 Pigskin Embossed Leather $66

PRIESTS Two sizes for trout and salmon. This handsome accessory has a polished brass head, a hardwood handle and leather wrist thong. Trout $32 Salmon $38

BRASS BALANCE Each brass balance has a large hook and micrometer adjustment. Finished in polished brass, these quality balances have dual markings in ounces and grams. 11 lbs. x 2 ozs. $44

LAPEL PIN The Hardy Corporate logo in brass with enamel applique. $15

NEOPRENE REEL POUCH Standard neoprene reel pouch embossed with Hardy logo. Size fits up to 3 3/4" reels or spools. $15

NEOPRENE FLY LINE RETAINER Simple and inexpensive method to keep fly lines in place on spare spools. One size fits all. $10

VINYL REEL POUCH Our standard reel case for the last 50 years with standard zip fastener and foam padded insert. Small $16 Large $16.50 Extra Large $17

PIN ON RETRACTOR High quality zinger made in our factory. Molded plastic with nylon cord. $20

-21-

Design Firm: Pattee Design, Inc. Art Director: Steve Pattee Designer: Trenton Burd Photographer: Andrew Russetti Client: Hardy U.S.A.

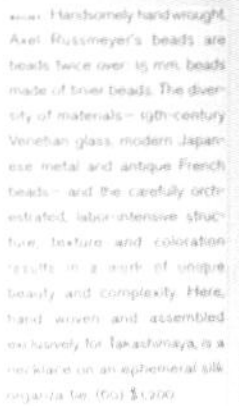

Design Firm: Design: M/W Creative Director: Allison Williams Designers: Allison Williams, Mats Hakansson, Yael Eisele Photographer: Anita Calero Copywriter: Laura Silverman Client: Takashimaya New York

Design Firm: Copeland Hirthler Design Creative Director: Brad Copeland Designers: Lionel Ferreira, Rebecca D'Attilio Illustrator: Lionel Ferreira Copywriters: Rodney Rogers, Juliet Sink Client: Miliken Carpet

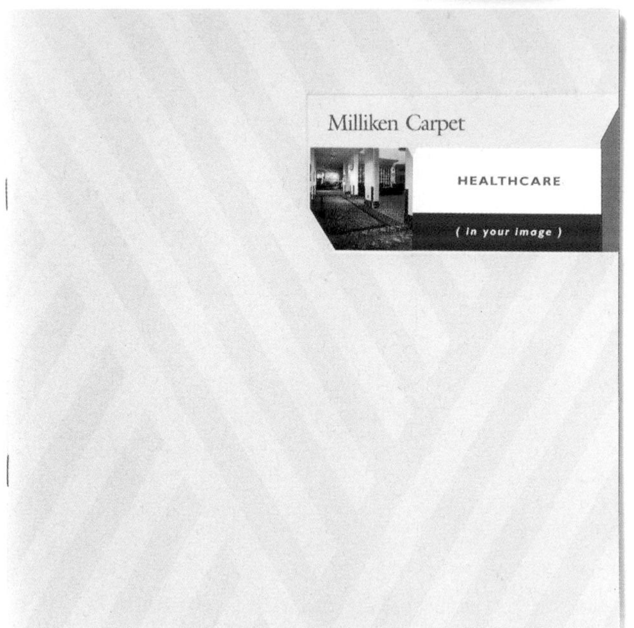

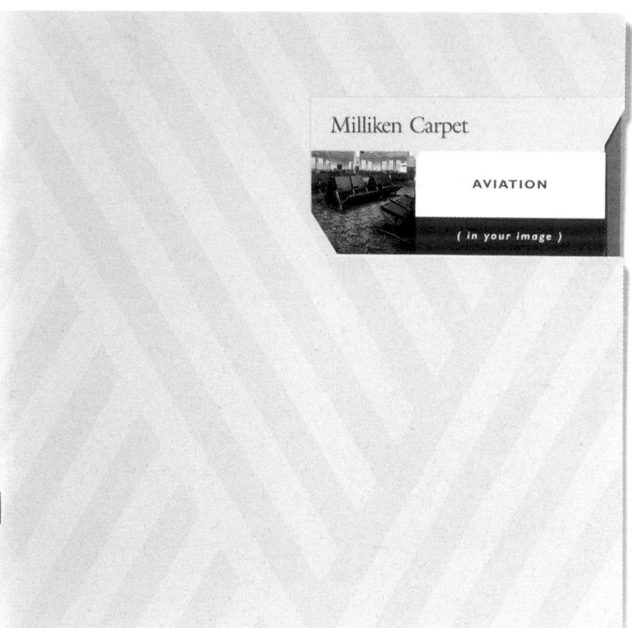

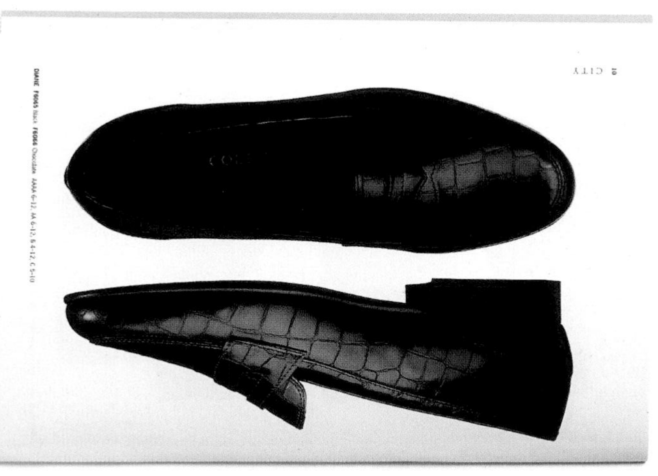

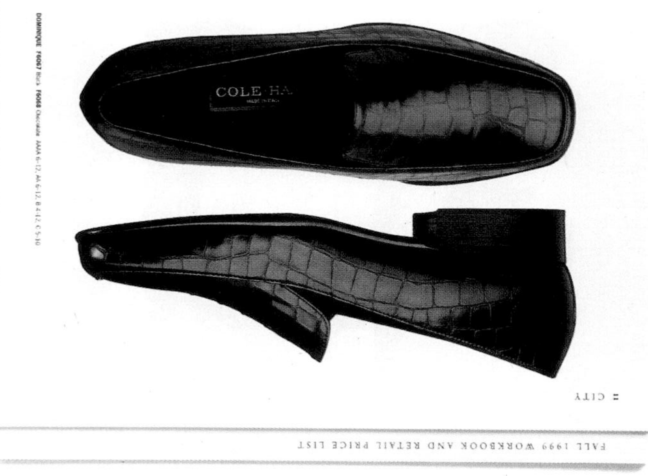

Design Firm: Concrete Design Communications Inc. Art Directors: Diti Katona, John Pylypczak Designer: Belinda Peres Photographers: Brian Sano, Ilan Rubin Client: Cole Haan

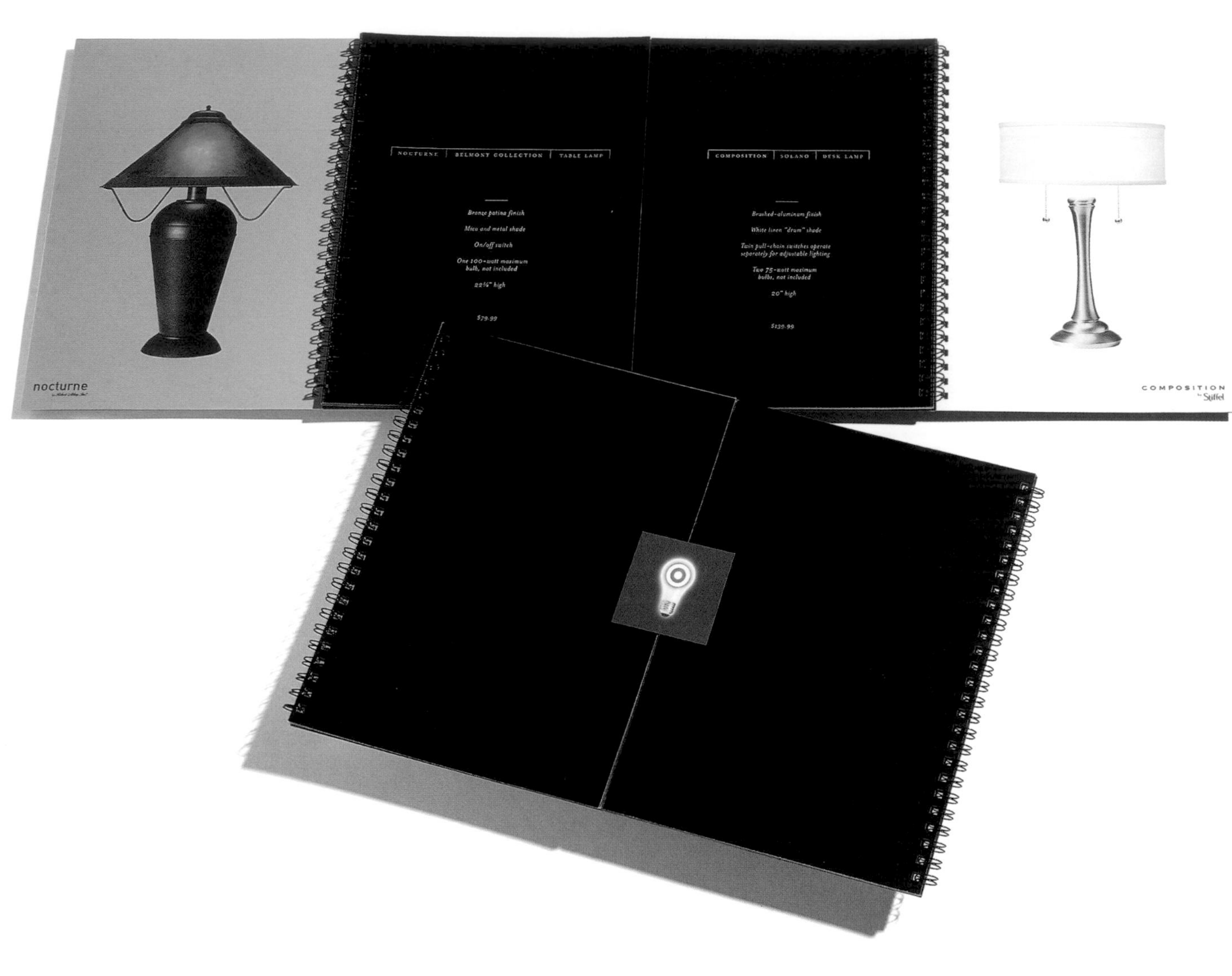

Design Firm: RBMM Designer: Tanya Freach Photographer: Joe Patronite Client: Joe Patronite

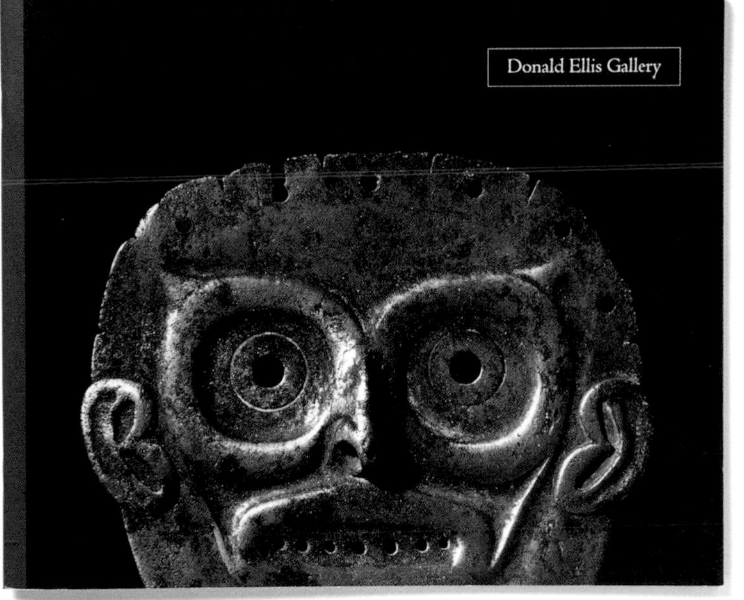

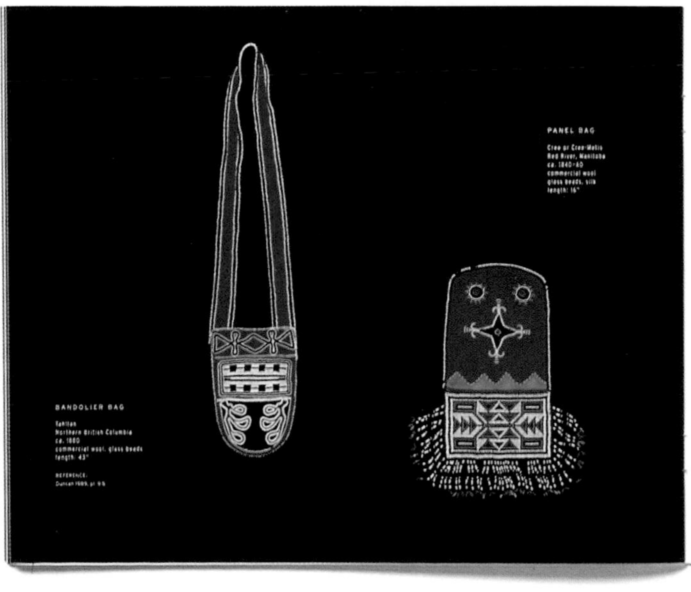

Design Firm: Hambly & Woolley Inc. Art Director & Designer: Barb Woolley Photographers: Frank Tancredi, John Bigelow Taylor Copywriter: Donald Ellis Client: Don Ellis Gallery

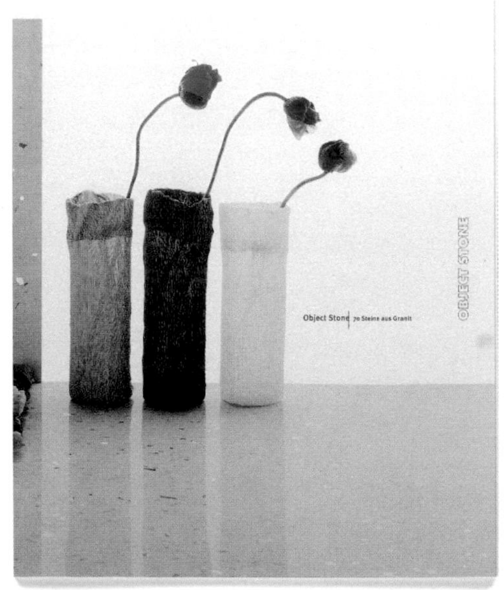
Object Stone | 70 Steine aus Granit
OBJECT STONE

OBJECT PARKETT

Kollektion | 15 Holzarten
K

DELEO CLAY TILE CO.

MADE IN THE USA
EST. 1984
THROUGHBODY CLAY TILES

MISSION

TUSCAN · ANTIQUE SAHARA · BUFFSTONE BELLA

When looks matter and craftsmanship counts.

MADE IN AMERICA

DELEO CLAY TILE COMPANY · 600 CHANEY STREET, LAKE ELSINORE, CALIFORNIA 92530 · WWW.DELEOCLAYTILE.COM.

Design Firm: Mires Design Art & Creative Director: Jose Serrano Designers: Miguel Perez, Gale Spitzley, Deb Hom, David Adey Client: Deleo Clay Tile Company

Design Firm: Templin Brink Design Creative Director: Gaby Brink Designers: Gaby Brink, Rishi Shourie Client: spinner.com

SPINNER
spinner.com
The Premiere Internet Music Service
SPINNER
.com
Where Music Lives Online
SPINNER
.com
Where Music Lives Online
SPINNER.COM
375 Alabama St., Suite 350
San Francisco, California 94110
scott@spinner.com
scott epstein
415-934-2703
415-703-0981
Senior Vice President, Marketing & Content
SPINNER.COM
375 Alabama Street, Suite 350
San Francisco, Ca 94110
(EST. 1996)
415-703-0980

YOU DON'T LAUNCH THIS CAR.

TT
YOU DON'T LAUNCH THIS CAR.

Corporate Identity 70,71

Design Firm: McKinney & Silver Art Director: Bob Ranew Creative Directors: David Baldwin, Bob Ranew Client: Audi North America

MARCUS

Design Firm: Pentagram Design Ltd. Art Director: David Hillman Designer: Simon Pickford Photographer: Nick Turner Client: Marcus (Time Products)

BASEBALL BLEND
SAVE 30%
ON SELECTED TULLY'S ITEMS
MARINER'S GREETING CARDS
$20.00
TUMBLER
$8.95
WHAT'S YOUR CALL?
SPIN
SHAKE
Swirkle
WHEN OUR TEAM WINS, SO DO YOU
SAVE 30% ON SELECTED TULLY'S ITEMS
HOME
7
VISITORS
2
TULLY'S
BASEBALL BLEND

Design Firm: Werkhaus Design Art Director: Steve Barrett Designers: Julie Poth, Teresa Forrester Illustrator: Julie Poth Copywriter: Hugh Saffel Client: Tully's

INTERNATIONAL

Design Firm: Duffy Design and Interactive Art Director, Designer & Illustrator: Tom Riddle Creative Director: Joe Duffy Copywriter: John Jarvis Client: International Transportation Corp.

PAPER
WHERE THINGS STA
2000
Annual Report
A GUIDE TO THE BEST OF
OUR TWISTED TOWN
N.Y.C.
PLUS
HipTips FOR:
Los Angeles
San Francisco
Miami
Chicago
Seattle
Portland
FOOD
BARS
CLUBS
MUSIC
FILM|VIDEO
STAGE,ART
BOOKS,GAY
BEAUTY,ACTION
SHOP,HOTELS
$3.50US $4.50CAN
01>
0 71486 03659 3
KAREN ELSON SPARKS

PURE
POWER

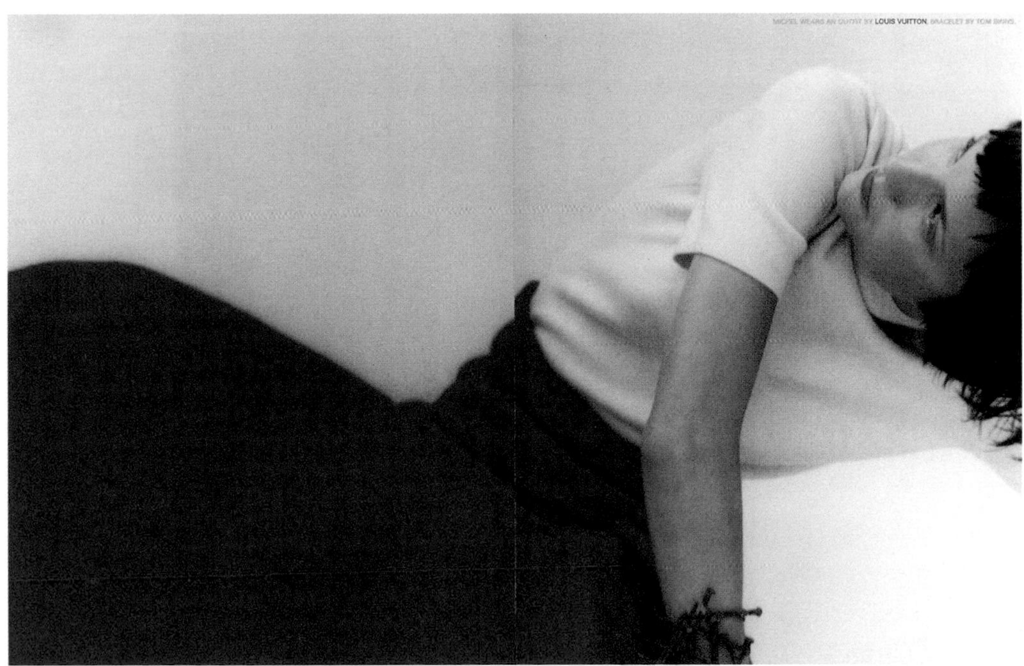
LOUIS VUITTON

MICHEL WEARS A DRESS AND SHOES BY MILA SCHÖN, NECKLACE BY TOM BINNS.

Design Firm: Socio X Creative Director: Bridget de Socio Designer: Dan Chen Photographer: Catherine Servel

DEEP
END

Harper's
BAZAAR
THE HOME FASHION ISSUE
BEST ACCESSORIES TO LIVE WITH
COURTENEY COX'S HOME IMPROVEMENT
LIFE IN THE FUTURE: YOUR HOUSE,
YOUR MAKEUP, YOUR HEALTH
WITH CHRISTY TURLINGTON
YOHJI YAMAMOTO
ANTHONY HOPKINS AND
KATE CAPSHAW
JUNE $3.00

Art Director: Caroline Jones Designer: Florentino Pamintuan Photo Editor: Dennis Golonka Client/Publisher: Harper's Bazaar

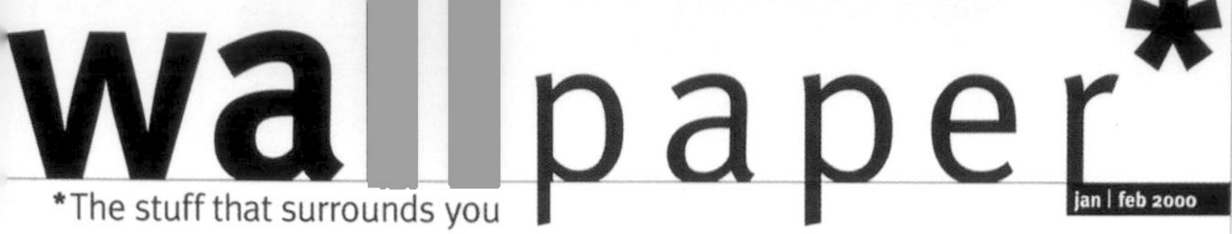

feeling better?

wallpaper* plays doctor

INTERIORS * ENTERTAINING * TRAVEL

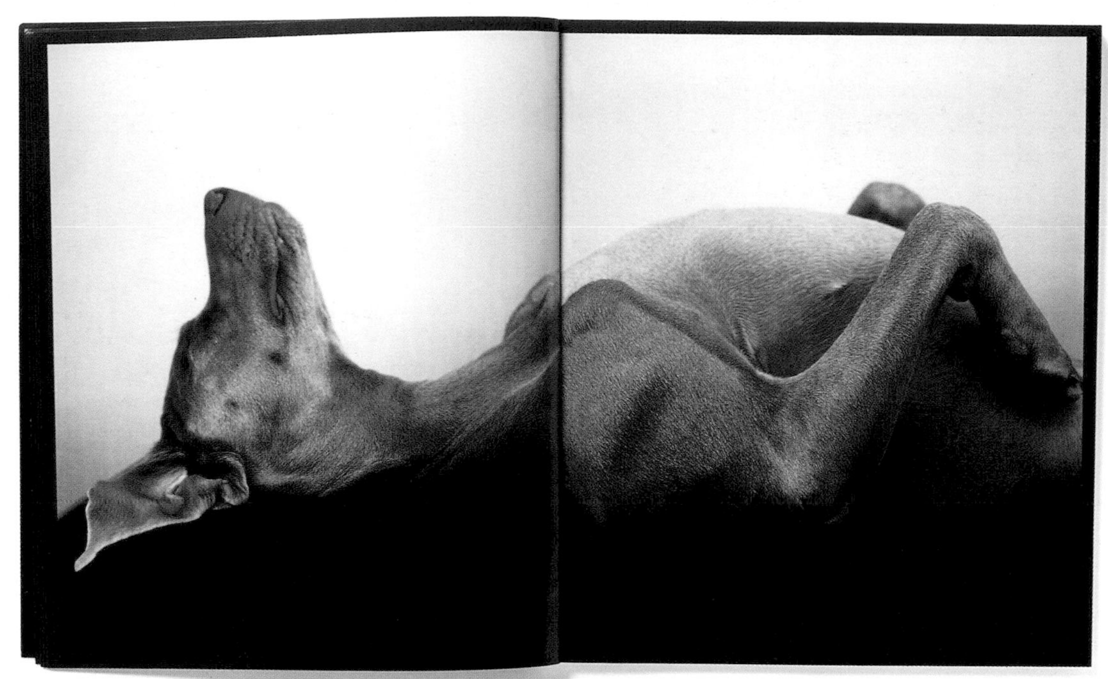

BLIND
SPOT
ISSUE FOURTEEN $14
JOHN BALDESSARI
ZEKE BERMAN
DOUGLAS COUPLAND
ROBBERT FLICK
JONATHAN FRANZEN
MASAHISA FUKASE
PER MANNING
EDWARD RUSCHA
WILLIAM WEGMAN

On Saturday, Manhattan Beach, 11:30 am to 12:15 pm All Photographs Courtesy Craig Krull, LA and Robert Mann, NY
ROBBERT FLICK

Designer: Kim Zorn Caputo Client/Publisher: Blind Spot Photography, Inc.

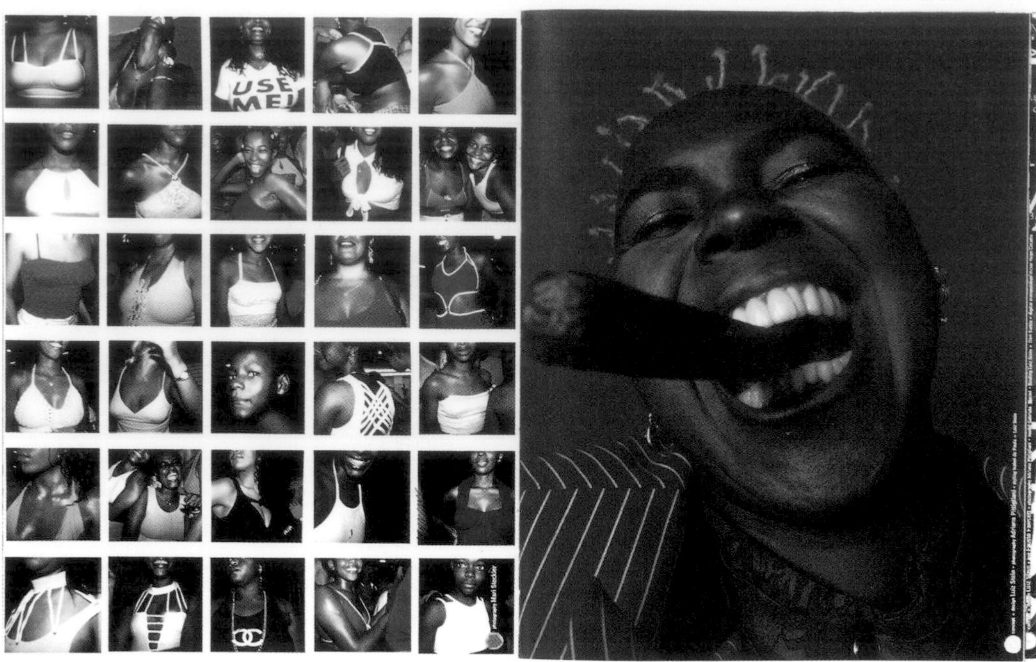

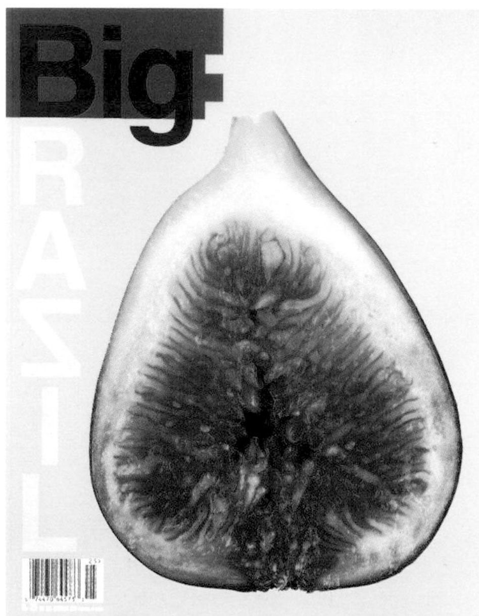
Big
BRAZIL

Big
France

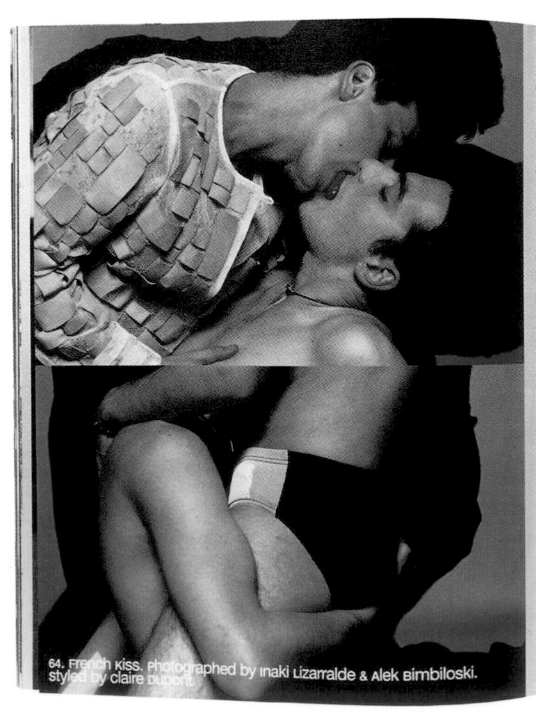
64. French kiss. Photographed by Inaki Lizarralde & Alek Bimbiloski.
styled by claire Dupont

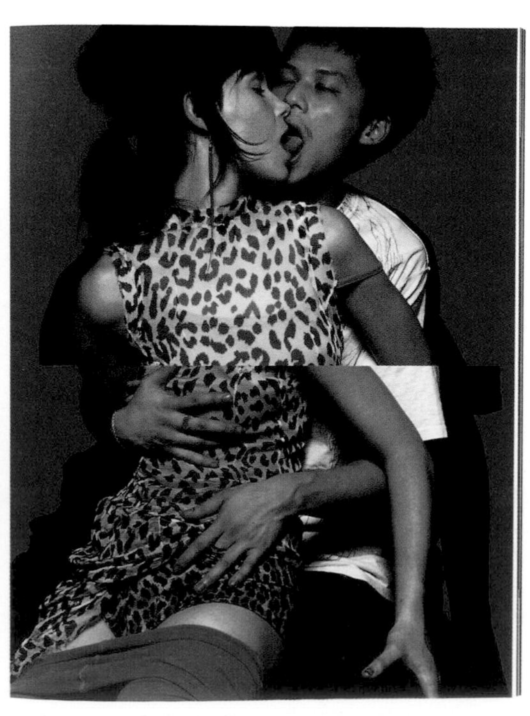

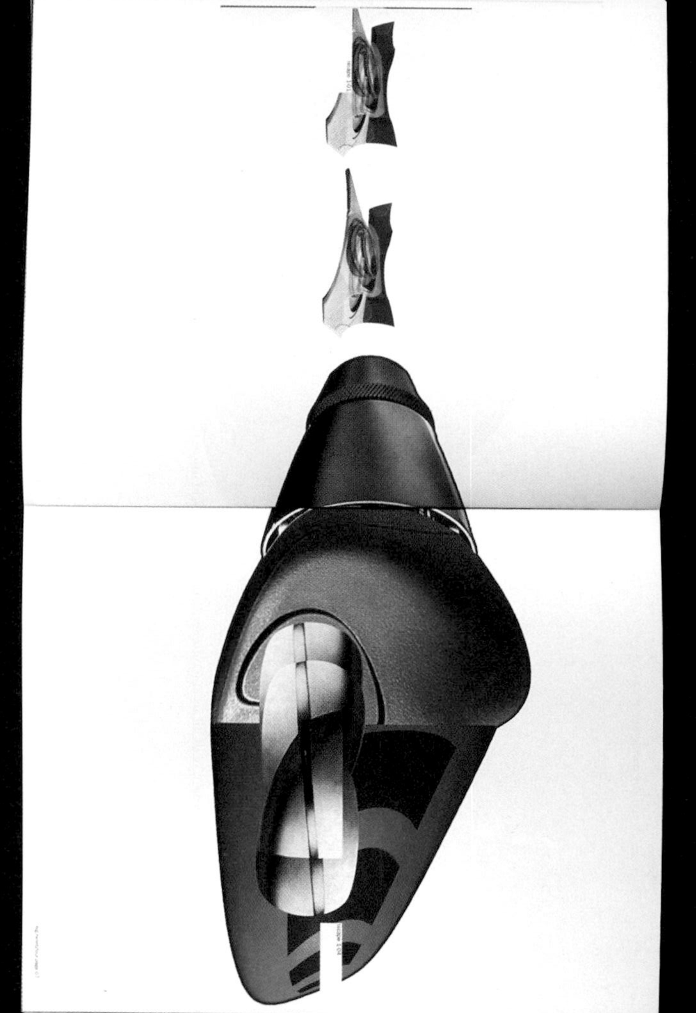

Creative Director: Marcelo Junemann Art Director: Doug Lloyd Designer: Ting Ting Lee Client/Publisher: Big (Design for Big Brazil by Rico Lins Studio; Cover of Big France by Jenny Van Sommers)

70. Huître fine de claire spéciale, cuisses de grenouille sauvage Française. Photographed by Guido Mocafico. styled by Emmanuel Turiot

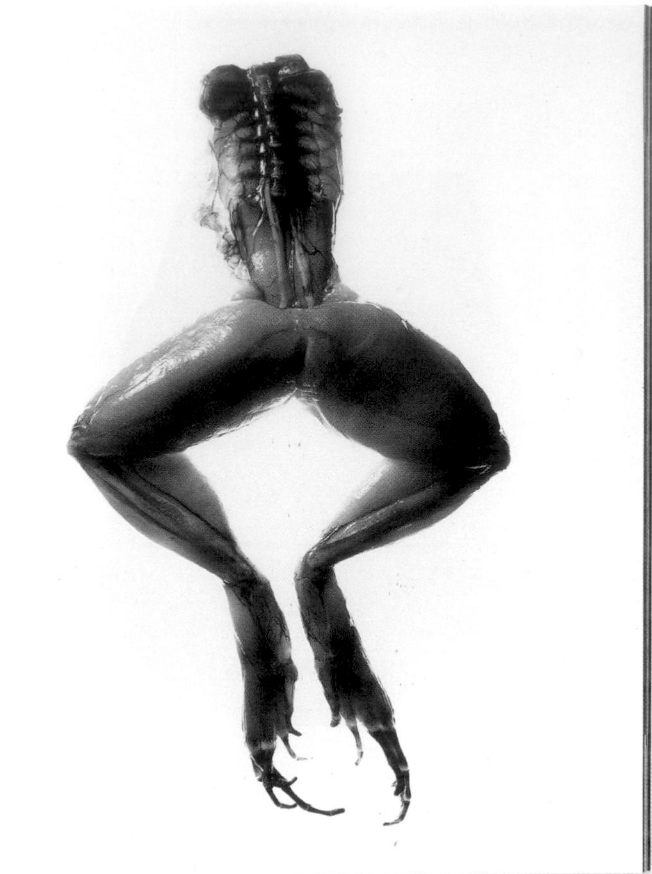

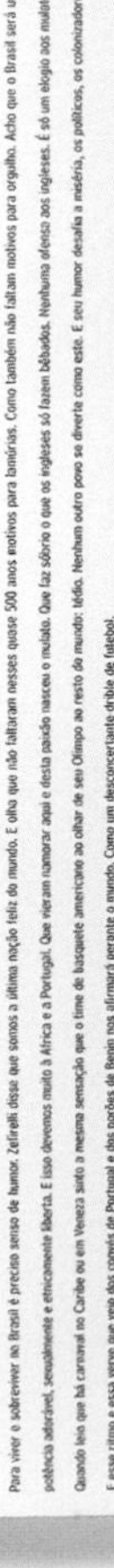

Para viver e sobreviver no Brasil é preciso senso de humor. Zefirelli disse que somos a última nação feliz do mundo. E olha que não faltaram nesses quase 500 anos motivos para lamúrias. Como também não faltam motivos para orgulho. Acho que o Brasil será uma potência adorável, sexualmente e etnicamente liberta. E isso devemos muito à África e a Portugal. Que vieram namorar aqui e desta paixão nasceu o mulato. Que faz sóbrio o que os ingleses só fazem bêbados. Nenhuma ofensa aos ingleses. É só um elogio aos mulatos.

Quando leio que há carnaval no Caribe ou em Veneza sinto a mesma sensação que o time de basquete americano ao olhar de seu Olimpo ao resto do mundo: tédio. Nenhum outro povo se diverte como este. E seu humor desafia a miséria, os políticos, os colonizadores.

E esse ritmo e essa verve que veio dos conveses de Portugal e dos porões de Benin nos afirmará perante o mundo. Como um desconcertante drible de futebol.

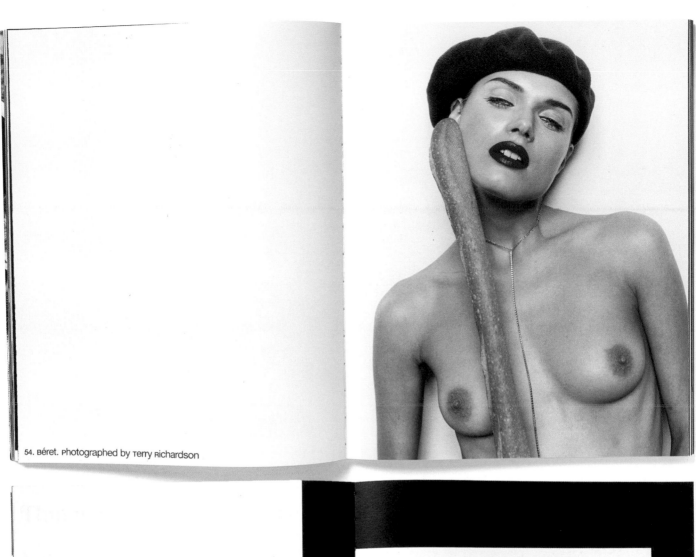

54. Béret. Photographed by Terry Richardson

Creative Director: Marcelo Junemann Art Director: Doug Lloyd Designer: Ting Ting Lee Client/Publisher: Big

(top) Art & Creative Director: Fred Woodward Client/Publisher: Rolling Stone (bottom) Art & Creative Director: Fred Woodward Photographer: David LaChapelle Client/Publisher: Rolling Stone

E R G I N D I A C N V U E L V E
N P I E C O D V I D H G J A B B
R U C C N G C H C M A D O N N A
I E A R K S M A R T I N S J A L
Q R L I O Y L R O C O G H U N K
U T A C U A H A L L A B H Q D F
E O T O R N O T L D V E Y K S C
A R I E C Q S A I E I L C N P O
S F N T H E P Y N G D O C A I L
C E O R L J I O G O A C U N D L
G D X O I N T Q Y K B A P C O I
R O B I L S A M Z I C E O Y L N
O W O C V R L P A K L I F E P S
S X A I N T E R V I E W P F S L
A M E N U D O D T G R A M M Y S

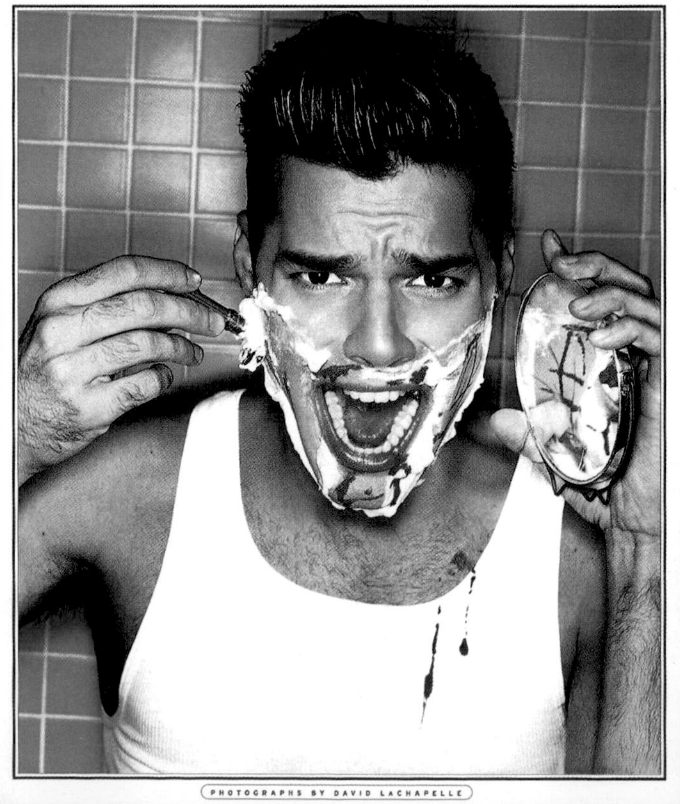

PHOTOGRAPHS BY DAVID LACHAPELLE

Editorial 88.89

Cherry Poppin'

Mama Jennifer Aniston

By Nancy Collins

says, "LIFE'S NEVER BEEN BETTER" as she turns thirty with a little help from her FRIENDS and a new love in BRAD PITT

Photographs by MARK SELIGER

Photographs by Peter Lindbergh

THE PASSION OF NICOLAS CAGE

THE OSCAR-WINNING ACTOR WHO SAYS HE BUILT A CAREER ON BEING "UNPREDICTABLE AND FRIGHTENING" REVEALS A SIDE NOBODY KNOWS

BY FRED SCHRUERS

Creative Director: Fred Woodward Photographer: Mark Seliger Client/Publisher: Rolling Stone (bottom) Art & Creative Director: Fred Woodward Photographer: Peter Lindberg Client/Publisher: Rolling Stone

Design Firm: Toda Art Director: David Raccuglia Creative Director: Marcos Chavez Designers: Karin Hug, Milton Melendez, Aimec Sealfon Photographers: David Raccuglia, Tim Tucker Copywriters: David Raccuglia, Kurt Kuethener, Rachel Orrino, Terry Lome, Craig Hanson, Leslie Lynch Jablonski Client: American Crew

Duo the word by definition refers to duplicity or the presence of duplicate or double elements (duet, duologue). The Duo Desic collection represents Desic 2000 in a form composed of two separate elements. The elements range from aggressively short scalp exposure combined with solid geometry to separate, but identifiable perimeter lines. The Duo Desic collection is most applicable to a youthful demographic (ages 10-24). With "Duo Desic," influences from the skateboard culture to the technopop music scene have been combined with a futuristic feeling found in Japanese comic book art. This hybrid of influences has created a collection both challenging and original.

DUO

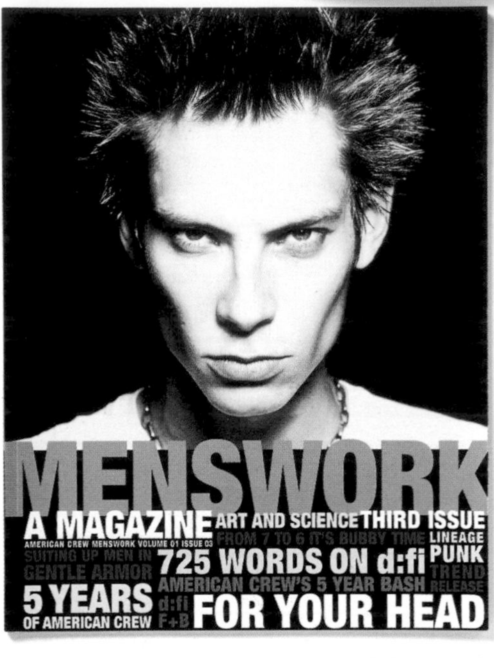

MENSWORK
A MAGAZINE
ART AND SCIENCE
THIRD ISSUE
AMERICAN CREW MENSWORK VOLUME 01 ISSUE 03
FROM 7 TO 6 IT'S BUBBY TIME
LINEAGE
SUITING UP MEN IN GENTLE ARMOR
725 WORDS ON d:fi
PUNK
TREND RELEASE
AMERICAN CREW'S 5 YEAR BASH
5 YEARS OF AMERICAN CREW
d:fi F+B
FOR YOUR HEAD

MENSWORK
A MAGAZINE
ONE DAY IS 86,400 SECONDS 1,440 MINUTES OR 24 HOURS
FOURTH ISSUE
ON GENERATION d:fi: BENEATH THE SURFACE
PORTRAITS OF A CULTURE IN EXILE
FILM CREW
DESIC 2000
TREND RELEASE
FASHIONING A CAUSE: MIGMAR TSERING'S CLIMB FOR FREE TIBET
AMERICAN CREW MENSWORK VOLUME 02 ISSUE 04
FOR YOUR HEAD

Oxy the word by definition refers to shapes that are acute, sharp, pointed, pungent, and severe (the shape of an oxygen molecule). The Oxy Desic collection is the aggressively short interpretation of Desic 2000. The design elements of the Desic collection are the most readily identifiable because the shapes are cut so close to the head. Extreme amounts of scalp exposure, blending into total scalp coverage are signatures of Oxy Desic. The acute or pointed element runs through the crown and occasionally in to the back of the profile. Oxy Desic combines conventional, technically demanding short haircutting techniques, with a new perspective on form, to create an entirely contemporary and futuristic shape.

(left) Designer: Ivan Chermayeff Client/Publisher: Domus (right) Designer: Yoichiro Kawaguchi Client/Publisher: Domus

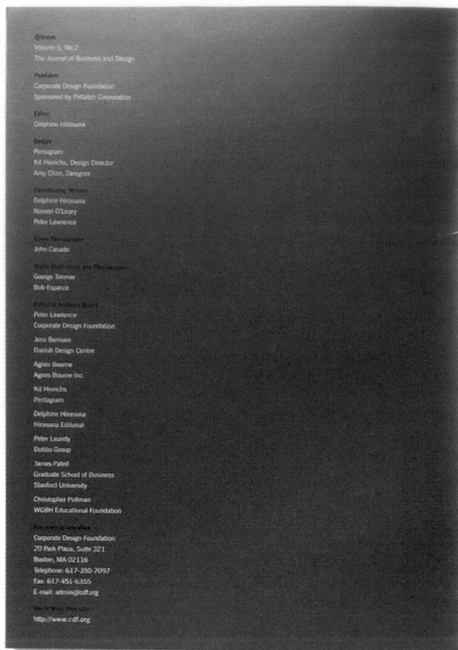

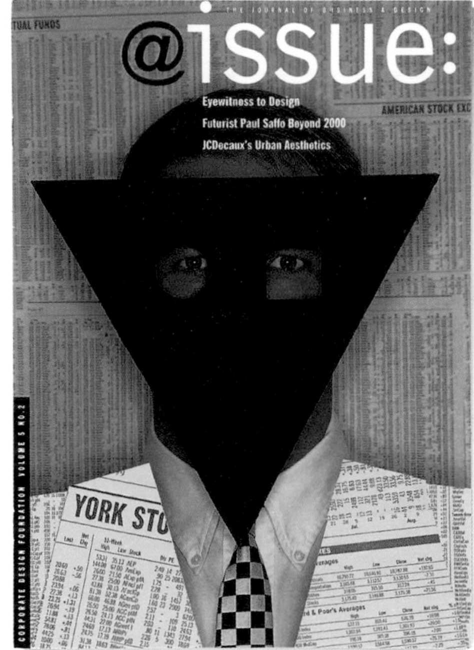

Jean-Claude Decaux
Chairman
JCDecaux S.A., Paris

As a young man more than 35 years ago, Jean-Claude Decaux made a living posting bills on buildings around Paris. His modest livelihood came to an abrupt halt after the local government declared this practice illegal. That's when Decaux came up with a better idea – one that would allow him to continue posting bills and do it in a way that would contribute to the quality of life and beauty of the city.

Decaux's inspiration came one stormy day when he noticed people getting soaked while waiting for a city bus to come by. Why not offer to build bus shelters for free in exchange for the right to sell advertising on them, Decaux thought. He took his proposal to the Mayor of Lyon and got permission to go ahead. That rainy day marked the start of the world's largest street furniture company – with projected revenues in 1999 of $1.4 billion, primarily generated from advertising.

Today the street furniture of JCDecaux S.A. is installed in more than 1,200 cities around the world. In early 1999, it acquired Havas Media Communication-Outdoor Advertising, Europe's largest billboard advertising firm, extending the company's presence into 31 countries and more than 11,000 cities.

Over the years, the company has expanded its street furniture offerings from bus shelters and kiosks to news racks, traffic signage, light posts, litterbins, benches, interactive information panels and automatic public toilets. "When I created the first advertising bus shelter, free of charge to local authorities, I wanted to remedy the problem of dilapidated equipment; to fight against surplus and unsightly advertising, and, by revaluing it, make known the lively role that quality advertising can play," says Decaux, who still manages the privately owned company along with his sons, Jean-Francois and Jean-Charles. "Our main concern has been the cleanliness of cities and the setting up of public services essential to the comfort of city dwellers."

Although the field of private contractors vying for city contracts has become crowded, JCDecaux has distinguished itself by producing street furniture that is as attractive as it is functional. In addition to its own in-house talent, it has commissioned some 30 of the world's best architects and designers to create a wide array of street furniture that is sensitive to the cultural urban nuances of their native countries. Jean-Michel Wilmotte, Philippe Starck, Mario Bellini, Sir Norman

Jean-Francois Decaux
Chief Executive Officer
JCDecaux S.A., Paris

Foster, Massimo Vignelli, Martin Szekely, Charles Gwathmey, Robert Stern, Peter Eisenman, Knud Holscher and James Polshek are among the legendary names who have contributed to JCDecaux's furniture line. Porsche's design department, Style Porsche, also used its affinity for the street to come up with striking designs, as did the Mackintosh School of Architecture in Glasgow, Scotland.

JCDecaux sees its role as designing what French architect Jean-Michel Wilmotte calls a city's "interior architecture," deserving of "as much thought as that given to private spaces." It believes that bus shelters,

Design Firm: Pentagram Design Creative Director: Kit Hinrichs Designer: Amy Chan Photographer: John Casado Client/Publisher: @issue

VOGUE

DEC
£3.00

SPECIAL
MILLENNIUM
ISSUE

THE FUTURE STARTS HERE

THE NEW BODY

THE NEW CLOTHES

THE NEW YOU

VOGUE

DEC
£3.00

SPECIAL
MILLENNIUM
ISSUE

A CENTURY OF STYLE

THE COOLEST PEOPLE

THE LOOKS THAT MATTERED

THE BEST OF TIMES

BRITISH EDITION
USA$7.75 CAN$9.95

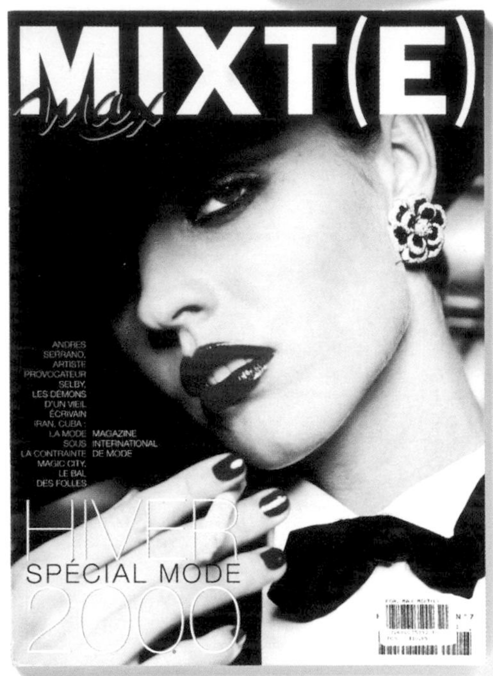
MIXT(E)
ANDRES SERRANO, ARTISTE PROVOCATEUR
SELBY, LES DÉMONS D'UN VIEIL ÉCRIVAIN
IRAN, CUBA : LA MODE SOUS LA CONTRAINTE
MAGIC CITY, LE BAL DES FOLLES
MAGAZINE INTERNATIONAL DE MODE
HIVER
SPÉCIAL MODE
2000

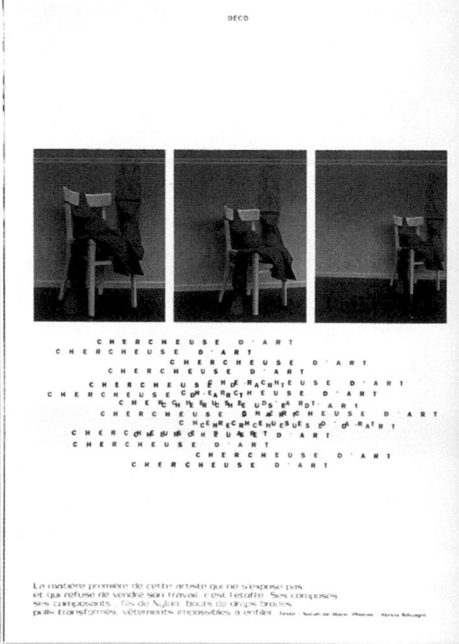

DECO
CHERCHEUSE D'ART
La matière première de cette artiste qui ne s'expose pas
et qui refuse de vendre son travail, c'est l'étoffe. Ses composés
ses composants : fils de Nylon, bouts de draps brodés
pulls transformés, vêtements impossibles à enfiler.

Art Directors: Christian Ravera, Guy Guglieri Client/Publisher: Max Mix(e)

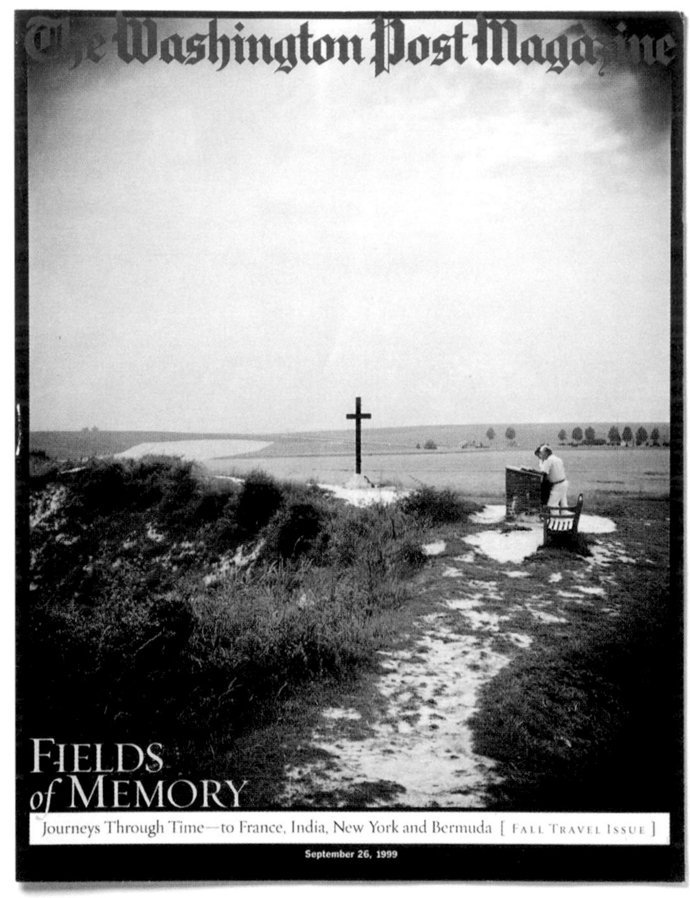

(left) Design Firm: Hirano Studio Inc. Art Director: Mitsuo Katsui Designer: Keiko Hirano Photographer: Yasuo Saji Client: Morisawa & Company Ltd. (right) Art Directors: Kelly Doe, Lisa Schrieber Designer: Karen Tanaka Photo Editor: Keith W. Jenkins Client: Washington Post Magazine

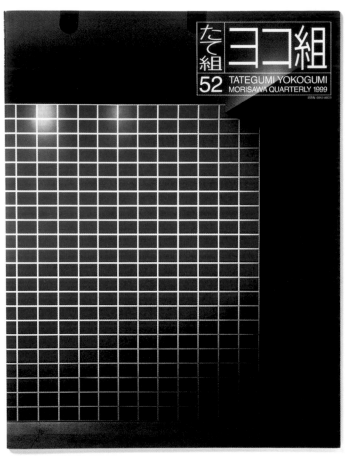

Design Firm: Frost Design Ltd. Art & Creative Director: Vince Frost Designers: Vince Frost, Melanie Mues Client: British Design & Art Direction

Design Firm: Sussman/Prejza & Co., Inc. Art Director & Designer: John Johnston Creative Director: Deborah Sussman Photographers: Jim Simmons, Annette Del Zoppo, Everett & Soule Client: Universal Creative, Orlando Florida

UNIVER
CINEPLEX
LOEWS
THEATRES

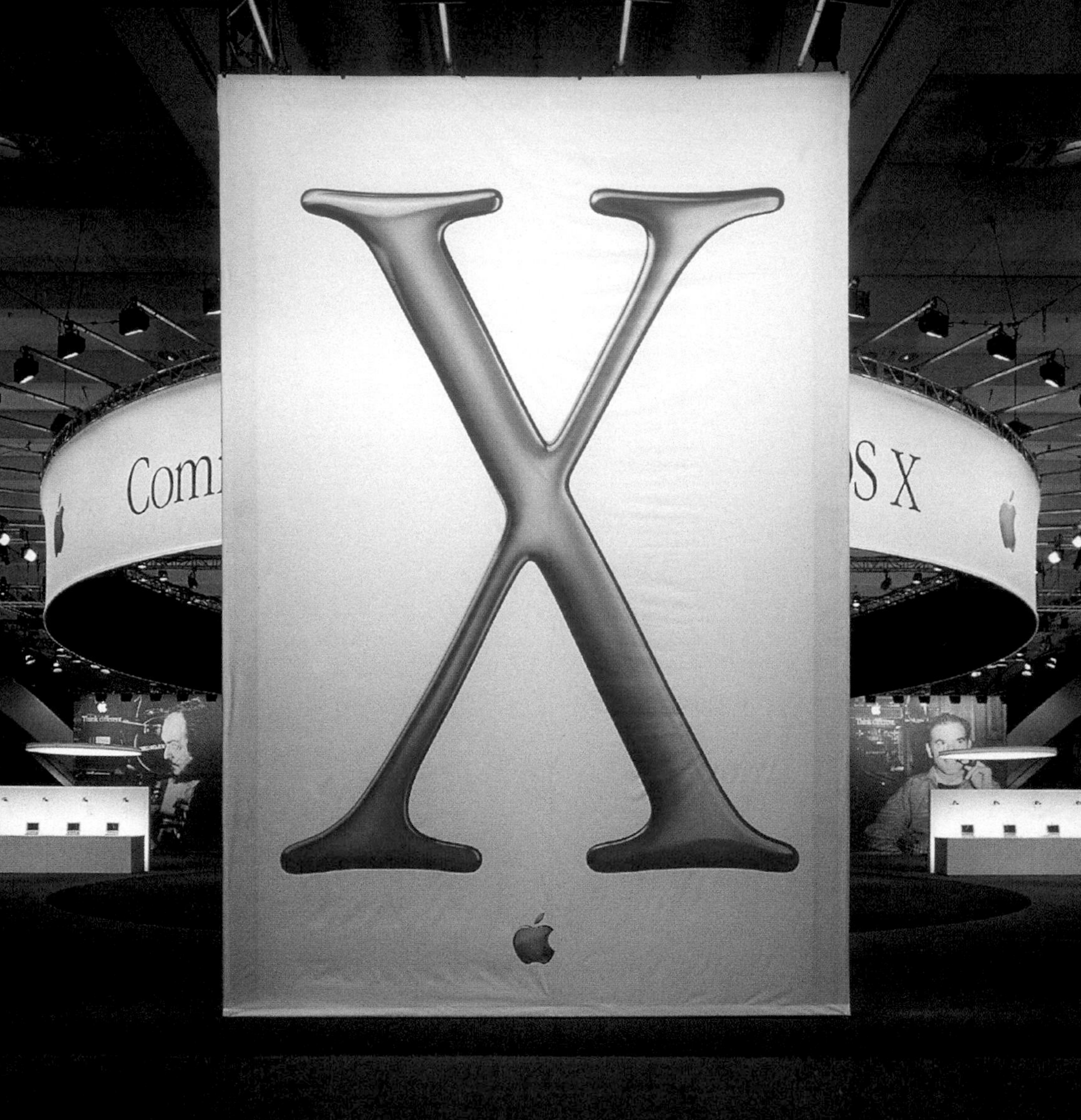
X

Design Firm: USWeb/CKS Creative Director: Andy Dreyfus Designers: Patti Glover, Aki Shelton, Amy Wyler, Dana Ahlfeldt, Eric Wendt, Tim Kobe, Mike Dolan, Wilhelm Oehl Client: Apple Computer

Design Firm: Duffy Design and Interactive Art Director: Kobe Suvongse Creative Director: Joe Duffy Designers: Kobe Suvongse, Craig Duffney, Tom Kelley, Ron Gallas Photographer: Dana Wheelock Illustrators: Kobe Suvongse, Craig Duffney, Jim Holmberg, Dan Michiel, Andy Powell, Leon Huscha Client: Zelo (Rick Webb Restaurants)

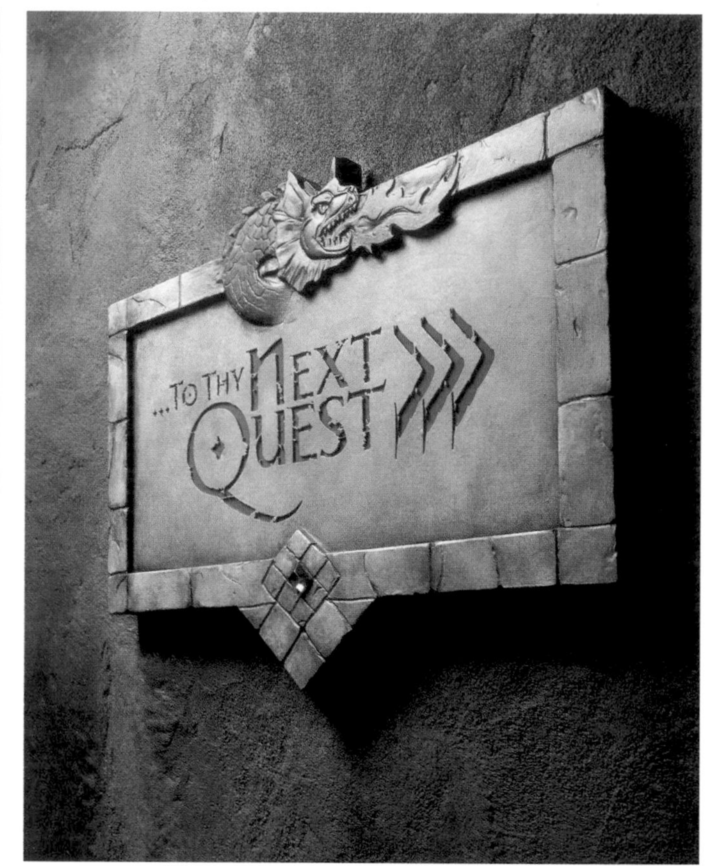

Design Firm: David Carter Design Art Directors: Joe Marrs, Eric Jany Creative Directors: Lori B. Wilson, Mark Woodbury, Steve Leff Designers: Tien Pham, Steve Oliver Photographer: Rich Klein Client: Universal Studios

Design Firm: Vanderbyl Design Art & Creative Director: Michael Vanderbyl Designers: Michael Vanderbyl, Peter Fishel, Jeremy Regenbogen Photographer: Hedrich Blessing Client: Teknion, Inc.

Design Firm: Lorenc & Yoo Design Art & Creative Director: Jan Lorenc Designers: Chung Youl Yoo, Veda Sammy, Steve McCall Architect: Steve Hepler Photographer: Rion Rizzo Illustrators: Michelle Scott, Veda Sammy Client: McWane Center

MOVIES cafe

TICKETS
ADVENTURE HALLS
STORE
IMAX DOME
JOHN W. WOODS THEATER

Design Firm: Graphics & Designing Inc. Art Director & Designer: Toshihiro Onimaru Creative Director: Takanori Aiba Client: Cube Foods

Design Firm: Lippa Pearce Design Ltd. Art & Creative Director: Harry Pearce Designers: Harry Pearce, Jeremy Roots Illustrator: Jeremy Roots Client: Halfords Ltd.

Client: Lifetime Television NYC

Design Firm: Lorenc & Yoo Design Art Director: Jan Lorenc, Rory Myers Creative Director: Jan Lorenc Designer: David Park, Gary Flesher, Steve McCall, Chung Youl Yoo Photographer: Rion Rizzo Illustrator: Rory Myers Copywriter: Matthew Porter

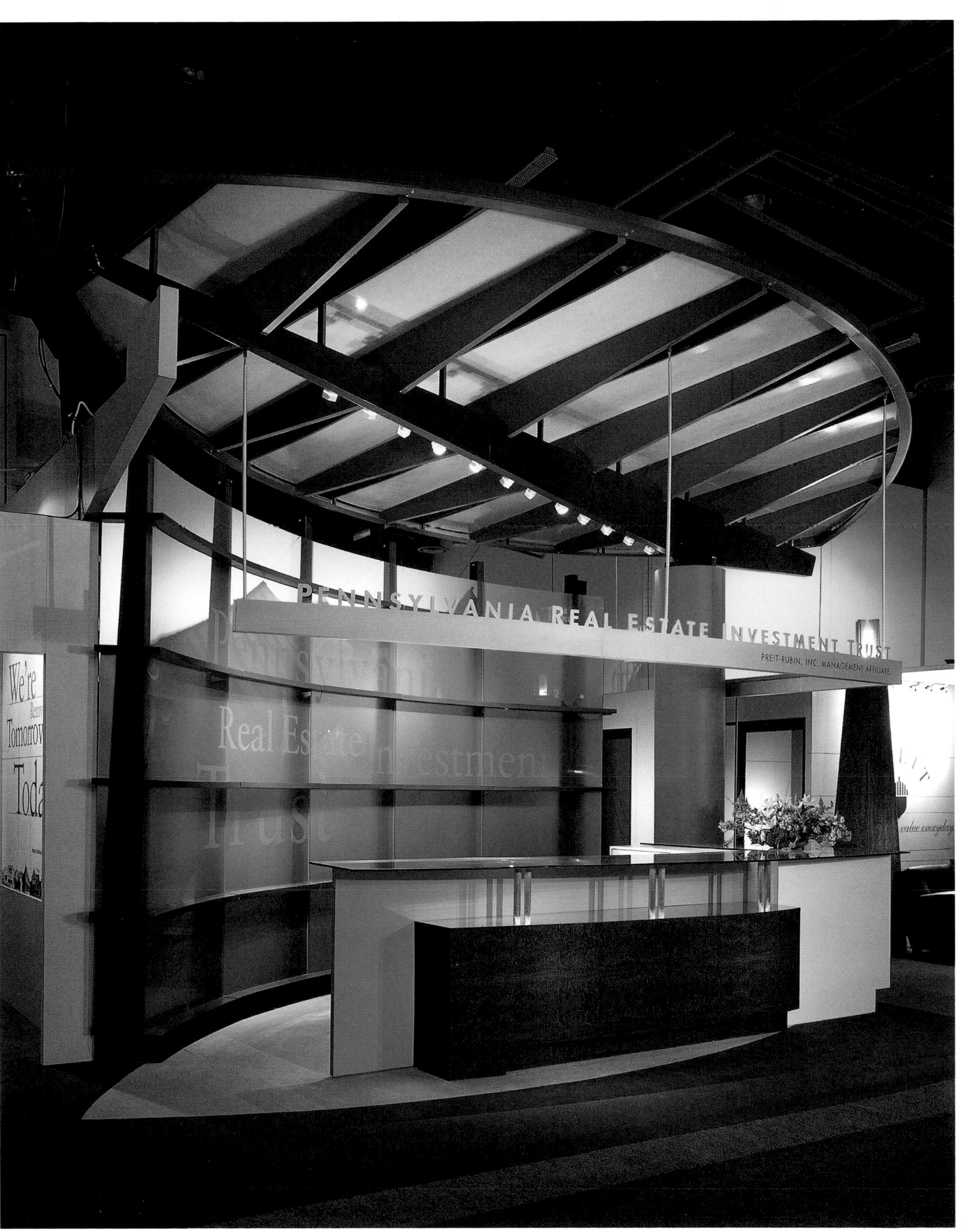

Design Firm: Lorenc & Yoo Design Art Director: Jan Lorenc Creative Directors: Jan Lorenc, Beth Cochran Designers: David Park, Veda Sammy, Steve McCall, Chung Youl Yoo Photographer: Rion Rizzo Illustrator: Veda Sammy Copywriter: Beth Cochran Client: Pennsylvania Real Estate Investment Trust

FIRST UNION

FIRST UNION

Design Firm: Lorenc & Yoo Design Art Director: Jan Lorenc Creative Directors: Jan Lorenc, Beth Cochran Designers: David Park, Steve McCall, Veda Sammy Photographer: Rion Rizzo Illustrator: Veda Sammy Copywriter: Beth Cochran Client: First Union Management Exhibits 112,113

Exhibits 114,115

Creative & Art Director: Kit Hinrichs Photographer: Lucca Pioltelli Client: AIGA

Design Firm: Mauk Design Art Director: Mitchell Mauk Designer: Adam Brodsley, James Pennington-Kent Photographer: Andy Caulfield Client: Foote, Cone & Belding

Design Firm: Fullblastinc.com Creative Director & Designer: N. Todd Skiles Photographer: Bob Waldman Illustrator: Janice Emmerson Copywriters: Neil Webster, David Weigell, Perry Novelli Client: Chums

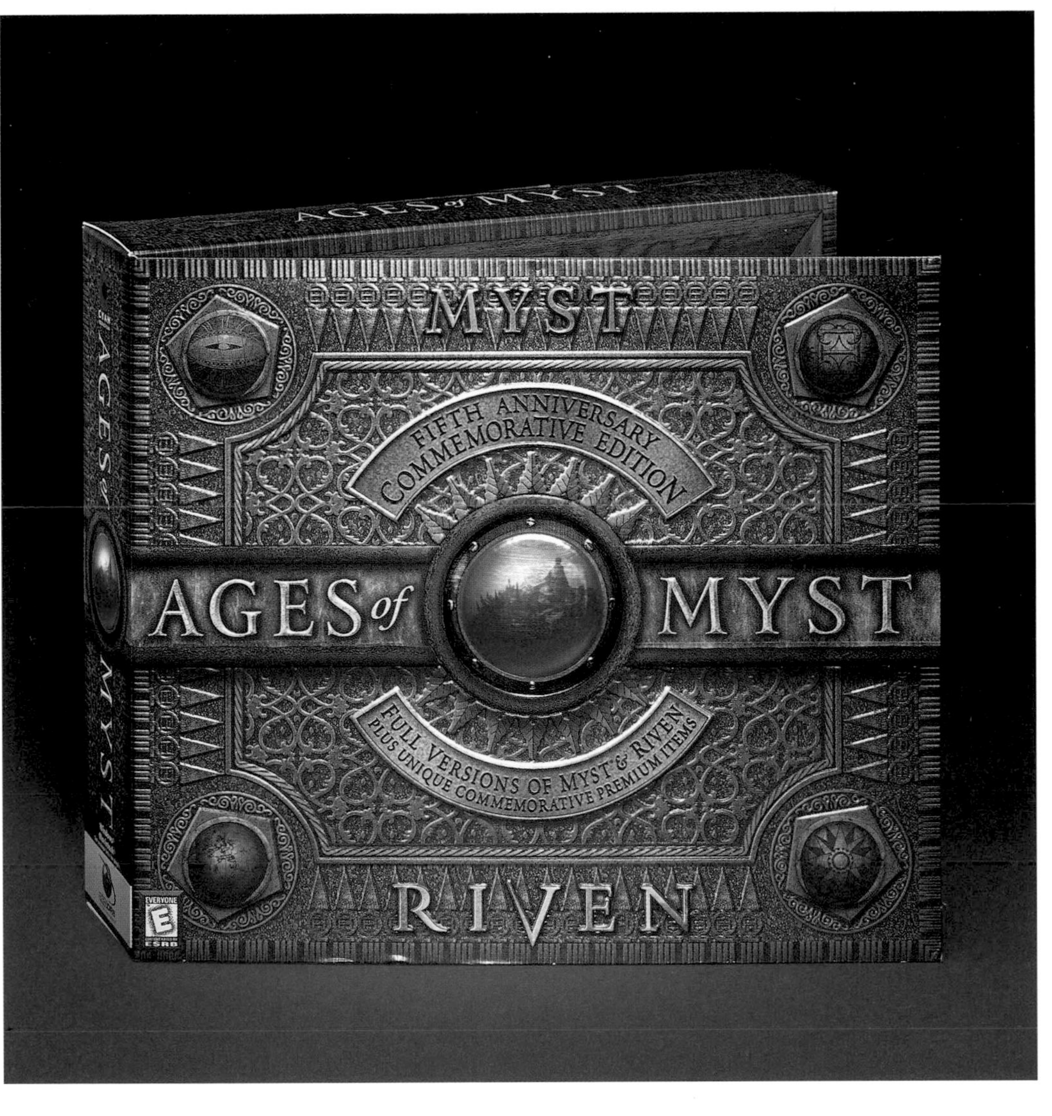

Design Firm: Deutsch Design Works Creative Director: Barry Deutsch Designers: Jacques Rossouw, Lori Wynn, Eric Pino, John Lucas Client: Red Orb Division of Broderbund Software

Design Firm: Karlic Design Associates Art & Creative Director, Designer: Ken Karlic Illustrator: Fol Turgeon Copywriter: Marlene England Client: ZC Sterling

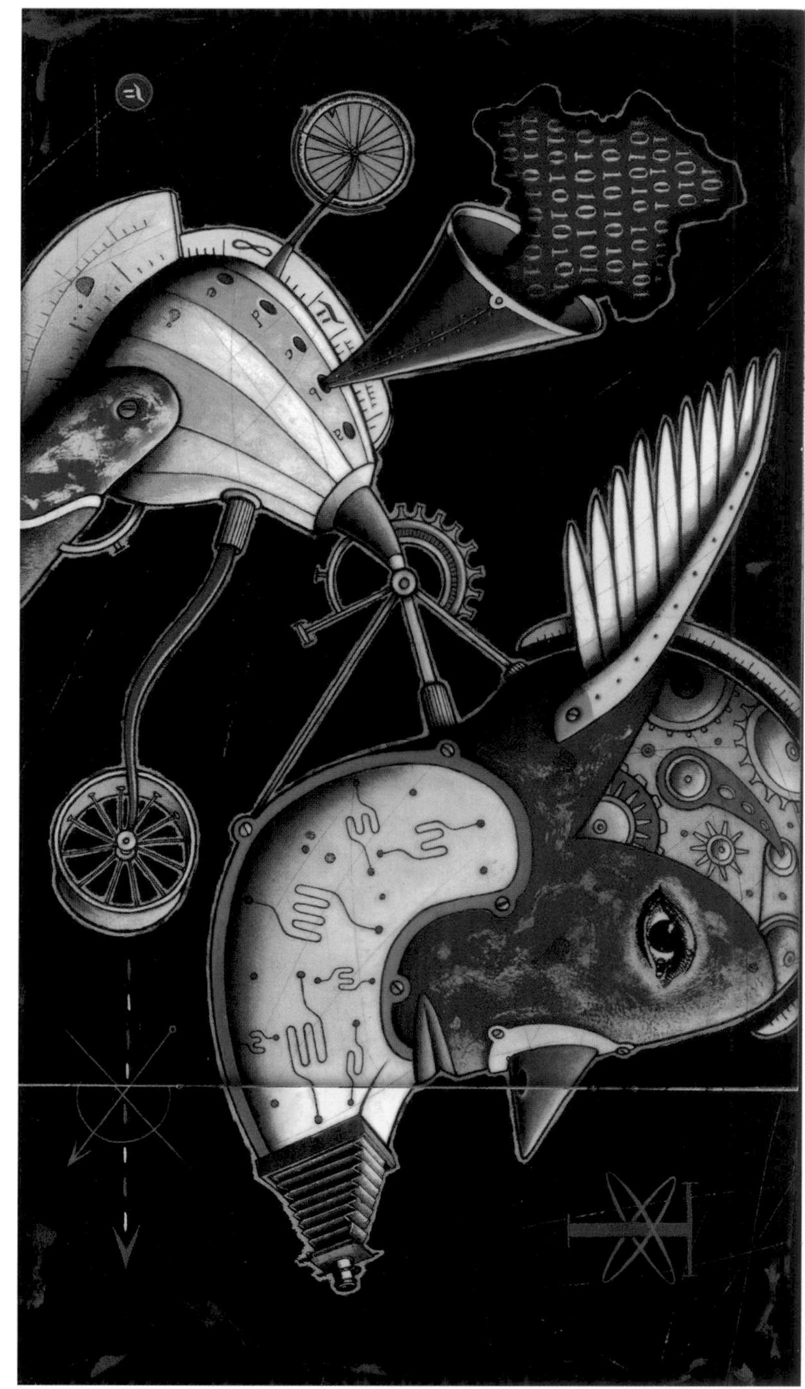

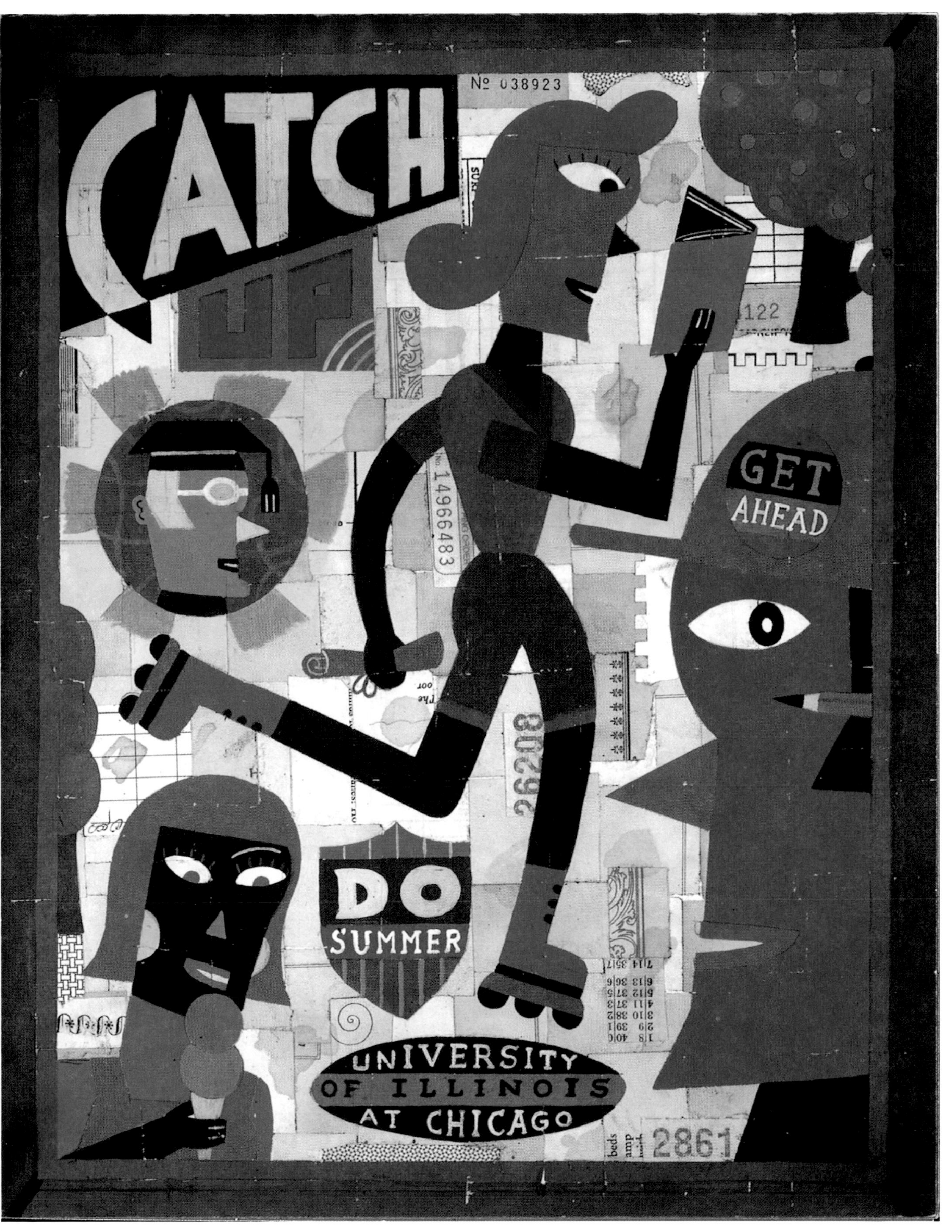

Design Firm: Group/Chicago Inc. Art & Creative Director, Designer: Barbara Lynk Illustrator: Noah Woods Copywriters: Rina Campbell, Cordelia Maloney Client: University of Illinois at Chicago

Design Firm: Gill Fishman Assocociates Creative Director: Gill Fishman Designer: Tammy Torrey Illustrator: Guy Billout Client: American Arbitration Association

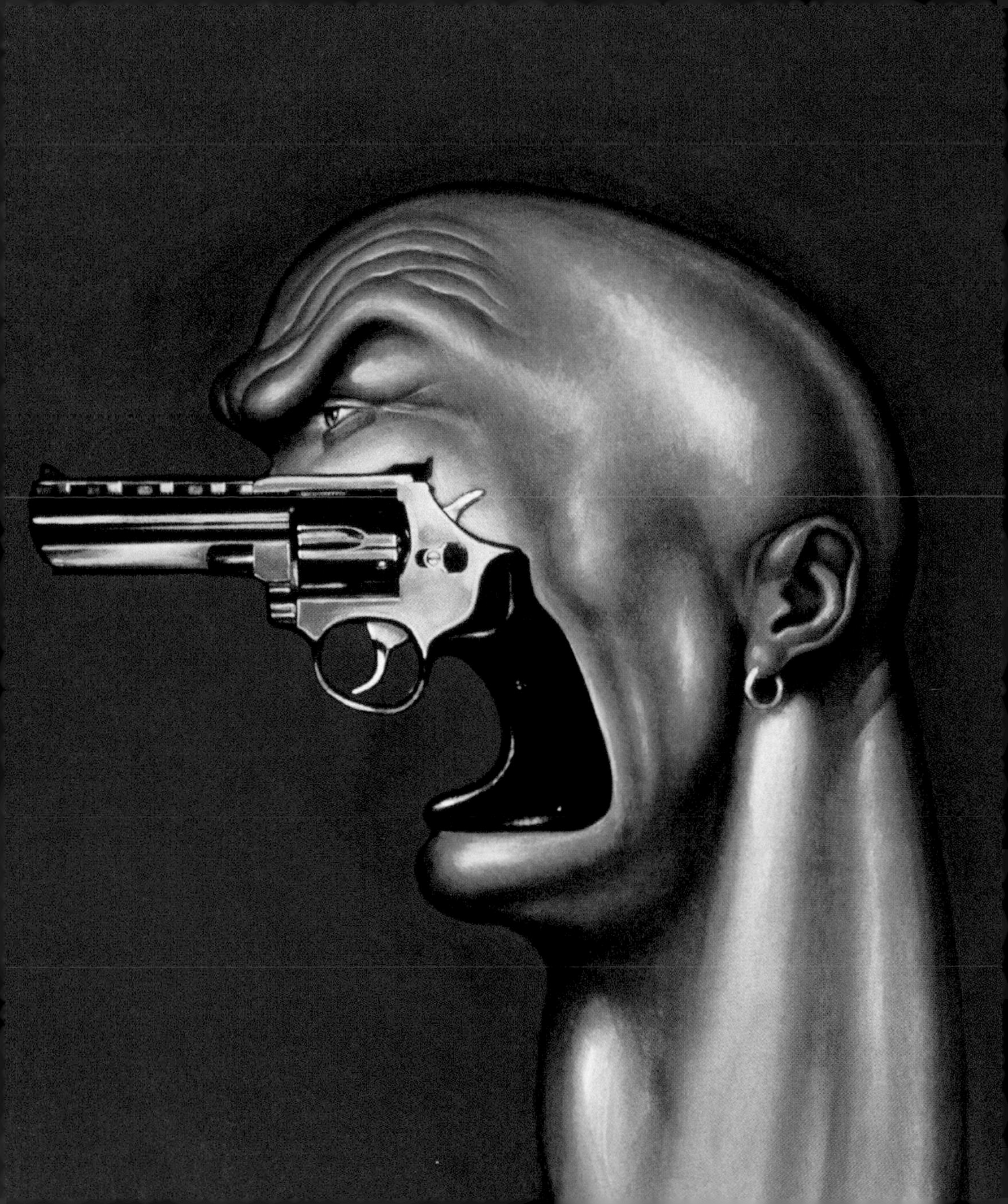

Design Firm: Olver Dunlop Associates Art Director & Designer: Patti Kowalczyk Client: Marlena Agency

Design Firm: Avon Books Art Director: Gail Dubov Illustrator: Cathleen Toelke Client: Avon Books

Design Firm: Rolf Jansson Design Illustrator: Rolf Jansson Client: Vart Land Publishing House

Design Firm: Laura Coe Design Associates Art & Creative Director, Designer, Illustrator: Ryoichi Yotsumoto Client: Ryoichi Yotsumoto

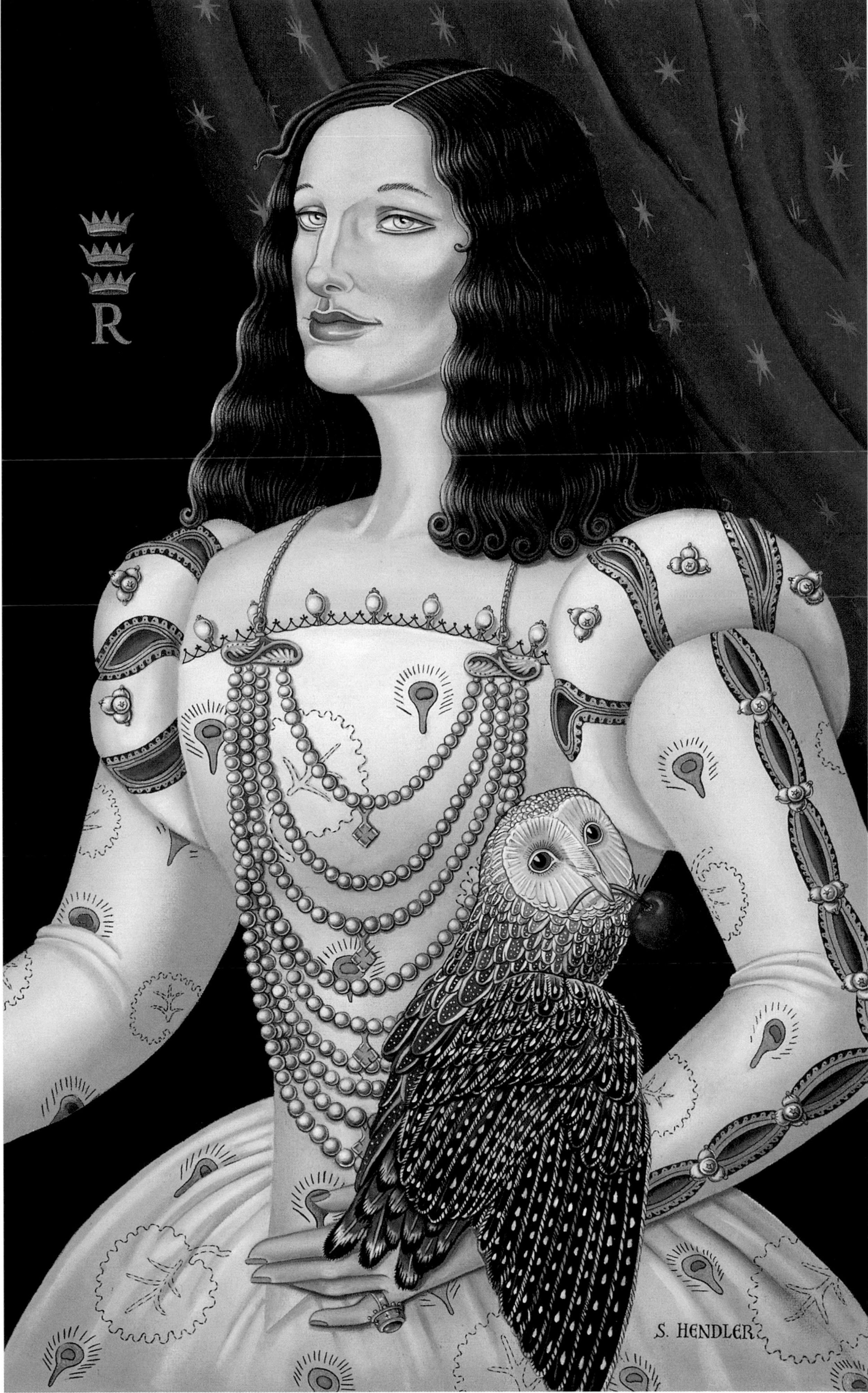

Design Firm: Sandra Hendler Designer & Illustrator: Sandra Hendler Client: S. Kooney

Design Firm: Templin Brink Design Creative Director & Designer: Joel Templin Client: KEA

KEA
INC.
KEITH E. ACKERT
PRESIDENT
612 386 5216
CELL PHONE
651 450 9958
OFFICE PHONE
651 455 3937
FACSIMILE
Mpls. St. Paul
MAILING INFORMATION
8795 RIVER HEIGHTS WAY • INVER GROVE HEIGHTS, MN 55076

Design Firm: Clockwork Apple Inc. Designer: Christo Holloway Illustrators: John McGarvey, John Kitses Client: Chris Collins

Chris Collins Studio 35 West 20th Street, NYC 10011 (212)633.1670 Fax:(212)727.1518

BONINI PHOTOGRAPHY
615 SE ALDER SUITE 300
PORTLAND OREGON 97214

T 503 239 5421
F 503 239 5621

STEVE BONINI
JAN HURST

BONINI PHOTOGRAPHY
615 SE ALDER SUITE 300
PORTLAND OREGON 97214

T 503 239 5421
F 503 239 5621

47

TO:

Design Firm: Sandstrom Design Art & Creative Director: Steven Sandstrom Designer: Starlee Matz Client: Bonini Photography

Design Firm: Hirano Studio Inc. Art Director & Designer: Keiko Hirano Client: Himeji Welcome 21 Executive Committee

The Food Bank

Keeping hunger at bay in Nebraska and western Iowa / Member of Second Harvest National Food Bank Network
6824 J St., Omaha, NE 68117-1016 / 402-331-1213 Fax: 402-331-6632 / www.discoveromaha.com/community/group/foodbank

The Food Bank

6824 J St., Omaha, NE 68117-1016

Design Firm: Bozell Art Director & Designer: Ron Sack Photographer: Bob Ervin Copywriter: Jackie Ostrowicki Client: The Food Bank

BOBMURPHYWRITER
150 Chestnut Street, Suite 700, Providence, Rhode Island 02903
phone: (401) 272-4613 email: murphycopy@aol.com
BOBMURPHYWRITER

Design Firm: Chris Herron Design Art Director, Designer & Illustrator: Chris Herron Creative Director & Copywriter: Bob Murphy Client: Bob Murphy, Writer

Design Firm: JOED Design Inc. Creative Director: Edward Rebek Designer: Tim Pressley Photographer: Howard Ash Client: Aumiller Youngquist P.C.

(top to bottom) Design Firm: Starkwhite Client: Dave Shafer Photography Design Firm: Woodpile Studios, Inc. Art & Creative Director: George Jacoma Designer & Illustrator: Peter Buttecali Client: Jacoma Design Design Firm: Templin Brink Design Creative Director: Joel Templin Designer: Paul Howalt Client: Warren Miller Entertainment Design Firm: Graphic Content Inc. Art Director & Designer: Art Garcia Client: Vipers Basketball Team Design Firm: Templin Brink Design Creative Director & Designer: Joel Templin Client: [illegible] Photography

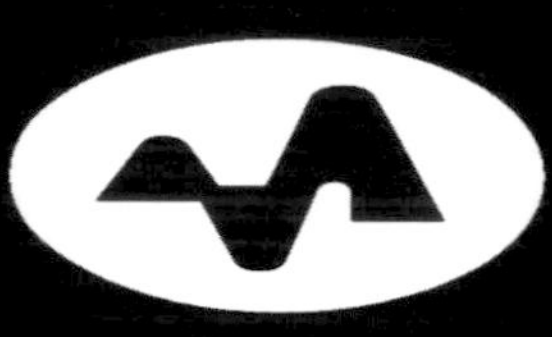

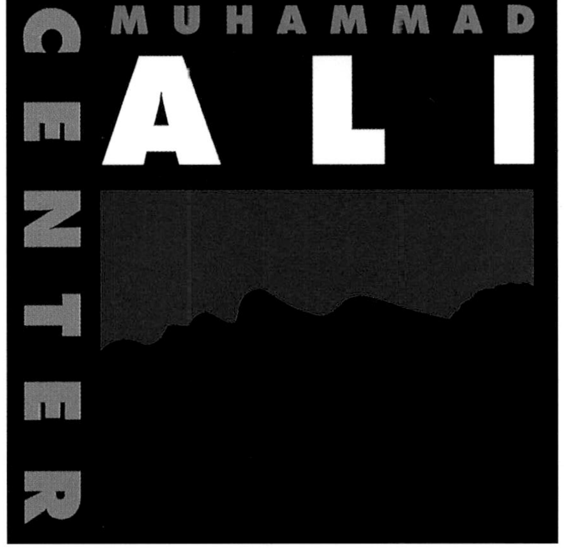

Design Firm: Jett Sport Art Director: Clare Jett Designer & Illustrator: Michael Schwab Client: Muhammad Ali Center

(top to bottom) Design Firm: Graphic Content Inc. Art Director: Art Garcia Designer: Art Garcia Client: Mothers Against Drunk Driving Design Firm: Design Edge Designer: Jane Brooks Client: Visionary Research Design Firm: Principia Graphica Art Director: Heidi Rickabaugh Designer: Clint Gorthy Client: Oregon Corporation for Affordable Housing Design Firm: Pentagram Design Art & Creative Director, Designer: Kit Hinrichs Client: Auto Web Design Firm: Iridium Marketing & Design Art Directors: Jean-Luc Denat, Mario L'Ecuyer Designer: Mario L'Ecuyer Illustrator: David Plunkert Client: Iridium Marketing & Design

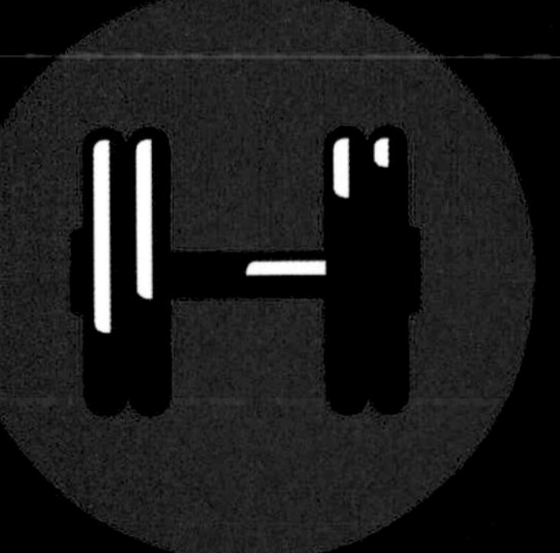

Design Firm: Sibley/Peteet Design Art Director & Designer: Mark Brinkman Creative Director: Matt Heck Client: Hyde Park Gym

Design Firm: Keith Harris Design Art Director, Designer & Illustrator: Keith Harris Client: Freunde Der Antonow Designer: Amy J. Nadaskay Client: Little Giants Design Firm: Duffy Design and Interactive Art Director & Illustrator: Tom Riddle Creative Director: Joe Duffy Designers: Tom Riddle, Nate Hinz Copywriter: John Jarvis Client: International Transportation Corp. Design Firm: Pentagram Design Inc. Creative Director

THE
OLD
KIRK

Design Firm: Pentagram Design Ltd. Art Director: Justus Oehler Client: The Old Kirk

Design Firm: Duffy Design and Interactive Art Director, Designer & Illustrator: Alan Colvin Creative Director: Joe Duffy Client: La Madeleine Designer: Amy J. Nadaskay Illustrator: Eric Larson Client: Insignia Restaurant Design Firm: Duffy Design and Interactive Art Director: Alan Colvin Client: Nordstrom Design Firm: Automatic Art and Design Art Director: Charles Wilkin Designer: Charles Wilkin Client: Planet Coffee

Logos 144,145

Design Firm: Kosaka Design Creative Director: Wayne Kosaka Designer: Jeff Welch Client: Kimpton Group/Atwood Cafe

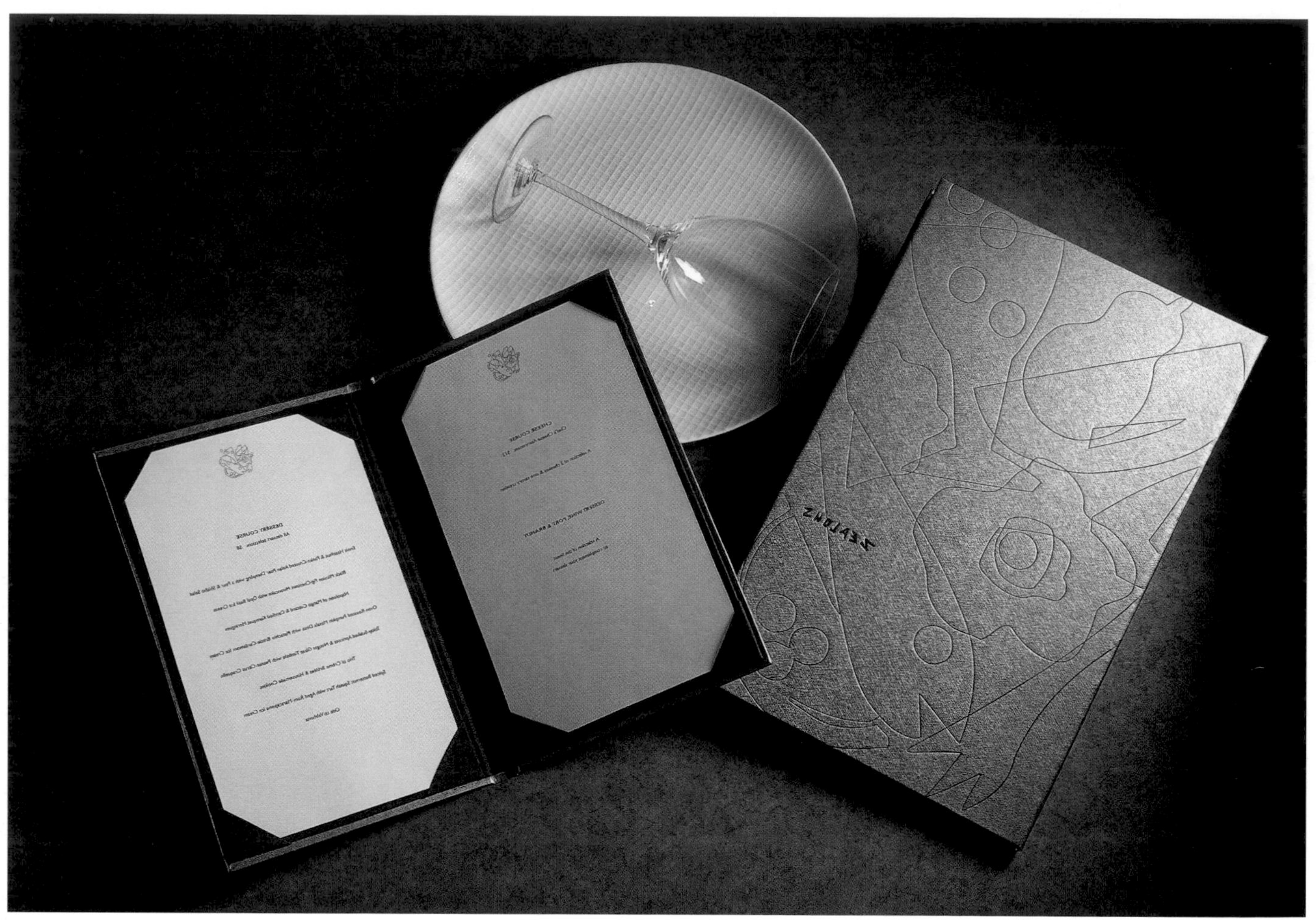

Design Firm: JOED Design Inc. Creative Director & Designer: Edward Rebek Client: Zealous Restaurant

Design Firm: Automatic Art and Design Art Director: Frank Gargulio Designer & Illustrator: Charles Wilkin Client: Capricorn Records

Art Directors: Keith Gold, Joe Vavra Creative Director: Keith Gold Designer & Illustrator: Joe Vavra Client: Time-Life Entertainment

Design Firm: Sagmeister Inc., NY Art Director: Stefan Sagmeister Designer & Illustrator: Motoka Hada Photographers: Danny Clinch, Dan Winters Client: Radioactive Records/Universal Mus

duke
ellington
the centennial edition
1
2
3
4
the SHOWMAN
5
6

(opposite page, top of this page) Design Firm: Red Herring Design Art Director: Carol Bobolts Creative Director: Janet DeMattes Designer: Rex Bonomelli Client: BMG Classics/RCA Victor (this page, bottom) Design Firm: World Circuit Client: WEA/Atlantic/Nonesuch Adapted by David Steinke

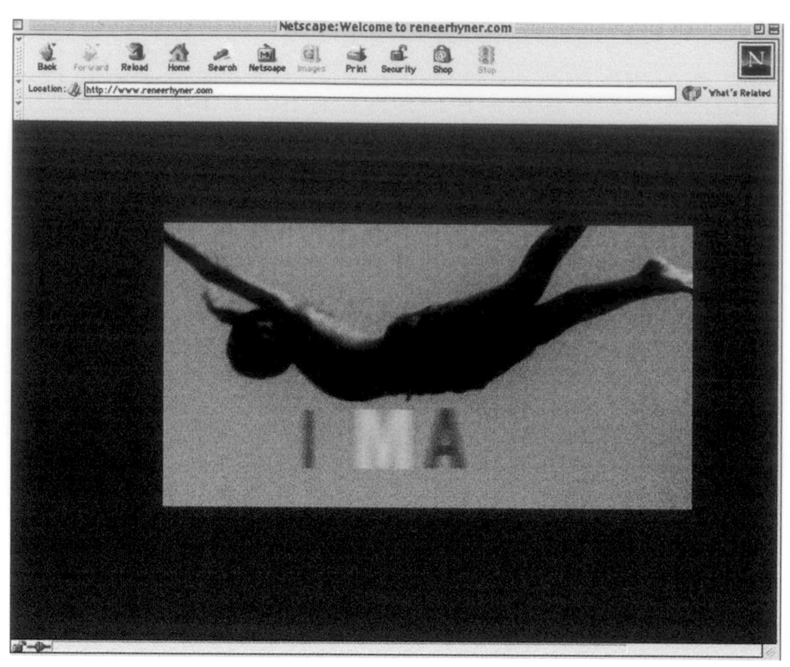
Netscape: Welcome to reneerhyner.com
Back
Forward
Reload
Home
Search
Netscape
Images
Print
Security
Shop
Stop
Location:
http://www.reneerhyner.com
What's Related
I MA

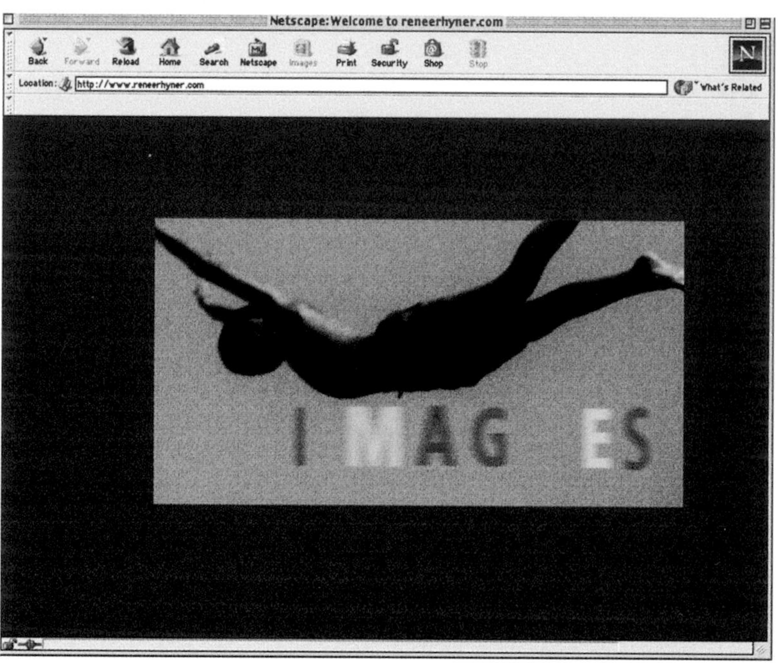
Netscape: Welcome to reneerhyner.com
Back
Forward
Reload
Home
Search
Netscape
Images
Print
Security
Shop
Stop
Location:
http://www.reneerhyner.com
What's Related
I MAG ES

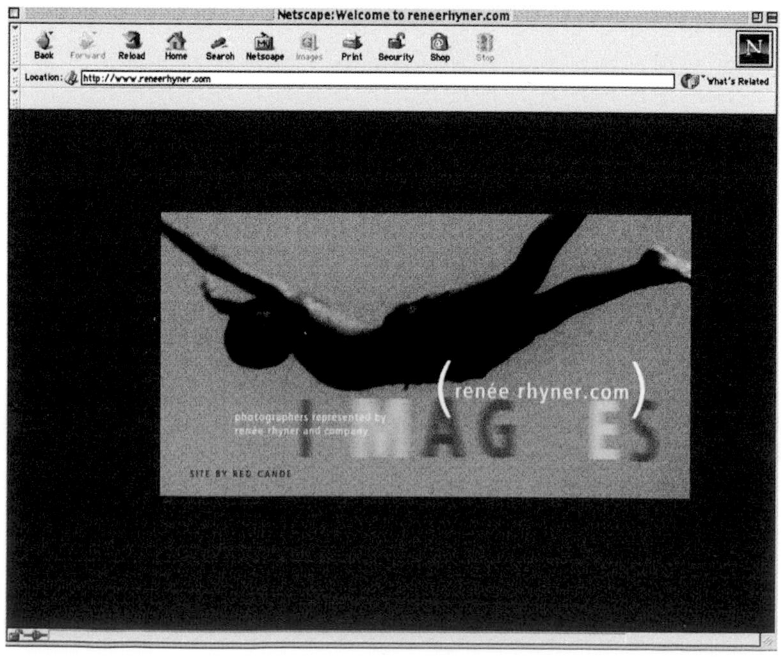
Netscape: Welcome to reneerhyner.com
Back
Forward
Reload
Home
Search
Netscape
Images
Print
Security
Shop
Stop
Location:
http://www.reneerhyner.com
What's Related
(renée rhyner.com)
photographers represented by
renée rhyner and company
I MAG ES
SITE BY RED CANDE

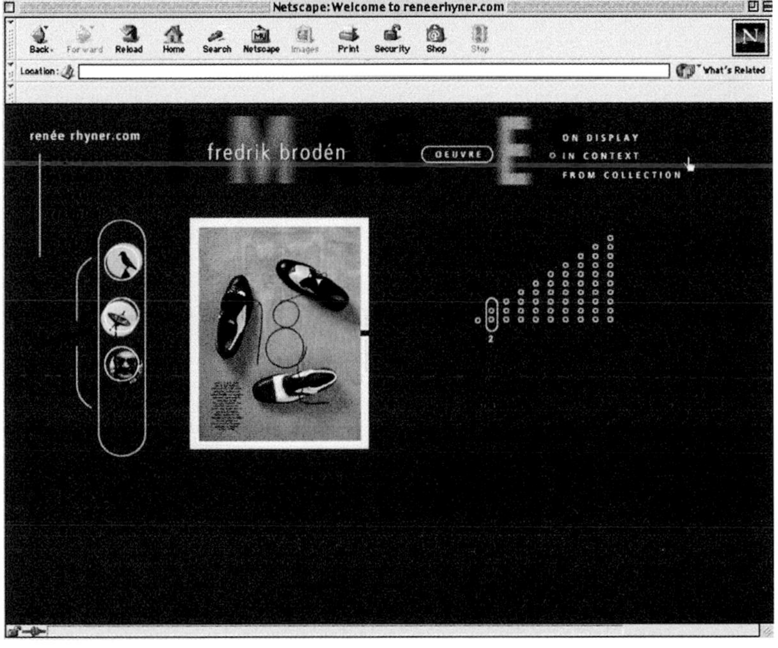

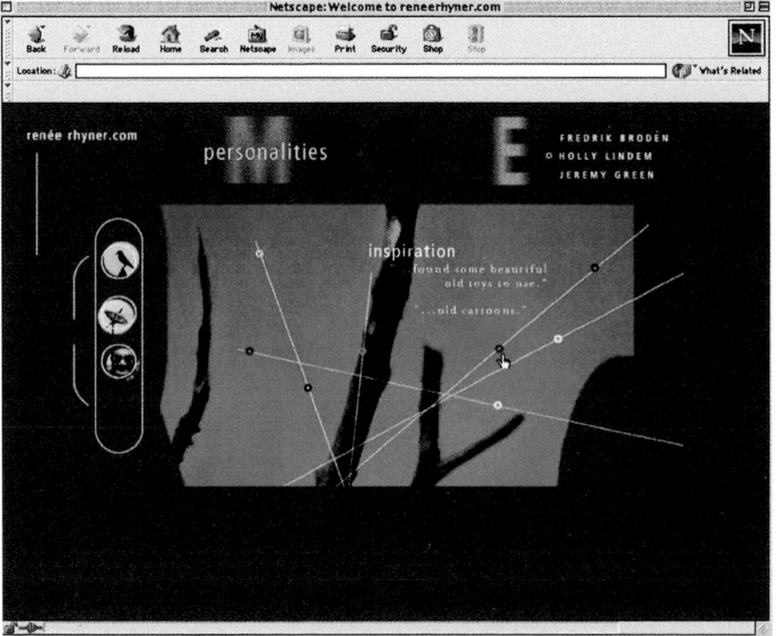

Design Firm: Red Canoe Art Director: Deb Koch Creative Director & Designer: Caroline Kavanagh Photographers: Fredrik Brodén, Holly Lindem, Jeremy Green Client: Renée Rhyner & Company

ISABELLA ROSSELLINI'S
MANIFESTO

I believe beauty can be of many kinds.

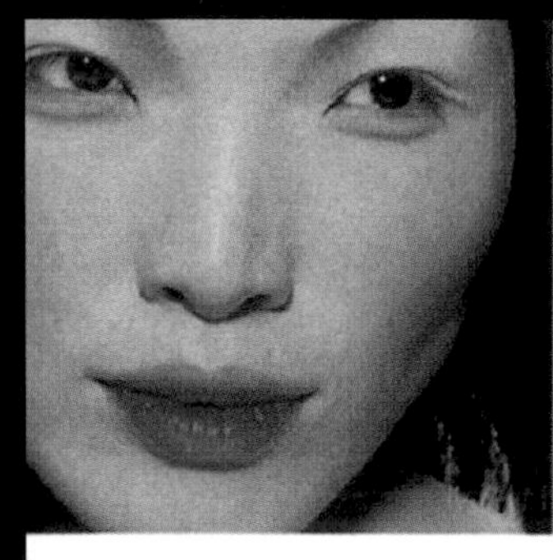

UNIQUENESS

The beauty I admire ... eness, our absolute singularity.

That for me is style.

That for me is style.

Design Firm: Design: M/W Art Director: Allison Williams Creative Directors: Allison Williams, J. Phillips Williams Designer: Yael Eisele Photographers: Miles Aldridge, Grant Peterson Client: Isabella Rossellini's Manifesto

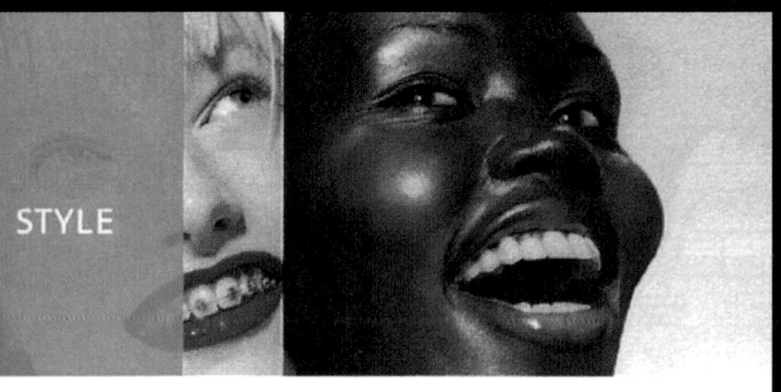

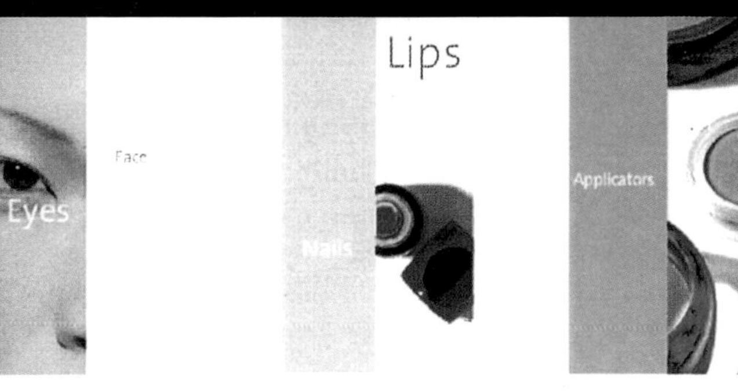

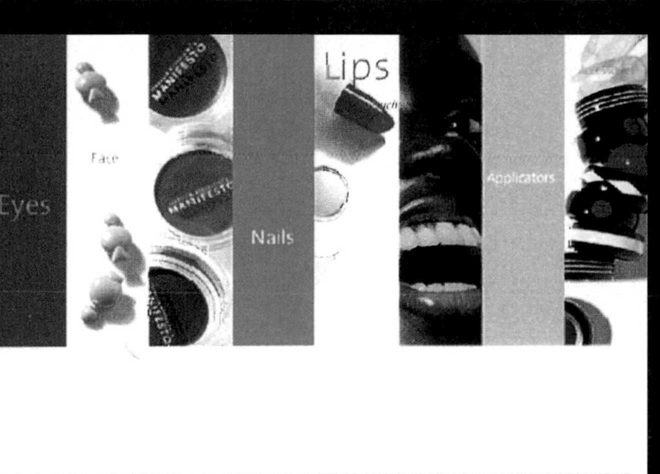

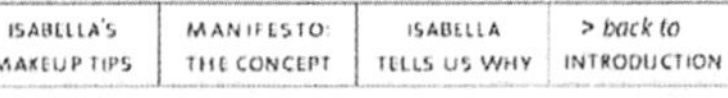

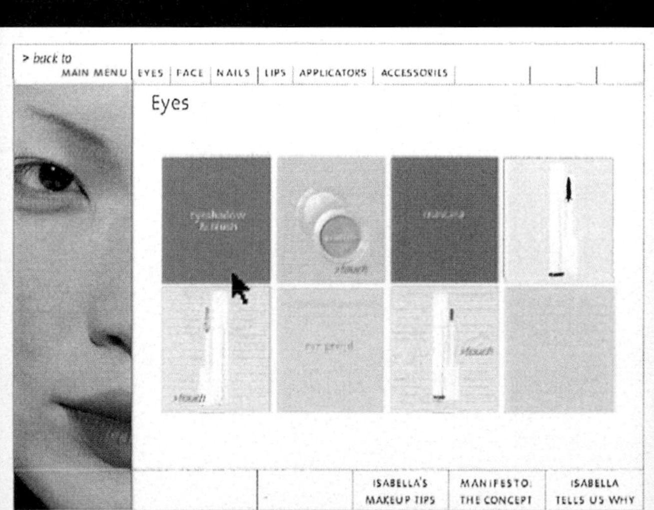

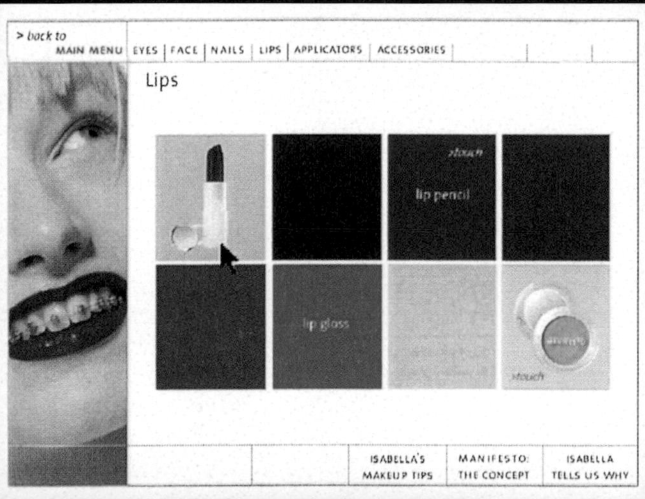

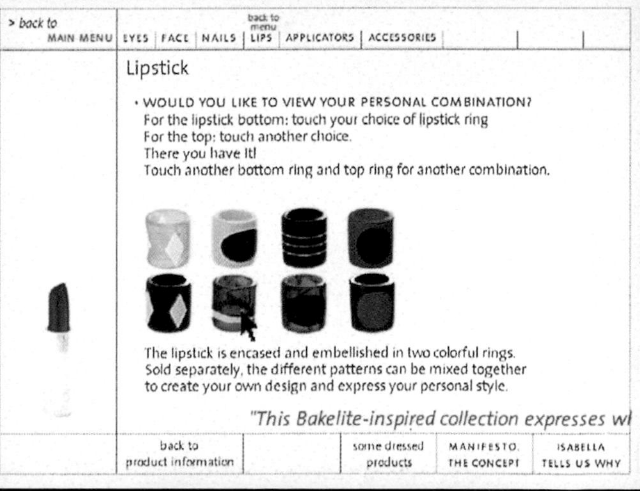

Netscape: Star Wars: Episode I: Racer on Nintendo 64
NINTENDO 64
STAR WARS EPISODE I RACER
Two engines. One racer. No limits and no fear.
It's Star Wars: Episode I: Racer, the game that lets you build and pilot your own Podracer.
With speeds up to 600 mph, a lineup of 23 Podracers, and the chance to race through more than 20 distinct tracks, it's time to bring home the movie's biggest thrill.
So fire up your Podracer and blast across the most treacherous tracks in the universe. Try not. Do.
STAR WARS RACER
NINTENDO 64 BUNDLE
PLAYERS GUIDE
PODRACERS
RACER TRACKS
HISTORY
STRATEGY
TRIVIA
RACER CARDS
GALLERY
PODRACER PIT STOP
Netscape: Star Wars: Episode I: Racer on Nintendo 64
NINTENDO 64
STAR WARS EPISODE I RACER
PODRACERS
BACK TO MENU
TOP VIEW
ANAKIN SKYWALKER
There's something special about young Anakin Skywalker. He has an amazing mechanical ability (he built his Podracer from scratch) and seems to have a natural skill for Podracing.
MODIFIED RADON-ULZER 620C RACING ENGINES
This home-built Podracer has great traction, good repair capabilities, and a great cooling system. It's not that fast, but when the Force is with you...who cares.
VEHICLE STATISTICS
TRACTION
TURNING
ACCEL
TOP SPEED
AIR BRAKE
COOLING
REPAIR
SIDE VIEW
BACK
NEXT
PODRACERS
RACER TRACKS
HISTORY
STRATEGY
TRIVIA
RACER CARDS
GALLERY
PODRACER PIT STOP
Netscape: Star Wars: Episode I: Racer on Nintendo 64
NINTENDO 64
STAR WARS EPISODE I RACER
RACER CARDS
Choose an e-mail communique to send to one of your friends, and share the entwined destinies of Watto, Anakin, and Sebulba.
With one Podrace, a journey begins...
Racer Cards require the Shockwave 7.0 plug-in.
GET PLUG-IN
WATTO
ANAKIN
SEBULBA
PODRACERS
RACER TRACKS
HISTORY
STRATEGY
TRIVIA
RACER CARDS
GALLERY
PODRACER PIT STOP

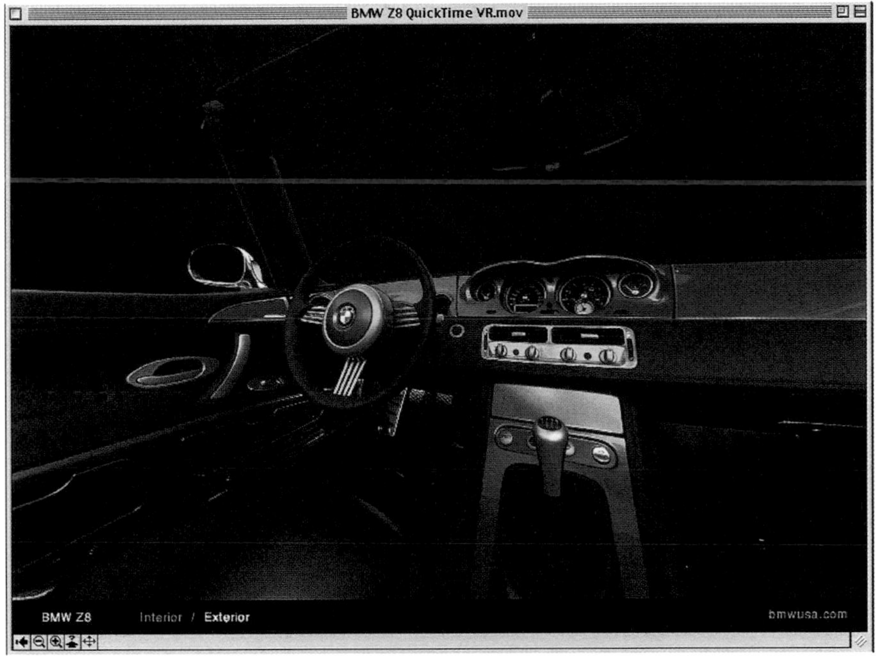

Design Firm: Duffy Design and Interactive Art Director: Kevin Flatt Creative Director: Joe Duffy Designers: Kevin Flat, Jason Strong, Dan Olson Photographer: Mark LaFavor Copywriter: Russ Stark Client: BMW of North America New Media 156,157

Design Firm: Margen Rojo, S.C. Comunicación Visual Art Director: Ofelia Martínez Garcia Creative Directors: Blanca Coss, Enrique Portillo V., Yessica Amanda Ledezma Rasillo Designer: Yessica Amanda Ledezma Rasillo Photographer: Carlos Alarcón Castillo Illustrator: Gerardo Portillo Venegas Client: Museo de las Californias CECUT, Tijuana

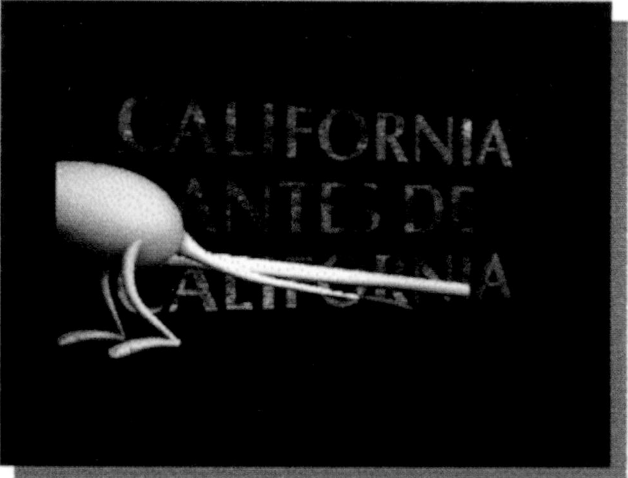

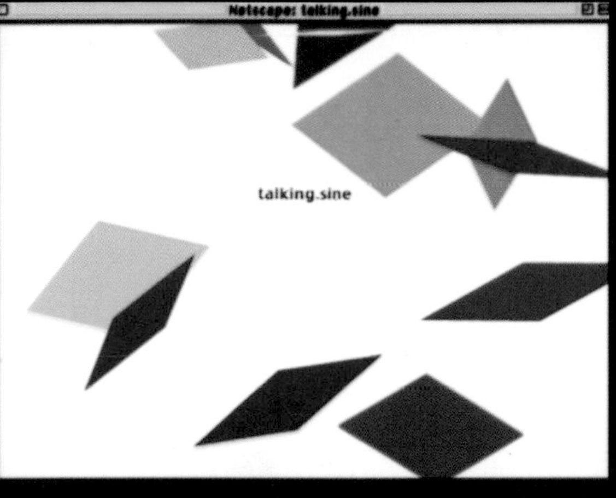

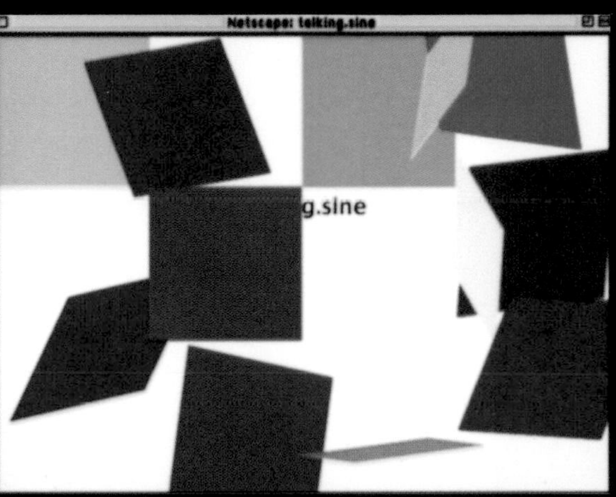

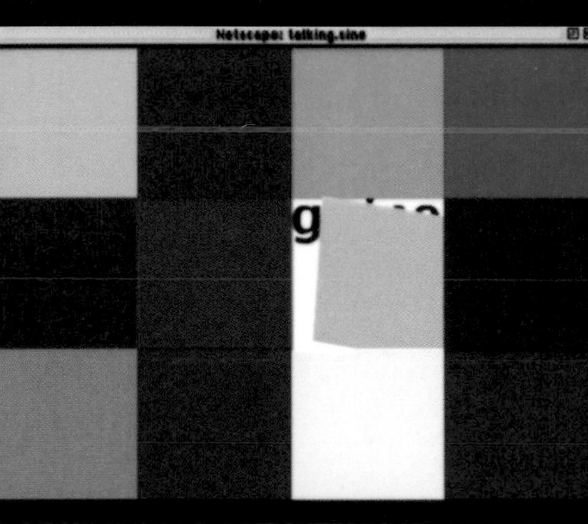

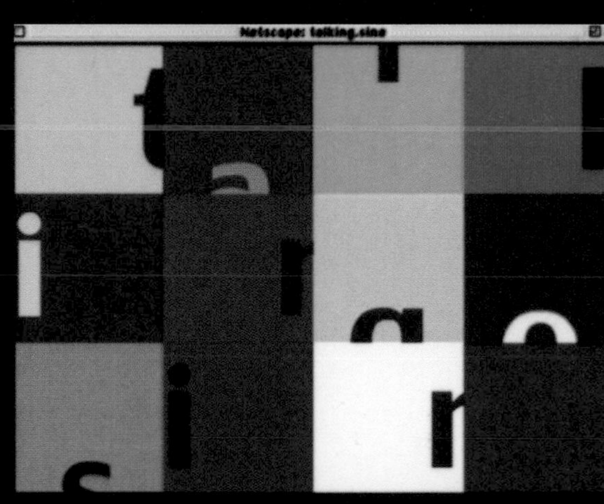

Design Firm: spiralegg.design Art & Creative Director: Sayumi Yoshida Designers: Sayumi Yoshida, Stefan Frank Client: talking.sine

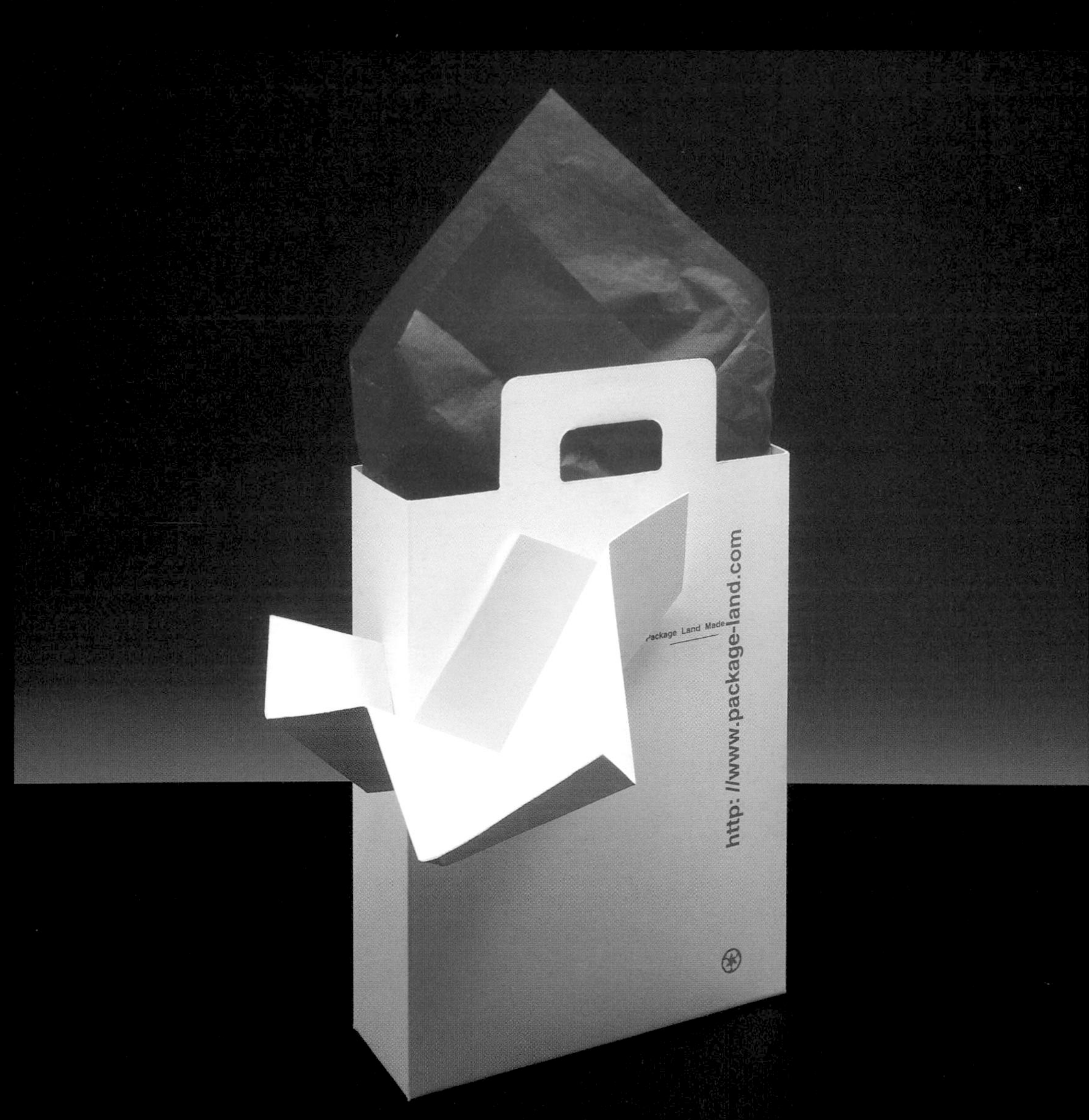
Package Land Made
http: //www.package-land.com

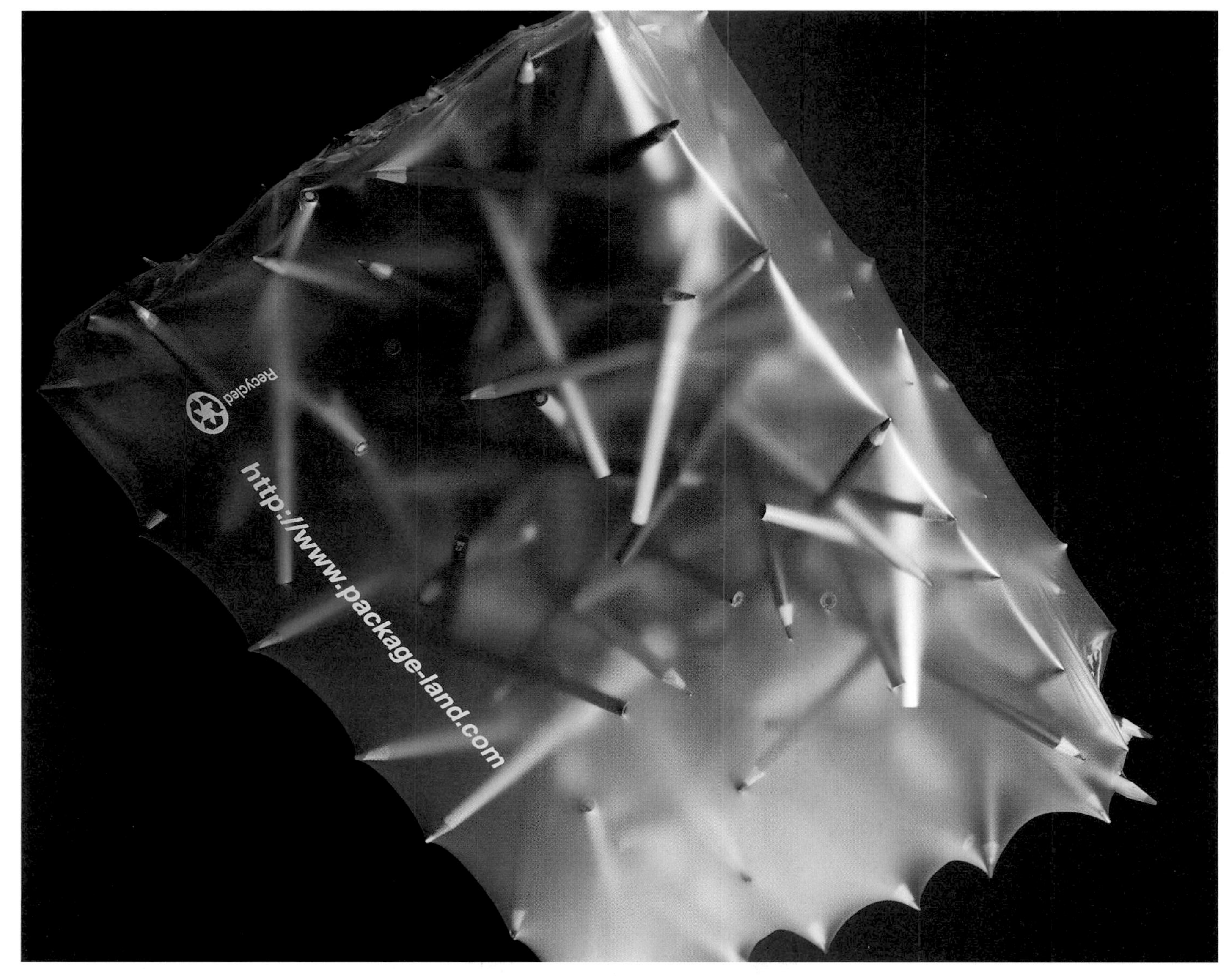

Design Firm: Package Land Co., Ltd. Art & Creative Director, Designer: Yasuo Tanaka Client: Package Land Co., Ltd.

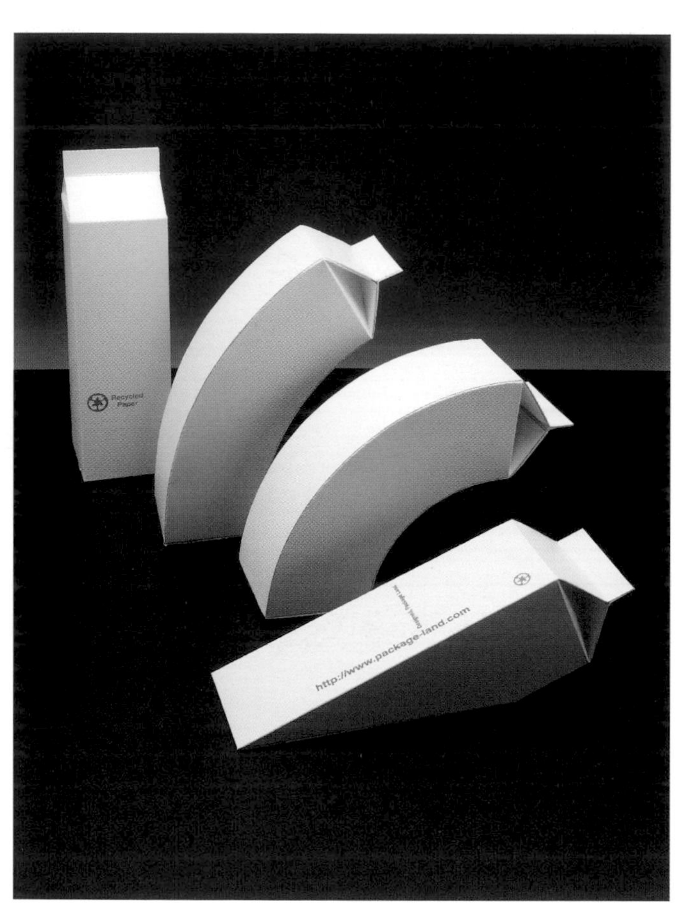
Recycled Paper
http://www.package-land.com

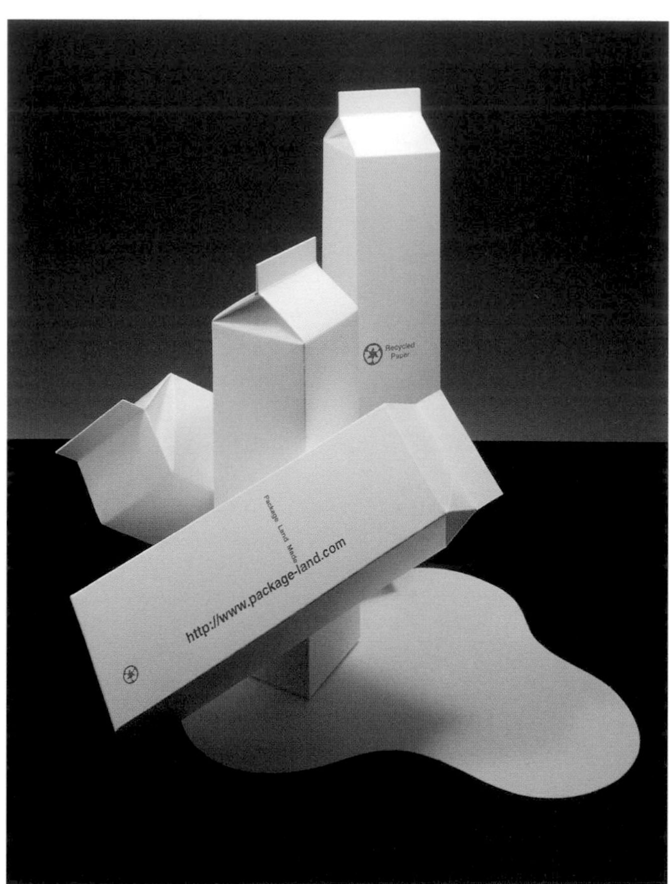
Recycled Paper
Package Land Media
http://www.package-land.com

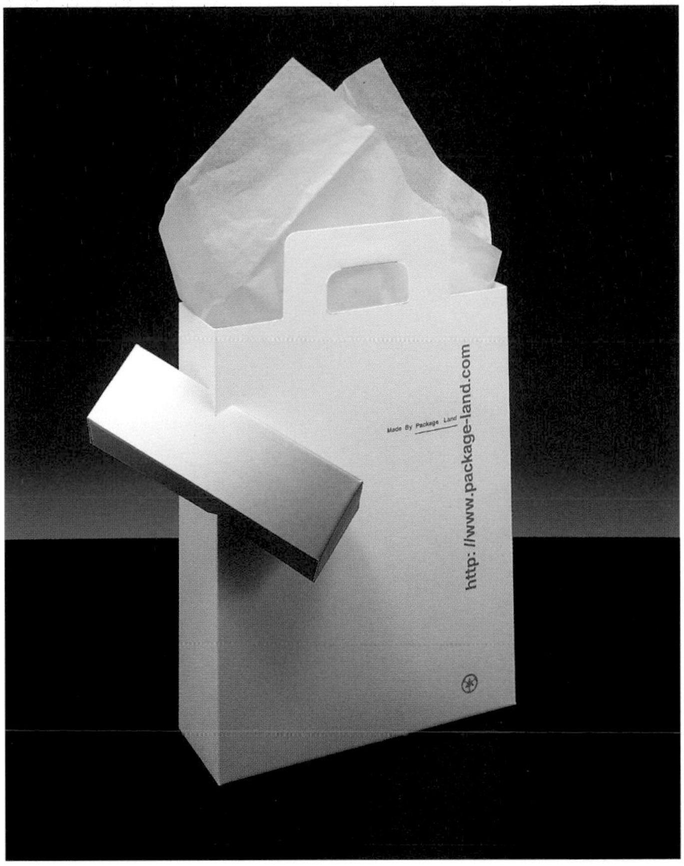

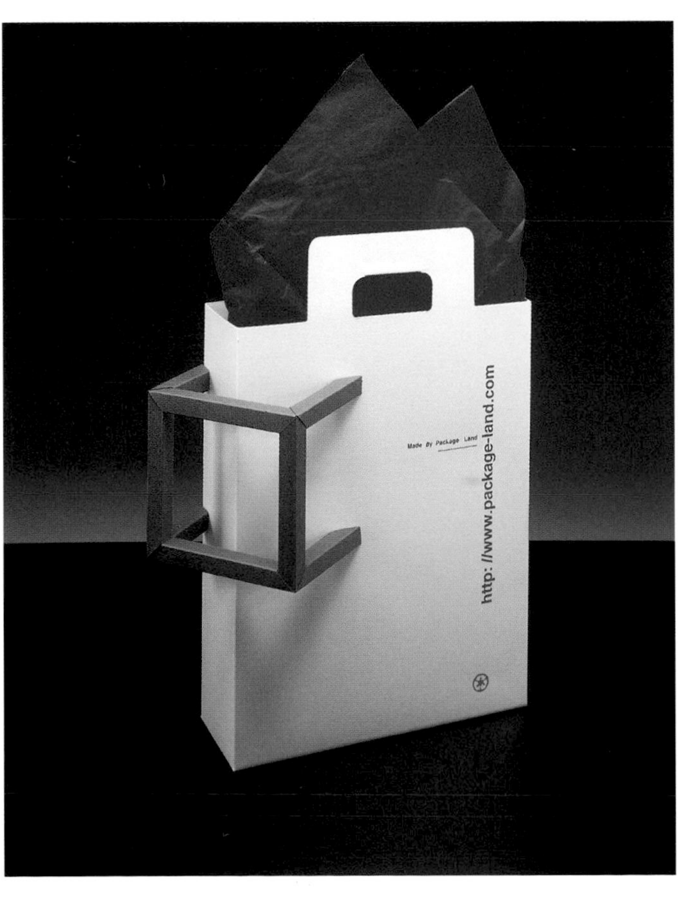

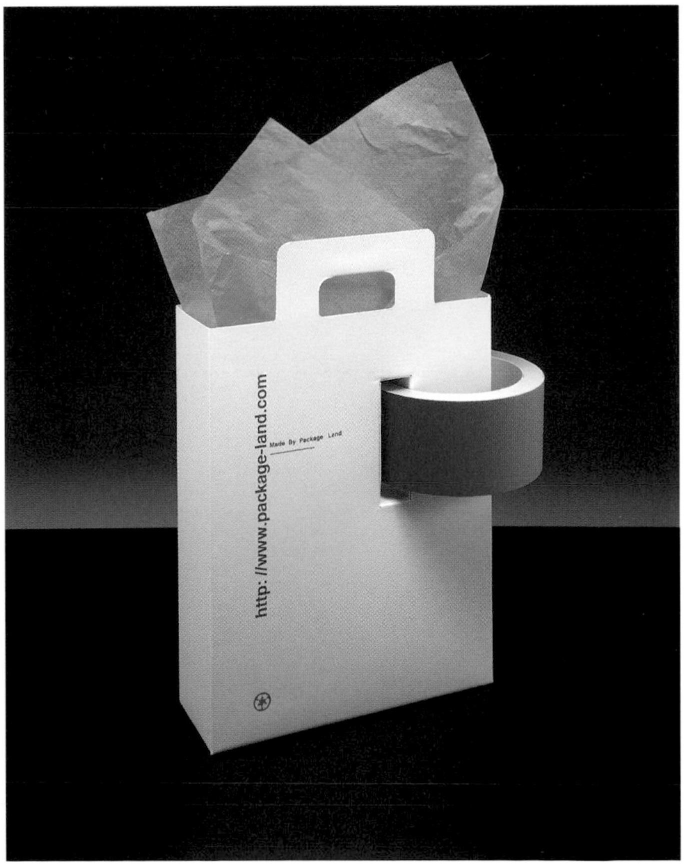

Design Firm: Package Land Co., Ltd. Art & Creative Director, Designer: Yasuo Tanaka Client: Package Land Co., Ltd.

0028

BALANCING

INFUSIONS

No/5

NOURISHE

NUTRITIVE HYDRATING
ALGAE TONER
No/5
NOURISHE
e 100 ml
No/5 
NOURISHE
No/5
NOURISHE

Design Firm: Turner Duckworth Creative Directors: David Turner, Bruce Duckworth Designers: Bruce Duckworth, Bob Celiz Client: Neal's Yard

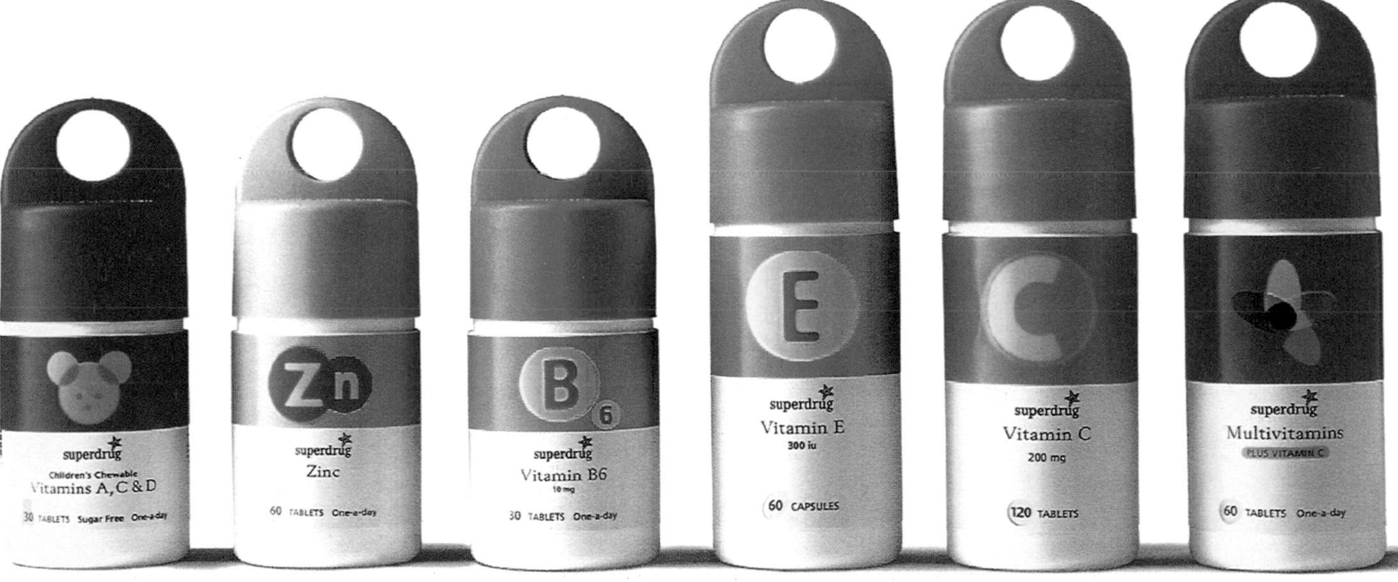

Design Firm: Turner Duckworth Creative Directors: David Turner, Bruce Duckworth Designer: Bruce Duckworth Illustrator: Justin Delavison Client: Superdrug

(Left) Design Firm: Karim Rashid Inc. Designer: Karim Rashid Client: Tommy Hilfiger (right) Design Firm: Karim Rashid Inc. Designer: Karim Rashid Clients: BPI, Parfums Issey Miyake

Design Firm: Shiseido Creation D.V.S. Art Director & Designer: Aoshi Kudo Client: Ipsa Co., Ltd.

(top) Design Firm: Sandstrom Design Art & Creative Director: Steve Sandstrom Designer: Amy Devletian Copywriter: Steve Sandoz Client: Tazo (bottom) Design Firm: RBMM Art Directors: Luis Acevedo, Dan Birlew Designer: Dan Birlew Illustrator: Robert Forsbach Client: Timpone's Fresh Food Corp.

Design Firm: Deutsch Design Works Creative Director: Barry Deutsch Designers: Lori Wynn, Jacques Rossouw Client: Napa Cigar Company

Telfort
Pak Bel
ABONNEMENT
MOTOROLA

Pak Bel
MOTOROLA

Agency: Pentagram Creative Directors: Woody Pirtle, John Klotnia Designers: Chris Dunn, Orville Kaiser Client: Callaway

THIS SIDE UP
total satisfaction
WORK BEER
OZ. BOTTLES
CLOCK OUT
POP A TOP
FOR A JOB WELL DONE™
YOU EARNED IT
WORK
BEER
CONTENTS
X 4
4/6 PAKS
24 TOPS TO POP
RICHMOND VA
USA
IN
OUT
6/12 Fluid Ounce Bottles
FORM B-1113

Design Firm: Work, Inc. Creative & Art Director: Cabell Harris Designer: Haley Johnson Photographer: Karl Steinbrenner Client: Work Beer

Design Firm: Turner Duckworth Creative Directors: David Turner, Bruce Duckworth Designers: David Turner, Allen Raulet Client: McKenzie River Corp.

(top) Design Firm: Turner Duckworth Creative Directors: David Turner, Bruce Duckworth Designers: David Turner, Allen Raulet Client: McKenzie River Corp. (bottom) Design Firm: Turner Duckworth Creative Directors: David Turner, Bruce Duckworth Designer: David Turner Illustrator: Tom Hennessey Client: McKenzie River Corp.

(top) Design Firm: WEGA Werbeagentun GmbH Art Director: Annette Mohr Creative Director: Heiderose Mohr Photographer: Peter Vogel Copywriter: Hans-Peter Theilig Client: Weldebräu (bottom) Design Firm: Sandstrom Design Art Director: Steve Sandstrom Designer: Starlee Matz Client: Seagrams

Design Firm: Templin Brink Design Creative Directors: Gaby Brink, Joel Templin Designer: Gaby Brink Illustrator: Elvis Swift Client: Kelham Maclean

Design Firm: Templin Brink Design Creative Director: Gaby Brink Designers: Gaby Brink, Jason Schulte Copywriters: Dann Wilkens, Jesse Zeifman Client: Dockers K-1 Khakis

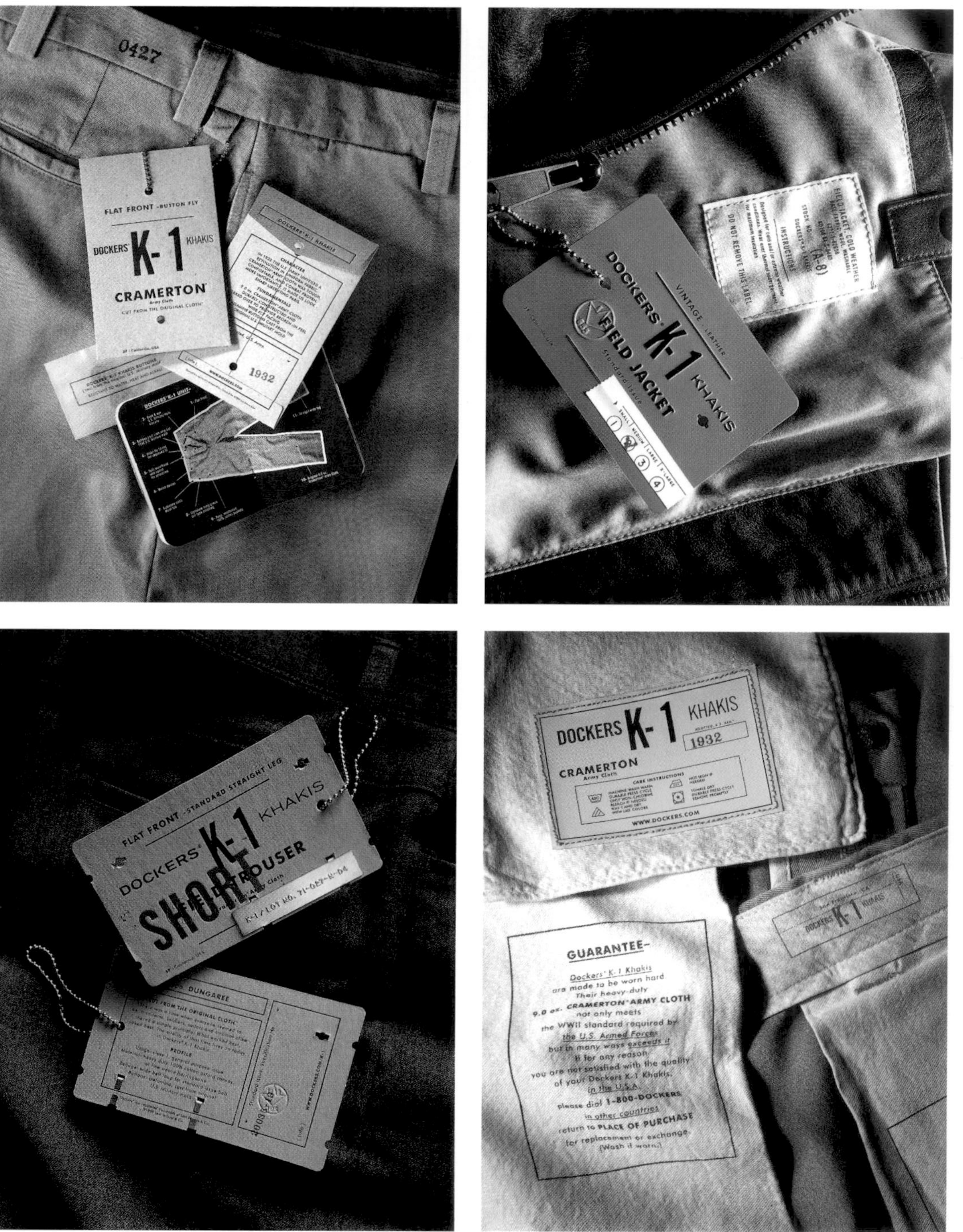

Design Firm: Matsumoto Inc. Creative & Art Director, Illustrator: Takaaki Matsumoto Designers: Takaaki Matsumoto, Kathryn Ham Client: Maharam

FPC frenchpaper.com
PAPER COMPANY
French
PAPER IS OUR MIDDLE NAME

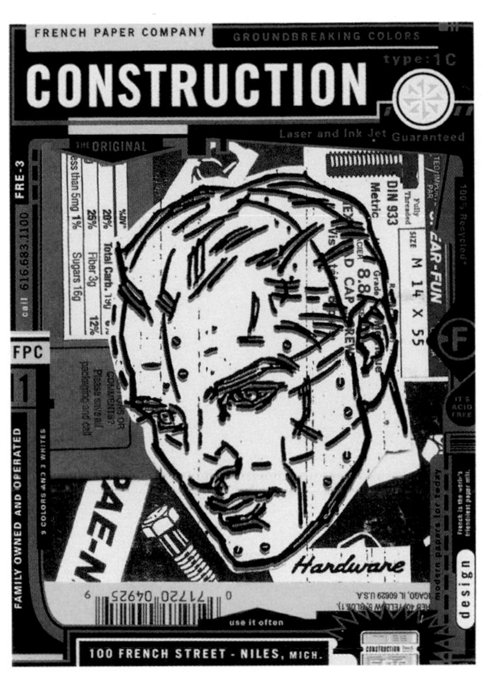

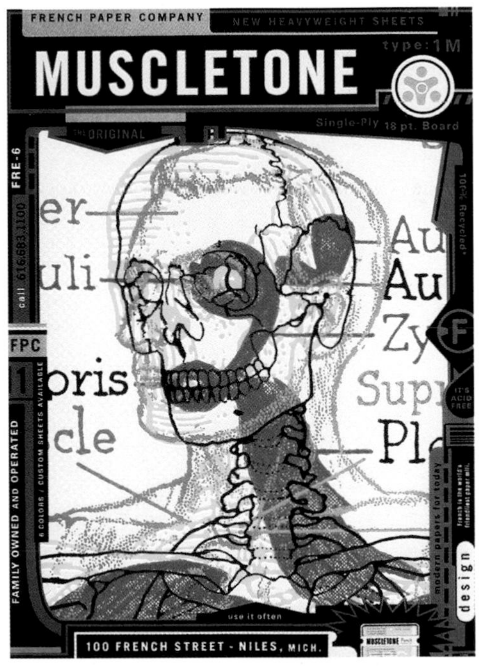

Design Firm: Charles S. Anderson Design Art Director: Charles S. Anderson Designers: Todd Piper-Hauswirth, Kyle Hames Illustrators: Charles S. Anderson, Kyle Hames Copywriter: Lisa Pemrick Client: French Paper Company

For our fourth and final volume of the American Design Century, we look at some of the objects and images that have become icons of the 20th century. It has been a fascinating exercise contemplating what has endured as meaningful and important to society, and what has ended up being more hype than substance. Some objects have come to symbolize an era, while others have come to define how we lived and played in the 20th century, and what we championed as our greatest achievements. Together these icons are our legacy to future generations – artifacts for them to ponder in amusement or to marvel at the tremendous strides we made. **M**ore than any other time in human history, the 20th century witnessed a rapid succession of changes, both technological and social. In America, the century dawned with the introduction of inventions that laid the foundation for everything that followed – the internal combustion engine, the electric motor, the telephone and assembly line production, to name a few. For the first time in history, it became possible to manufacture millions of identical copies of an object and promote them over the airwaves and sell them everywhere. Mass production led to mass marketing, which, in turn, led to mass consumerism. America unabashedly became a consumer society, and business actively pursued customers by using design to make their products more unique and appealing. Industrial design – a term coined in 1926 – emerged as a vital profession in the 1930s and graphic design – previously lumped under commercial arts – was recognized as a distinct discipline a few decades later. The combined impact resulted in everyday objects that exhibited greater style, physical appeal and functionality. Identical in appearance and cheap enough to own, these objects fostered a shared reality. Say the word "Rolodex" or "McDonald's" or "Weber Grill" and a scene, complete with sound and atmosphere, usually comes to mind. Iconic objects provided a kind of shorthand language for everything from work to leisure. **T**he 20th century is rich with American icons understood not only in the U.S. but all over the world. That has made choosing subjects for this book particularly hard. We surveyed several designers for suggestions, and we narrowed our criteria to "designed" objects, eliminating vast categories such as photojournalism, fine art and typography. Even so, space limitations and an inability to get our hands on certain images forced us to leave out many deserving icons. Undoubtedly, you'll think of things that should have been included. We readily agree. But our attempt here is simply to give you a representative look at the century to enhance your appreciation of who we were and how we're likely to be remembered.

America's infatuation with the automobile has never waned. Especially in the halcyon postwar days before gas shortages and commuter gridlock, car designs were extravagant and fanciful. Inspired by rocket science, GM's Harley Earl created America's ultimate dream car – the 1959 Cadillac Eldorado with dramatic tail fins and lots of chrome.
32

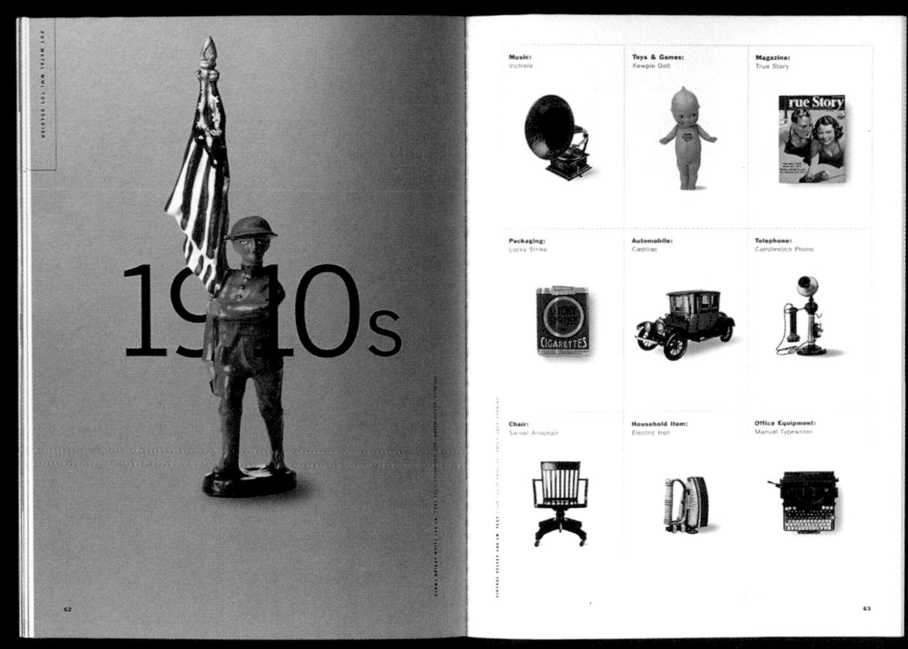

< Inverted in 1903 by Binney & Smith of Pennsylvania, Crayola has become the ubiquitous drawing tool for children worldwide. More than 100 billion crayons have been sold to date, and even adults recall favorite Crayola colors from their youth.

No matter how high-tech toys get or which beanie baby is in greatest demand, some toys never go out of favor. At 40, Barbie is as popular as ever with little girls, and 35-year old G.I. Joe still appeals to little boys. Toddlers find stuffed teddy bears (named for Teddy Roosevelt in 1902 after he refused to shoot a bear) irrepressibly cuddly. And Mr. Potato Head continues to offer great interactive fun.

15

Design Firm: Pentagram Design Art & Creative Director: Kit Hinrichs Designer: Brian Jacobs Copywriter: Daphaine Hirasuna Client: Potlatch

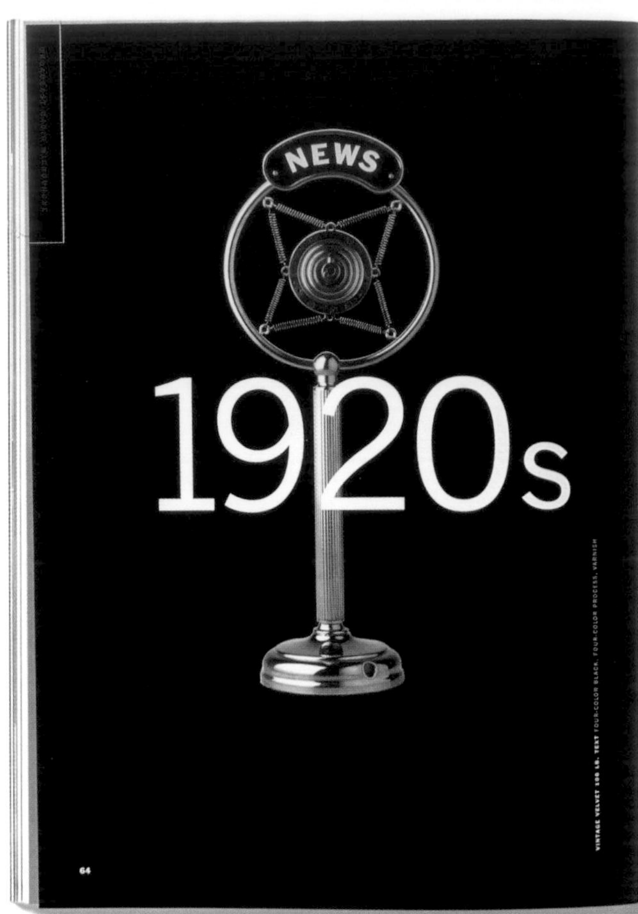

HARLEY-DAVIDSON MOTORCYCLE

No ordinary mode of transportation, the Harley-Davidson motorcycle, invented in 1903, has come to symbolize an unbridled love of the open road. Its cult-like following of customers even tattoo the corporate logo on their arms and make pilgrimages to the company's headquarters in Milwaukee, Wisconsin.

VINTAGE GLOSS 100 LB. TEXT FOUR-COLOR SEPIATONE, MATCH GREY, VARNISH

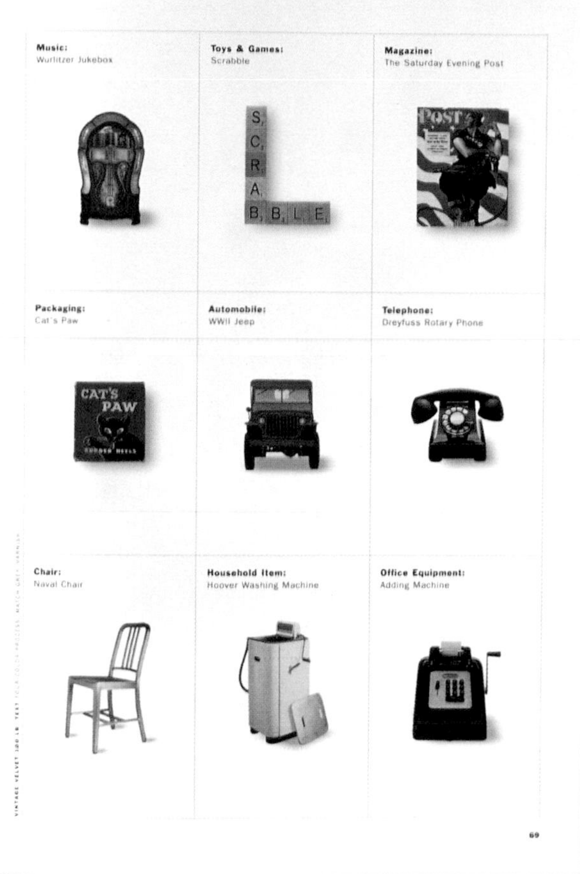

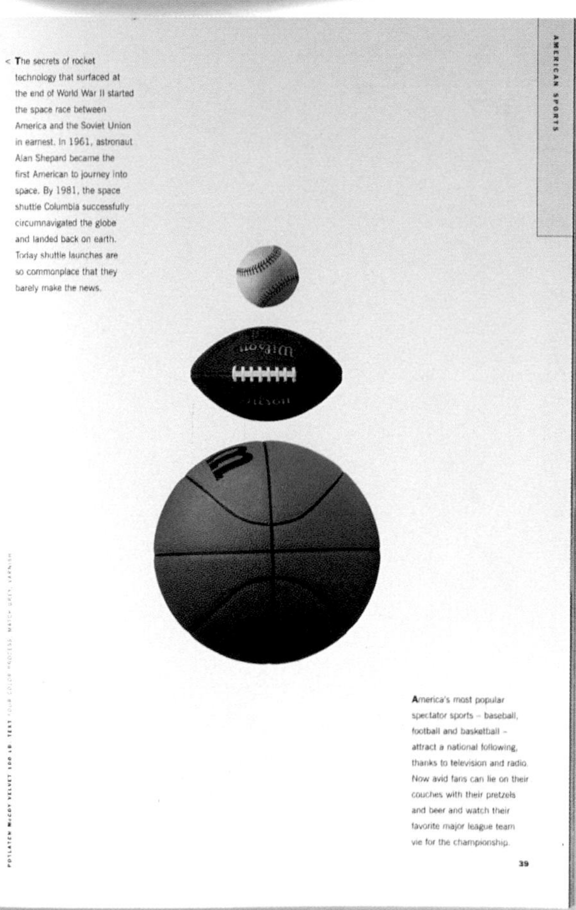

AMERICAN SPORTS
< The secrets of rocket technology that surfaced at the end of World War II started the space race between America and the Soviet Union in earnest. In 1961, astronaut Alan Shepard became the first American to journey into space. By 1981, the space shuttle Columbia successfully circumnavigated the globe and landed back on earth. Today shuttle launches are so commonplace that they barely make the news.
America's most popular spectator sports – baseball, football and basketball – attract a national following, thanks to television and radio. Now avid fans can lie on their couches with their pretzels and beer and watch their favorite major league team vie for the championship.
39

Design Firm: Pentagram Design Art & Creative Director: Kit Hinrichs Designer: Brian Jacobs Copywriter: Daphaine Hirasuna Client: Potlatch

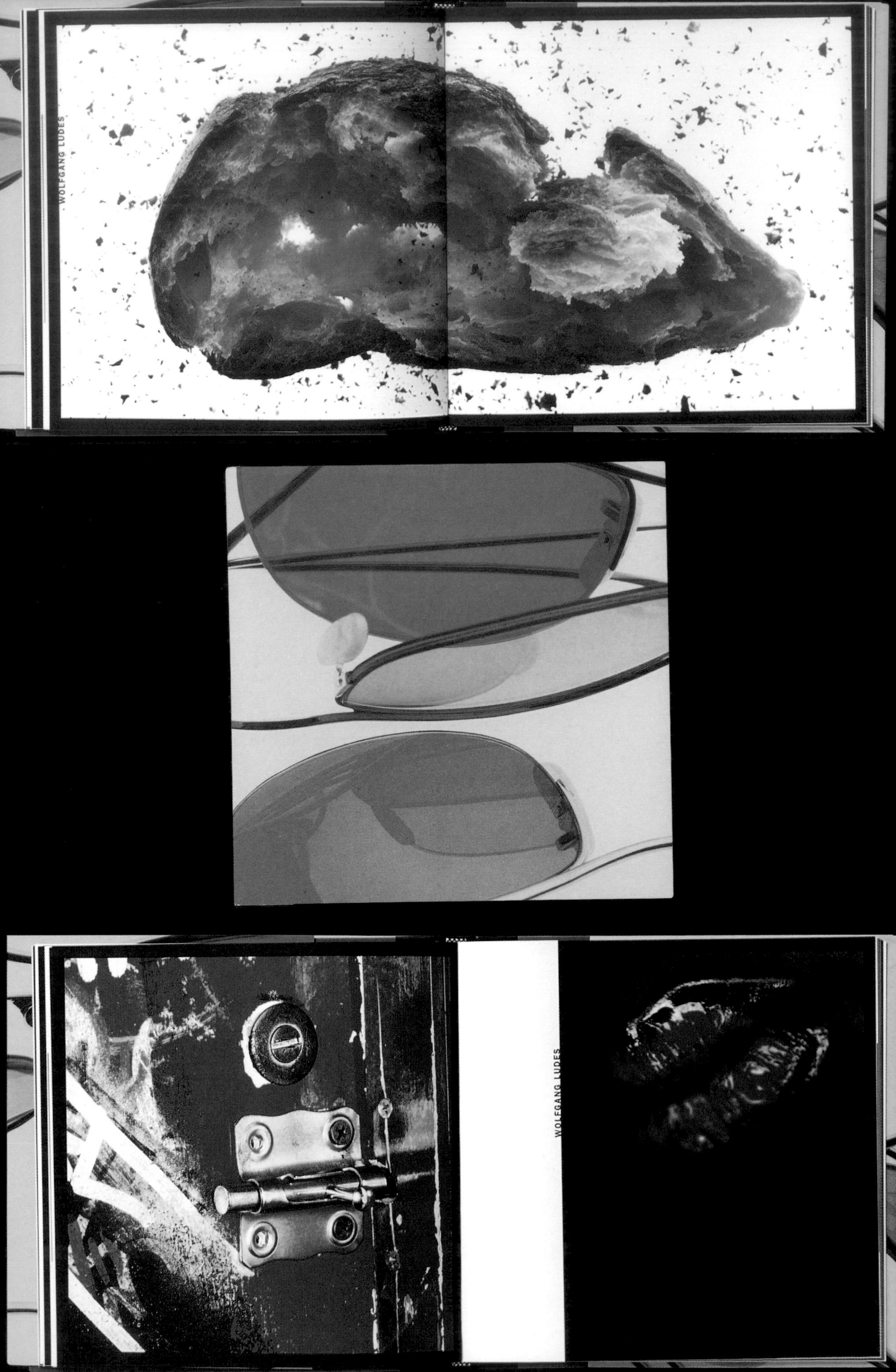
WOLFGANG LUDES
WOLFGANG LUDES

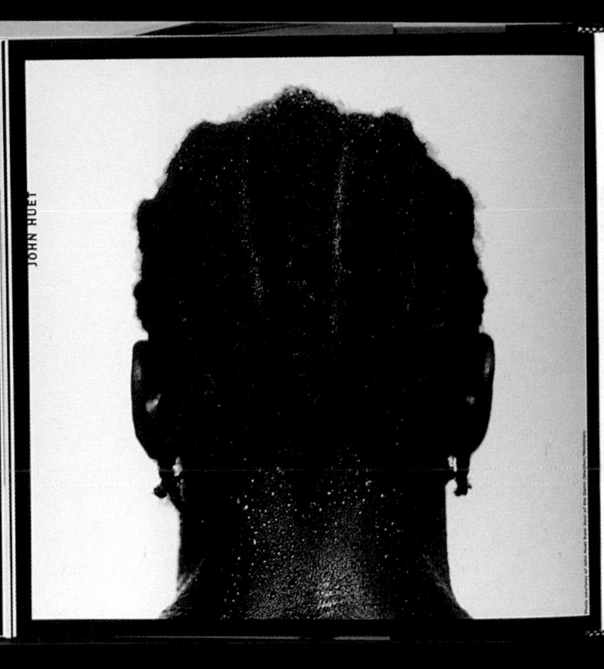

Meaning is something we acquire by collecting different pieces.

30 31

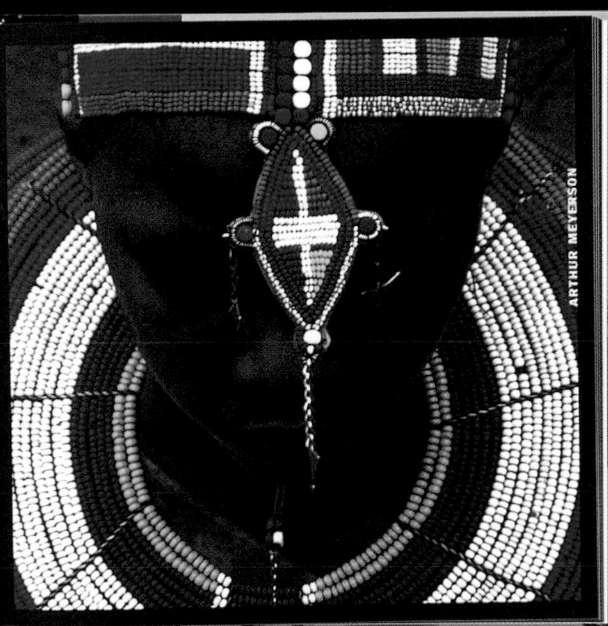

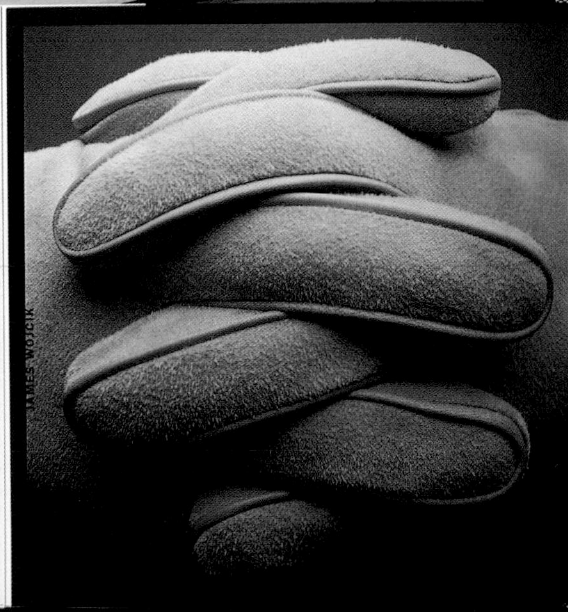

God, we have been told, is in the details. And it is the precise manner in which he—or she—has taken up residence there that interests us here.

46 47

Design Firm: Designframe Inc. Art Director: Michael McGinn Creative Director: James Sebastian Designer: Sharon Giresh Client: Strathmore Papers

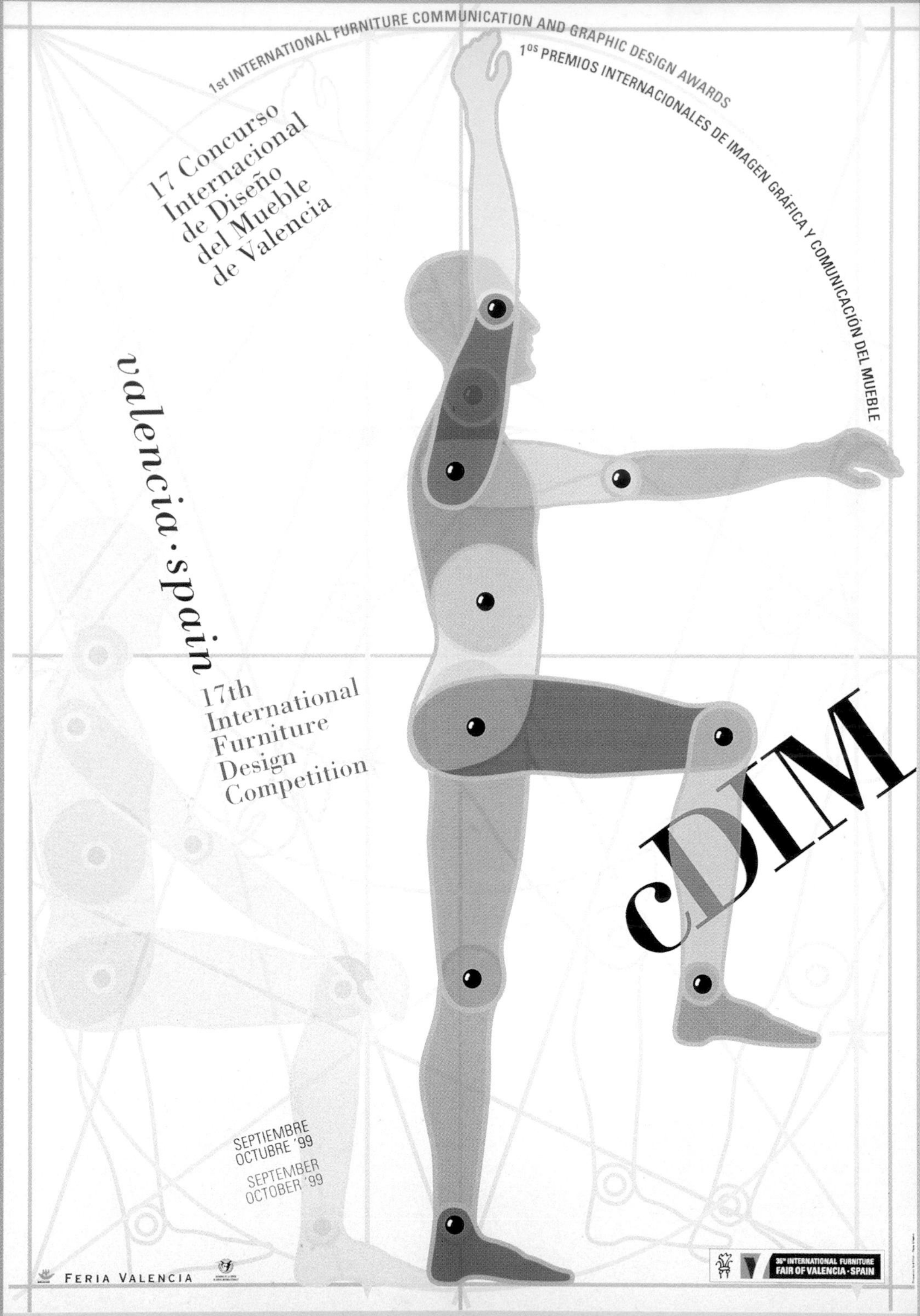

1st INTERNATIONAL FURNITURE COMMUNICATION AND GRAPHIC DESIGN AWARDS

1os PREMIOS INTERNACIONALES DE IMAGEN GRÁFICA Y COMUNICACIÓN DEL MUEBLE

17 Concurso Internacional de Diseño del Mueble de Valencia

valencia · spain

17th International Furniture Design Competition

cDIM

SEPTIEMBRE
OCTUBRE '99

SEPTEMBER
OCTOBER '99

FERIA VALENCIA

36th INTERNATIONAL FURNITURE FAIR OF VALENCIA · SPAIN

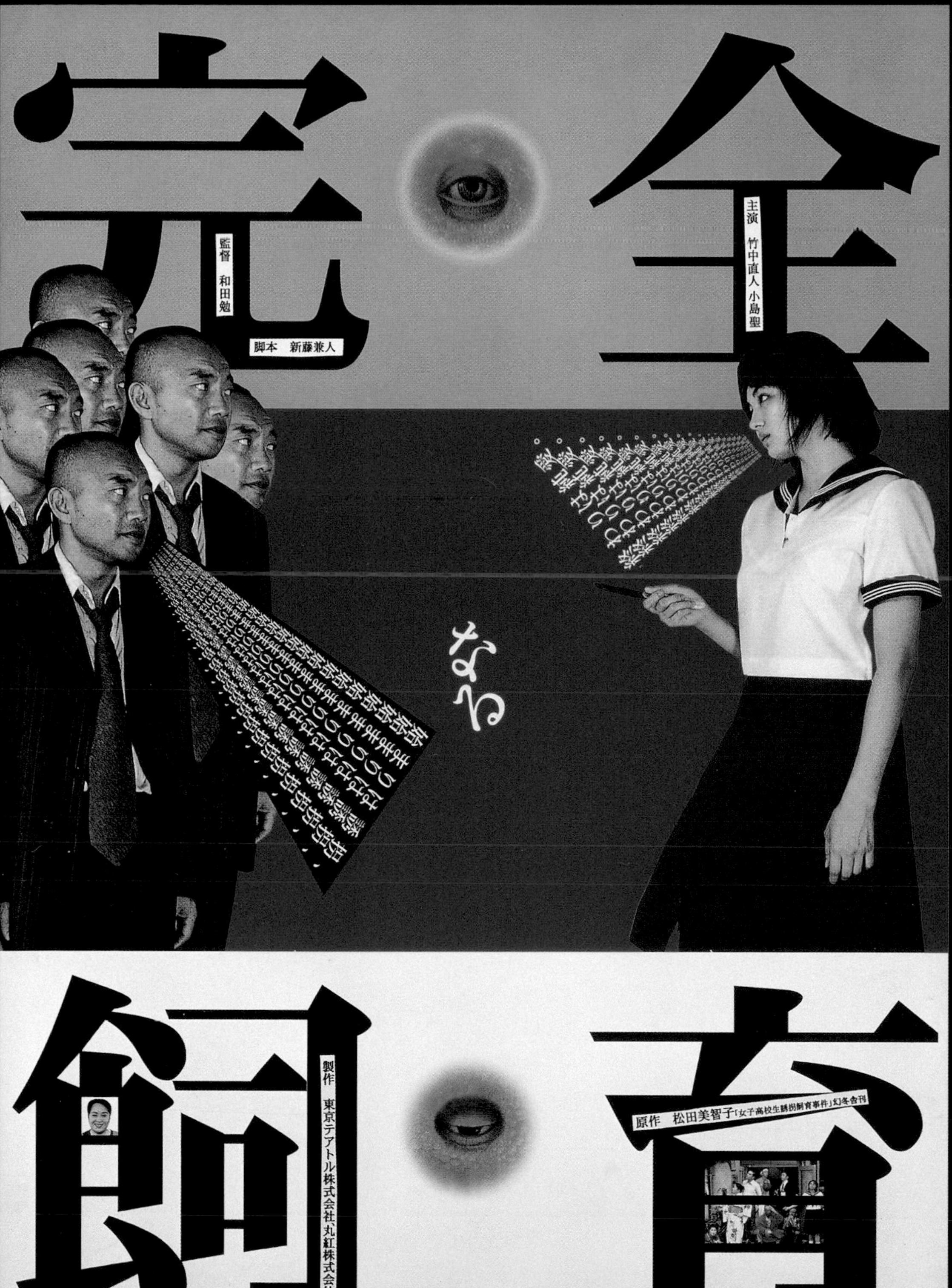

完全なる飼育

監督 和田勉

脚本 新藤兼人

主演 竹中直人 小島聖

製作 東京テアトル株式会社 丸紅株式会社

原作 松田美智子「女子高校生誘拐飼育事件」幻冬舎刊

R-15

Art & Creative Director, Designer: Tadanori Yokoo Photographer: Mitsuru Tabei Copywriter: Junko Narusawa Client: Tokyo Theatres Co., Ltd/Marubeni Corporation

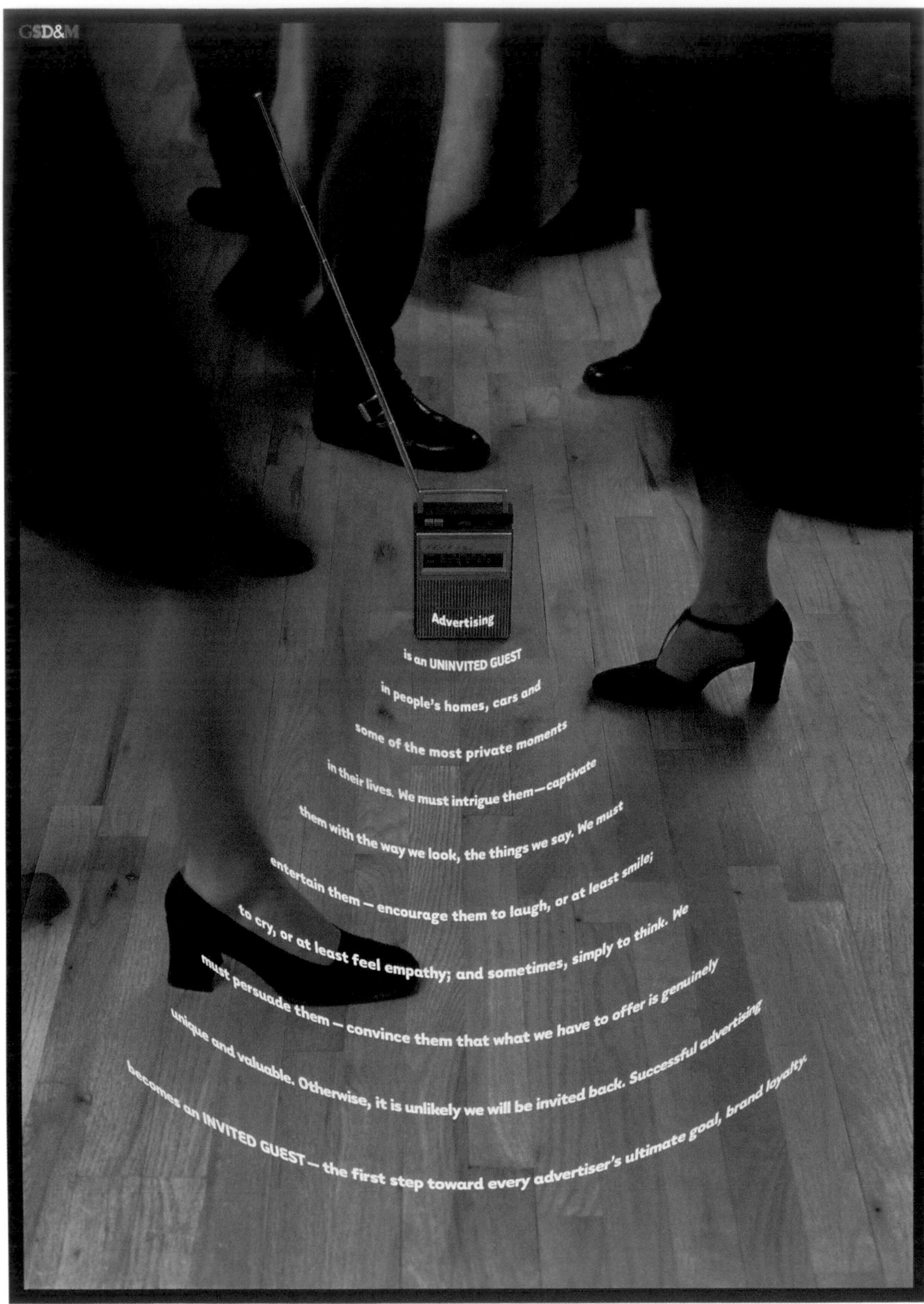
GSD&M
Advertising
is an UNINVITED GUEST
in people's homes, cars and
some of the most private moments
in their lives. We must intrigue them—captivate
them with the way we look, the things we say. We must
entertain them — encourage them to laugh, or at least smile;
to cry, or at least feel empathy; and sometimes, simply to think. We
must persuade them — convince them that what we have to offer is genuinely
unique and valuable. Otherwise, it is unlikely we will be invited back. Successful advertising
becomes an INVITED GUEST — the first step toward every advertiser's ultimate goal, brand loyalty.

Design Firm: GSD&M Art Director: Scott McAfee Creative Directors: David Crawford, Scott McAfee Photographer: Fredrik Broden Illustrators: Dale Minor, Kevin Peake Copywriter: Tim McClure Client: GSD&M

Design Firm: GSD&M Art Director: Scott McAfee Creative Directors: David Crawford, Scott McAfee Photographer: Fredrik Broden Illustrators: Dale Minor, Kevin Peake Copywriter: Tim McClure Client: GSD&M

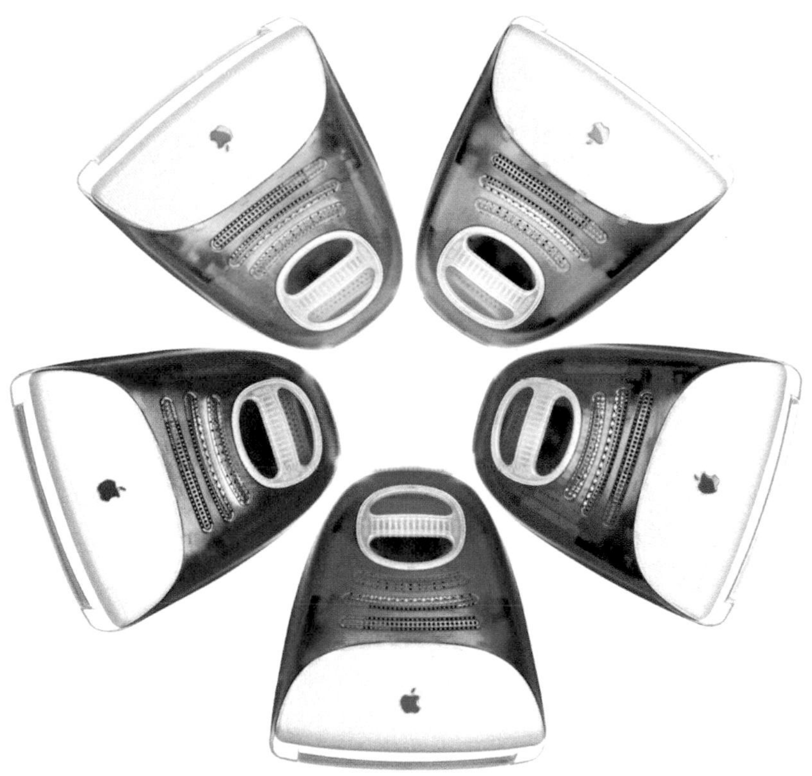

Yum.

Think different.

Firm: USWeb/CKS Art Director & Designer: Hiroki Asai Creative Director: Andy Dreyfus Photographer: Hunter Freeman Copywriter: David Belgar Client: Apple Computer

Design Firm: Wheaton Art Direction and Design Art & Creative Director, Designer: Michael Wheaton Photographer: Bob Carey Copywriter: Gene Payne Client: Beathouse Music

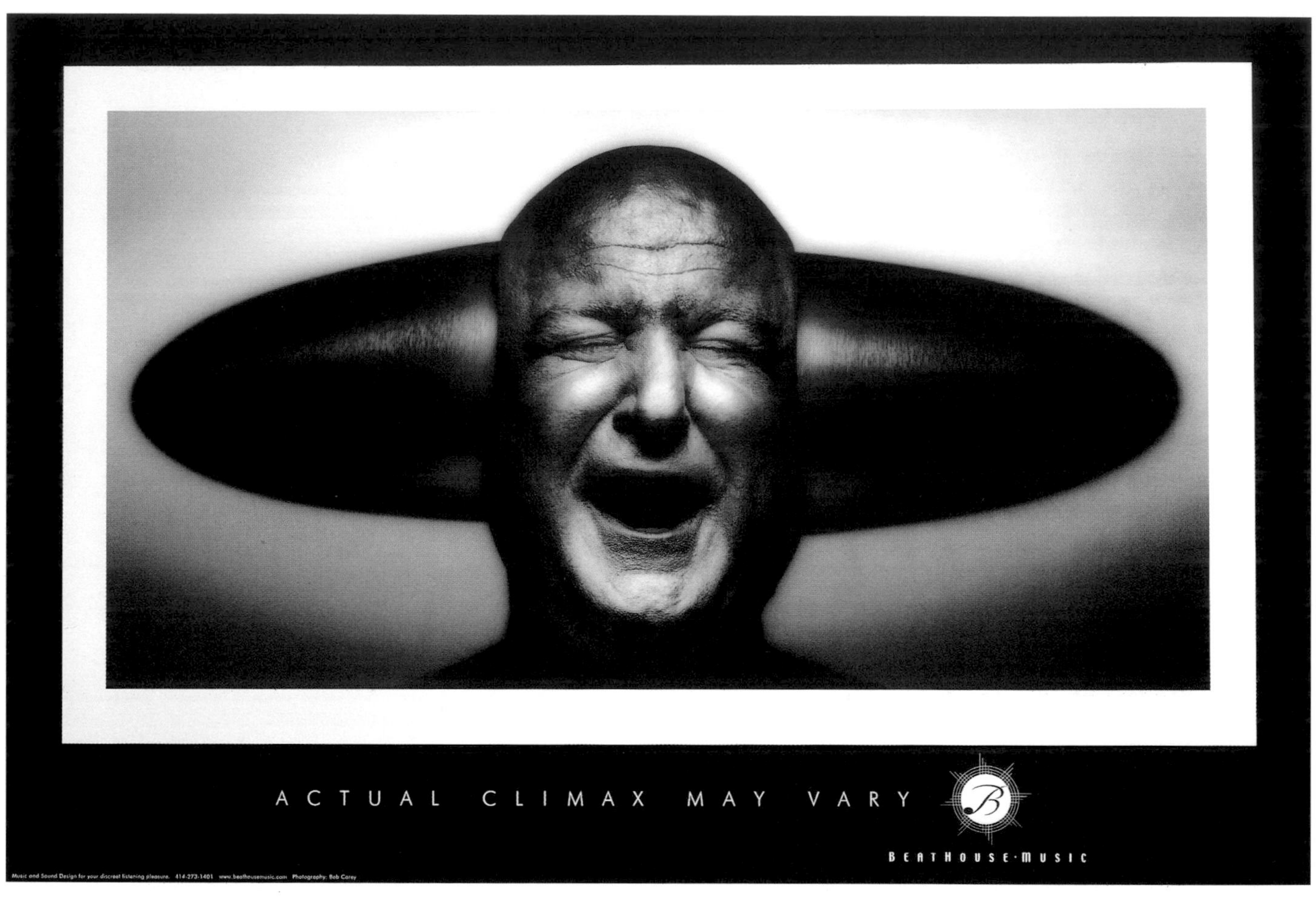

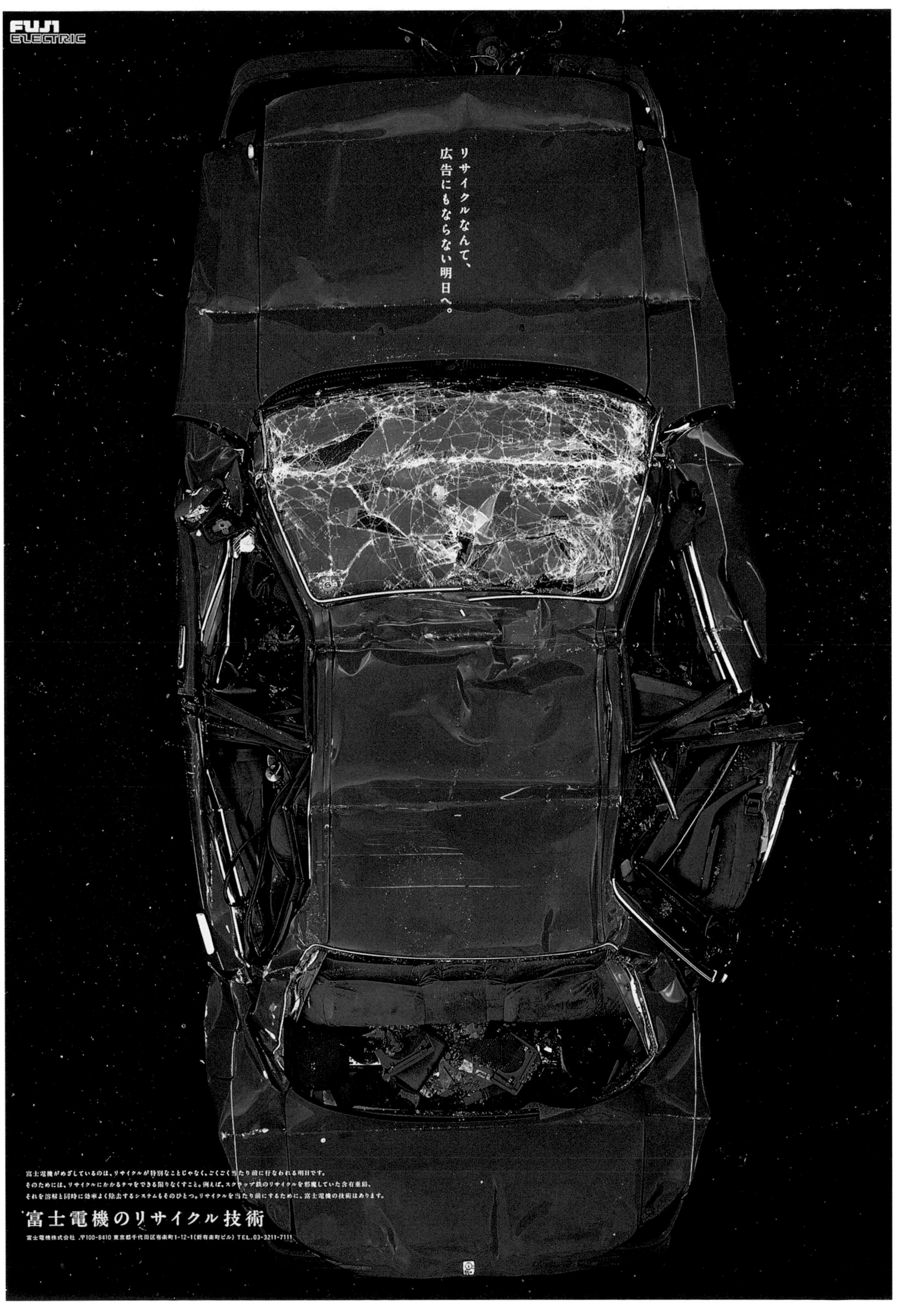

Design Firm: Strike Co., Ltd. Art Director & Designer: Norio Kudo Creative Director: Hiroshi Kyoto Photographer: Takahito Sato Copywriter: Azusa Kajita Client: Fuji Electric Co., Ltd.

CAUTION: CHILDREN AT WAR

Abolish the use of child soldiers worldwide. Children have the right to be children.

AMNESTY INTERNATIONAL

www.amnestyusa.org

Design defines the times

The JAGDA Poster Exhibition 2009-DESIGN

ke Co., Ltd. Art & Creative Director, Designer: Norio Kudo Photographer: Takahito Sato Copywriter: Juri Sakuma Client: Japan Graphic Designers Association, Inc.

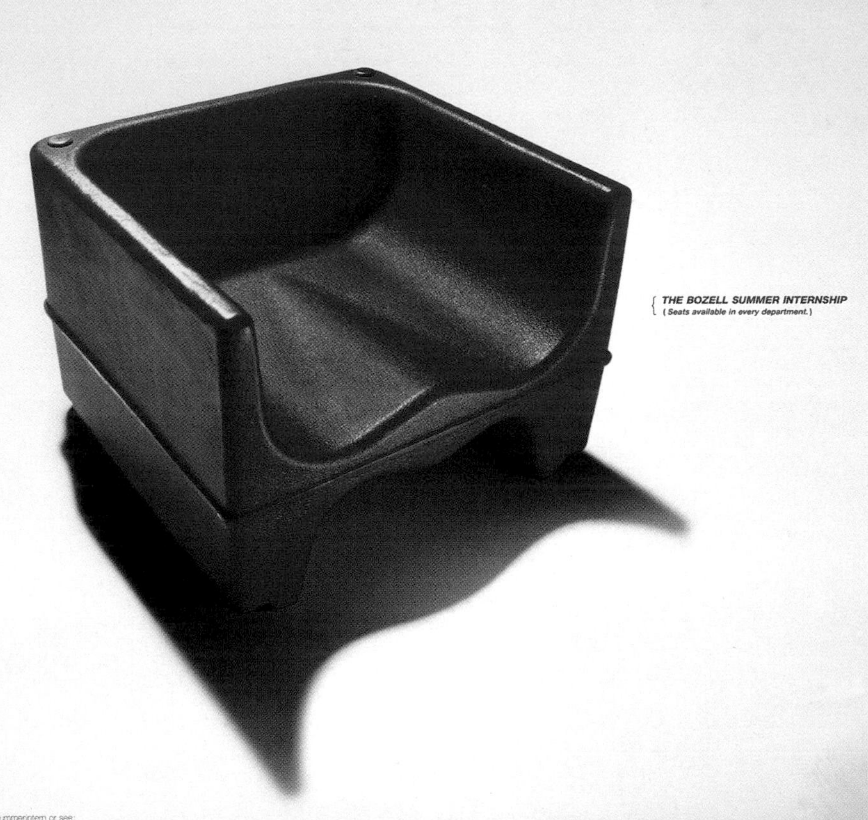

THE BOZELL SUMMER INTERNSHIP
(Seats available in every department.)
Application deadline: 3/1/2000. For more information, log on to www.bozell-omaha.com/summerintern or see:

Design Firm: Bozell Group Art Directors: David Steinke, Dustin Black Creative Director: David Moore Photographer: Bob Irvin Copywriter: Robin Fitzgerald Client: Bozell Group

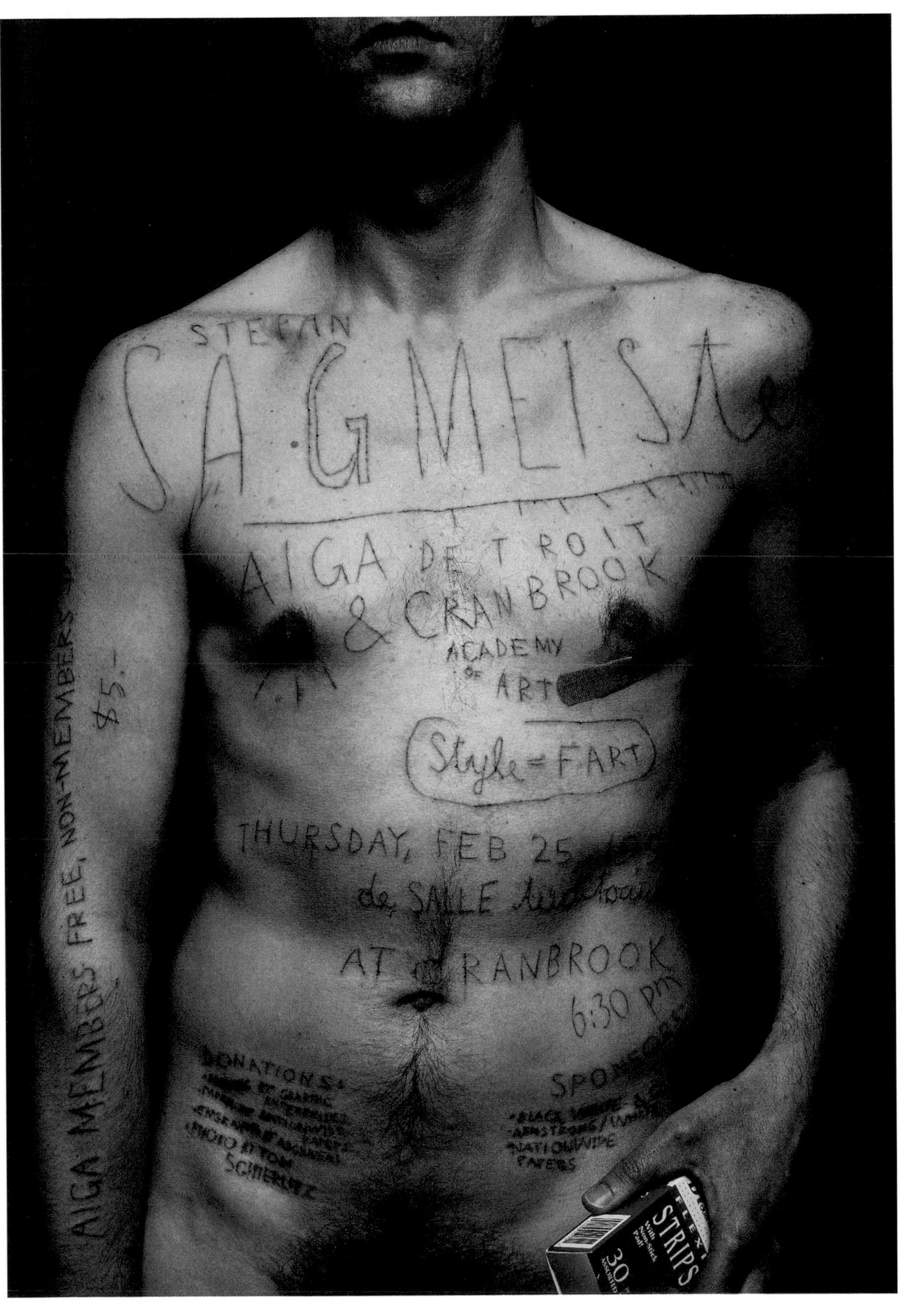

Design Firm: Sagmeister Inc. Art & Creative Director: Stefan Sagmeister Designers: Hjalti Karisson, Stefan Sagmeister Photographer: Tom Schierlitt Client: Aiga Detroit

Underwood
HALBERSTAM ON JORDAN.
THE SPOKEN WORD WITH DAVID HALBERSTAM FROM HIS UPCOMING BOOK PLAYING FOR KEEPS: MICHAEL JORDAN AND THE WORLD HE MADE. MONDAY, DECEMBER 7, 1998 6:00 P.M. THE ALGONQUIN OAK ROOM

Design Firm: Axiom Creative Group Art & Creative Director: Brian Hill Photographer: Mike Carroll Client: World T.E.A.M. Sports

Design Firm: Vanderbyl Design Art & Creative Director: Michael Vanderbyl Designers: Michael Vanderbyl, Jeremy Regenbogen Client: Exhibitor Magazine

Design Firm: Nippon Design Center, Inc. Art Director: Kazumasa Nagai Designer: Hitoshi Oikasa Client: Takeo Co., Ltd.

Our Mission: Identifying abilities. Increasing awareness and options. Opening opportunities. Achieving an individuals goals. These are the cornerstones of community rehabilitation programs for people with disabilities. Where does your staff find the wisdom and acquire the skills and knowledge needed to assist competently and professionally the individuals who seek help from your

community programs? The Continuing Education Center continues the legacy of the Stout Vocational Rehabilitation Institute, bringing proven technology, unmatched expertise and innovative practices to rehabilitation programs. Through CEC's training and on-site technical assistance, community-based staff and administrators acquire better ways, easier methods and more effective techniques.

Finding answers. Providing solutions. Ensuring futures.

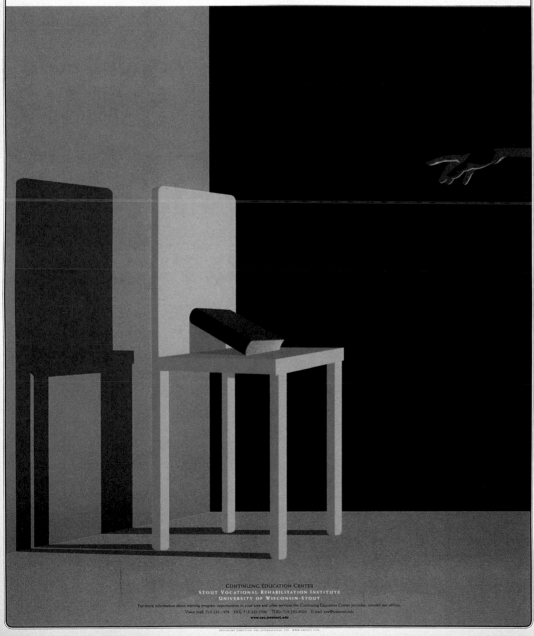

Continuing Education Center
Stout Vocational Rehabilitation Institute
University of Wisconsin-Stout

For more information about training program opportunities in your area and other services the Continuing Education Center provides, contact our offices.
Voice mail: 715-232-1379 FAX: 715-232-5396 TDD: 715-232-5025 E-mail: cee@uwstout.edu
www.cee.uwstout.edu

DESIGN/ART DIRECTION: DBD INTERNATIONAL, LTD. WWW.DBDINTL.COM

...nternational, Ltd. Art & Creative Director, Designer, Illustrator: David Brier Copywriters: Steve Ferry, David Brier Client: U.W. Stout - CEC

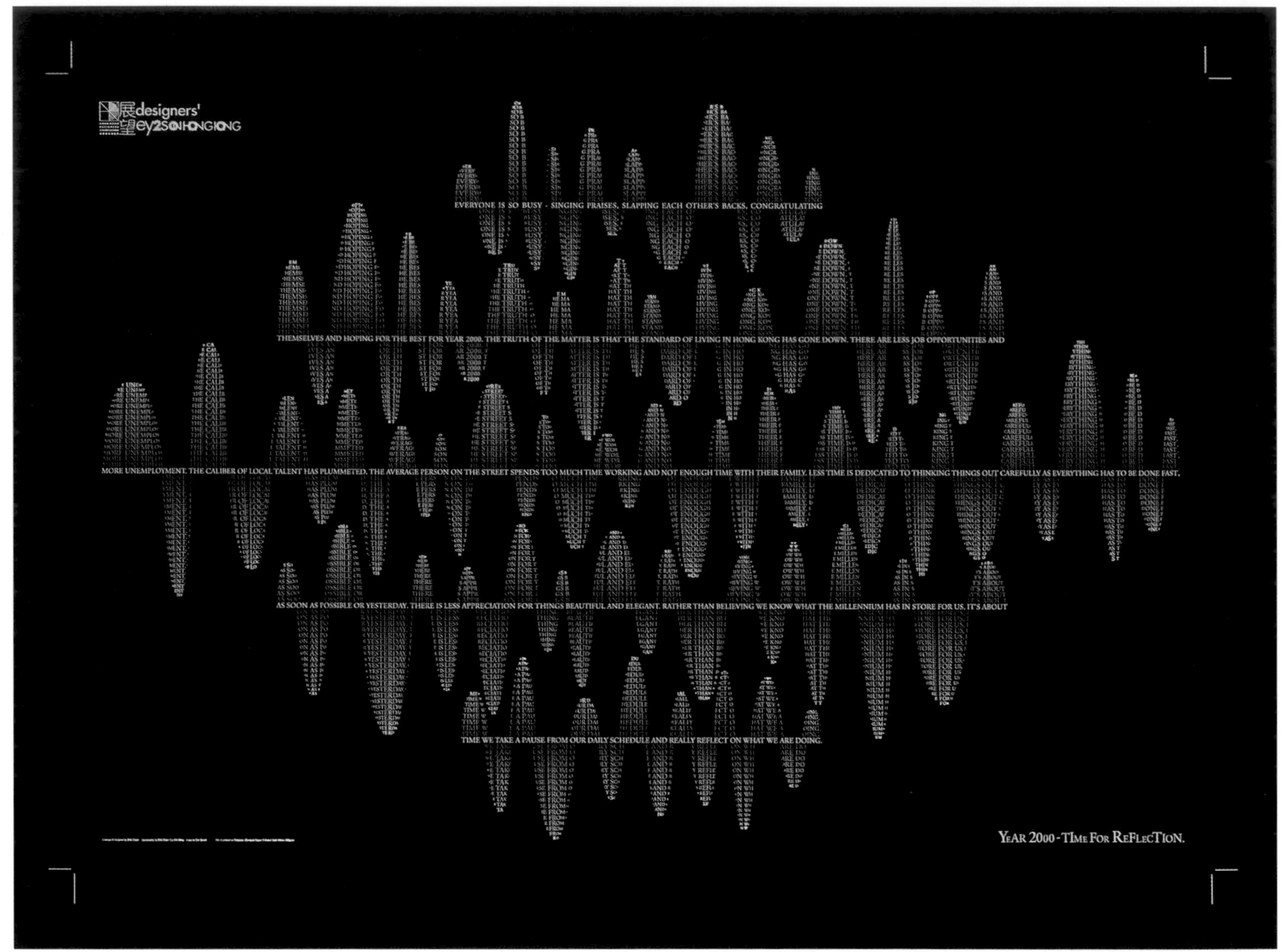

Design Firm: Eric Chan Design Co., Ltd. Creative Director, Designer & Copywriter: Eric Chan Client: Designer's Eyes on Hong Kong 2000

Design Firm: Frost Design Ltd. Art & Creative Director, Designer: Vince Frost Client: Chartered Society of Designers

WJCT
JACKSONVILLE
JAZZ FESTIVAL
20 SWINGING YEARS
JAZZ
GOLD

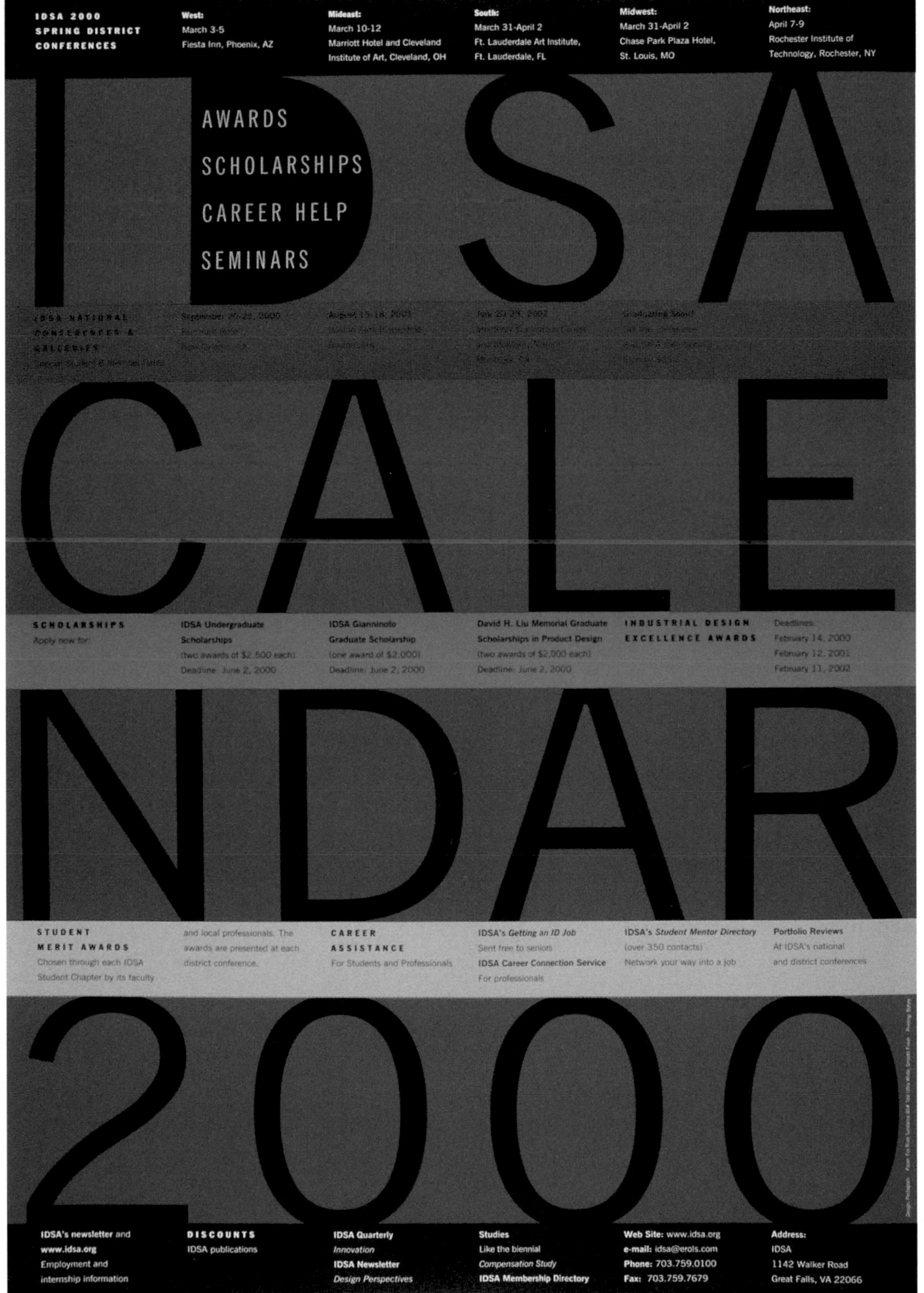

Design Firm: Pentagram Design Art & Creative Director: Kit Hinrichs Designer: Amy Anan Client: IDSA

Design Firm: Turner Duckworth Creative Directors: David Turner, Bruce Duckworth Designers: Allen Raulet, Jonathan Warner Photographer: Lloyd Hryciw Client: Nike

AIR GAUNTLET RUNNING

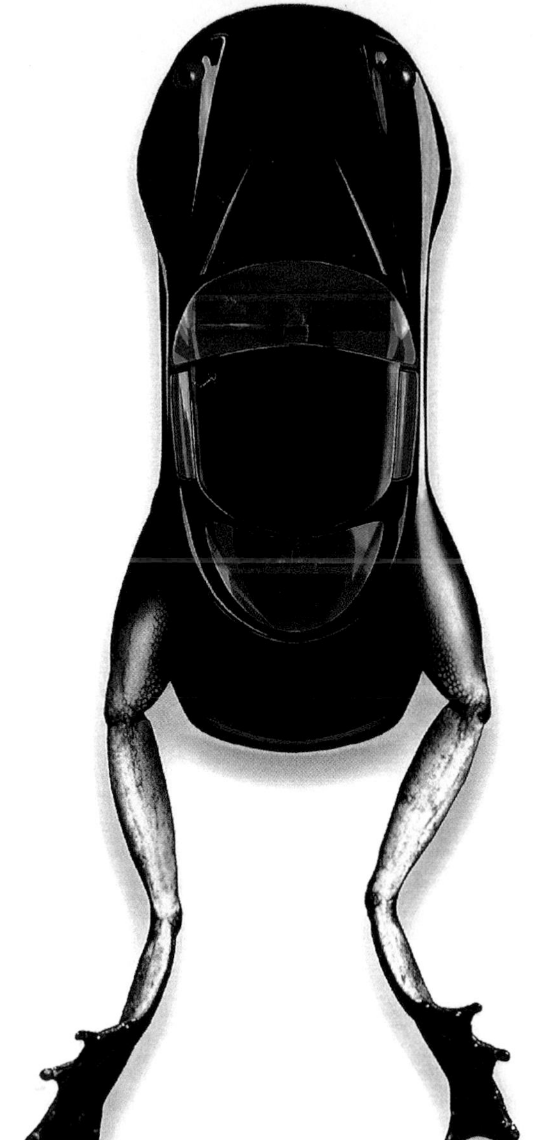

SUPER JUMP TRACTION · AUTOMOTIVE STYLING

AIR PIPPEN III BASKETBALL

Design Firm: RKS Design, Inc. Designers: Nashan Sheppard, Chris Glupker, Rob Englin Client: Intrigo

Firm: Herbst Lazar Bell Inc. Art Director: Todd Henreckson Designer: Greg Holderfield Client: General Binding Corporation

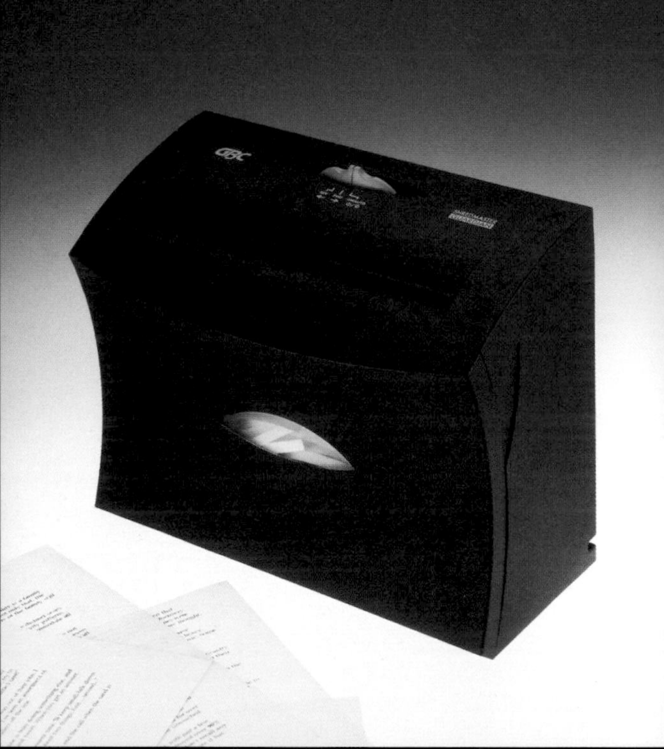

Design Firm: Jennifer Sterling Design Art & Creative Director, Designer, Copywriter: Jennifer Sterling Client: Spike

→ Shay, Shea, Hsieh & Skjei announce the release of *On the Cutting Edge*, a sly little chapbook juxtapositioning contrary and edgy remarks of renown designers. This 16 page limited edition is letterpressed in 2 colors with a hand-sewn gatefold cover and sells for $23.00 (includes postage). Send a check or money order to: Shay, Shea, Hsieh & Skjei, 806 Mt. Curve, Minneapolis, MN 55403. (Minnesotans add $1.40 for sales tax.)

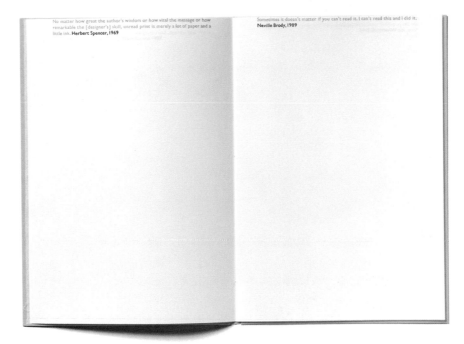

No matter how great the author's wisdom or how vital the message or how remarkable the [designer's] skill, unread print is merely a lot of paper and a little ink. Herbert Spencer, 1969
Sometimes it doesn't matter if you can't read it. I can't read this and I did it. Neville Brody, 1989

On the Cutting Edge

Most of the time people simply latch on to trends or freakish solutions they believe are creative but which have nothing to do with real problems — with right or wrong. Paul Rand, 1985
Don't trust anyone who pontificates about rights and wrongs... intuition is everything... let your heart spit it out. P. Scott Makela, 1995

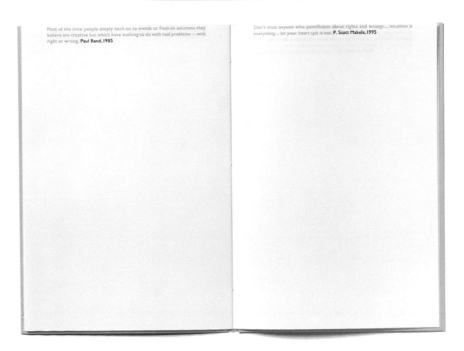

Design Firm: M. Skjei Design Co. Creative Director & Designer: Michael Skjei Client: Shay, Shea, Hsieh & Skjei Publishers

Design Firm: Vanderbyl Design Art & Creative Director: Michael Vanderbyl Designers: Michael Vanderbyl, Karin Myint Photographer: Hugh Kretschmer Copywriter: Penny Benda Client: Teknion, Inc.

[NO. OI IN A SERIES]

BOUNDARIES MARK THE PLACE WE START FROM, TRAVELING WITH NO FIXED DESTINATION OR EVEN A MAP, BUT RATHER TO EXPLORE THE MYSTERY, BRING BACK GLIMPSES OF THE POSSIBLE AND THE SOUVENIRS OF OUR COURAGE. THE GUGGENHEIM MUSEUM, DESIGNED BY FRANK LLOYD WRIGHT, CHANGED THE WAY WE LOOK AT ART AND INHABIT SPACE, REINSCRIBING THE BOUNDARIES OF ARCHITECTURE. IN THAT SPIRIT, TEKNION® INTRODUCES ALTOS,™ A FULL-HEIGHT WALL SYSTEM, DESIGNED TO CREATE NEW BOUNDARIES FOR A WORLD THAT WORKS TOGETHER. SEE US AT NEOCON 99. SPACE 1048.

TEKNION | ALTOS | WALL | SYSTEM

Teknion

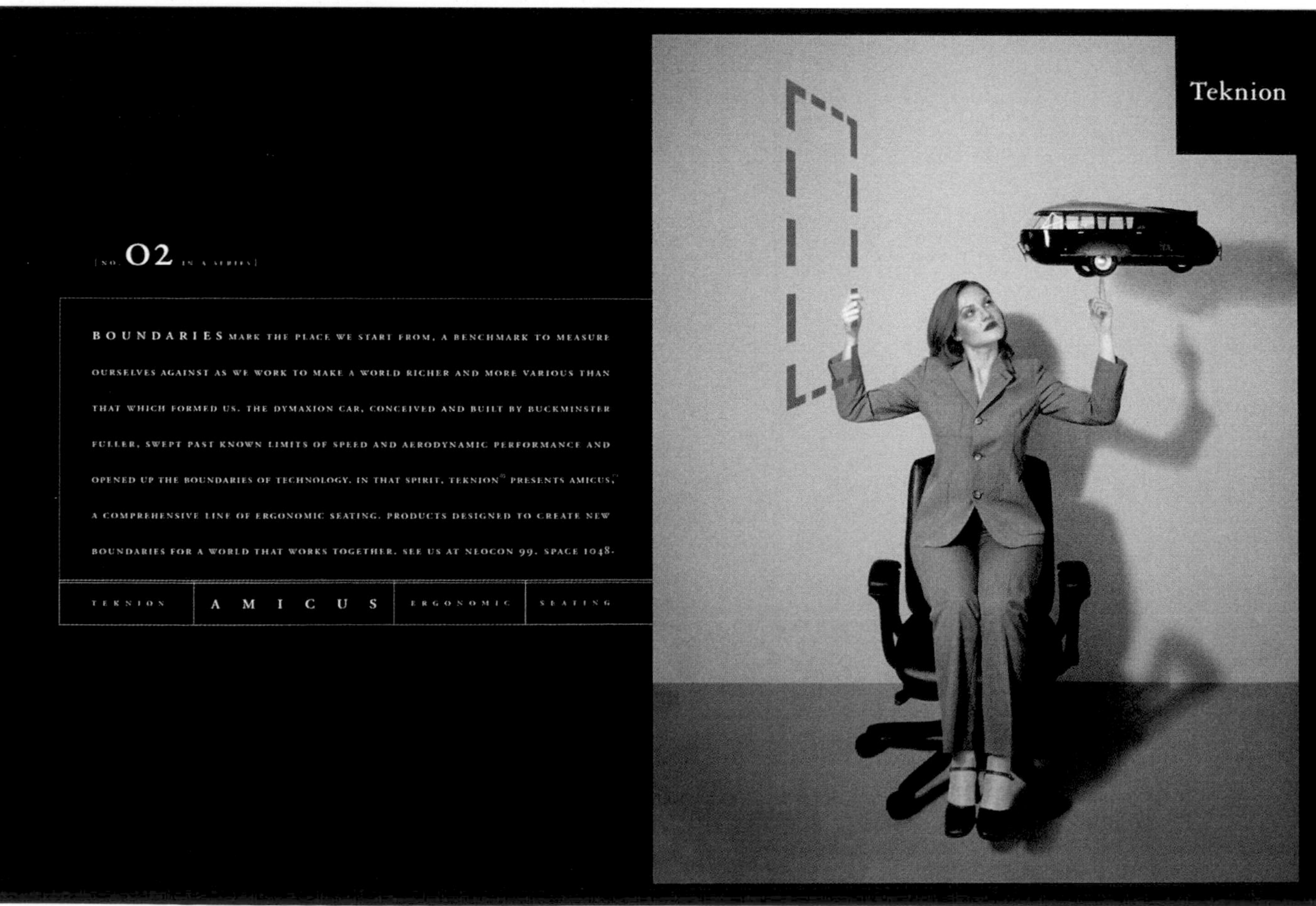

[NO. O2 IN A SERIES]
BOUNDARIES MARK THE PLACE WE START FROM, A BENCHMARK TO MEASURE OURSELVES AGAINST AS WE WORK TO MAKE A WORLD RICHER AND MORE VARIOUS THAN THAT WHICH FORMED US. THE DYMAXION CAR, CONCEIVED AND BUILT BY BUCKMINSTER FULLER, SWEPT PAST KNOWN LIMITS OF SPEED AND AERODYNAMIC PERFORMANCE AND OPENED UP THE BOUNDARIES OF TECHNOLOGY. IN THAT SPIRIT, TEKNION® PRESENTS AMICUS,™ A COMPREHENSIVE LINE OF ERGONOMIC SEATING. PRODUCTS DESIGNED TO CREATE NEW BOUNDARIES FOR A WORLD THAT WORKS TOGETHER. SEE US AT NEOCON 99. SPACE 1048.
TEKNION
AMICUS
ERGONOMIC
SEATING
Teknion

Design Firm: GSD&M Art Director: Anne Stevenson Creative Director: Brian Brooker Designer: Kris Newman Copywriter: Carlotte Stankiewicz Client: Southwest Airlines

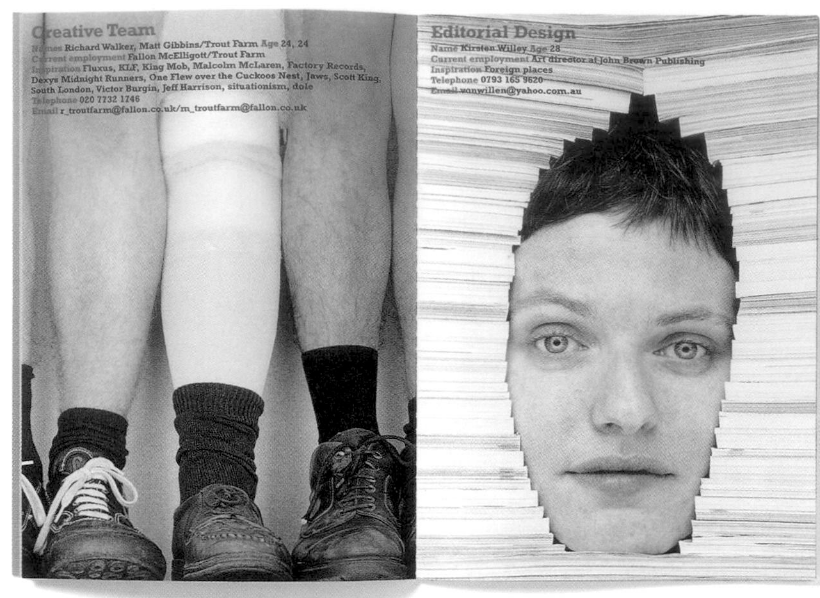
Creative Team
Names Richard Walker, Matt Gibbins/Trout Farm Age 24, 24
Current employment Fallon McElligott/Trout Farm
Inspiration Fluxus, KLF, King Mob, Malcolm McLaren, Factory Records, Dexys Midnight Runners, One Flew over the Cuckoos Nest, Jaws, Scott King, South London, Victor Burgin, Jeff Harrison, situationism, dole
Telephone 020 7732 1746
Email r_troutfarm@fallon.co.uk/m_troutfarm@fallon.co.uk
Editorial Design
Name Kirsten Willey Age 28
Current employment Art director at John Brown Publishing
Inspiration Foreign places
Telephone 0793 165 9620
Email vonwillen@yahoo.com.au

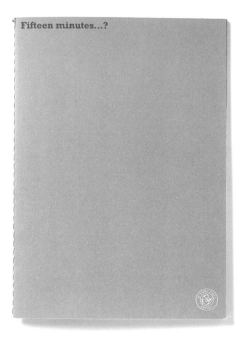

Fifteen minutes...?

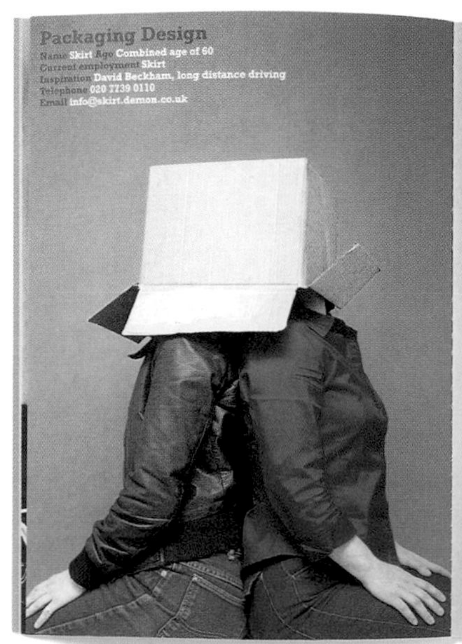
Packaging Design
Name Skirt Age Combined age of 60
Current employment Skirt
Inspiration David Beckham, long distance driving
Telephone 020 7739 0110
Email info@skirt.demon.co.uk

Advertising Photography
Name Richard Bush Age 26
Current employment Freelance
Inspiration Literature, people and everyday being
Telephone 020 7434 3202/Untitled Managment Ltd
Email richard@untitled.uk.com
Bold

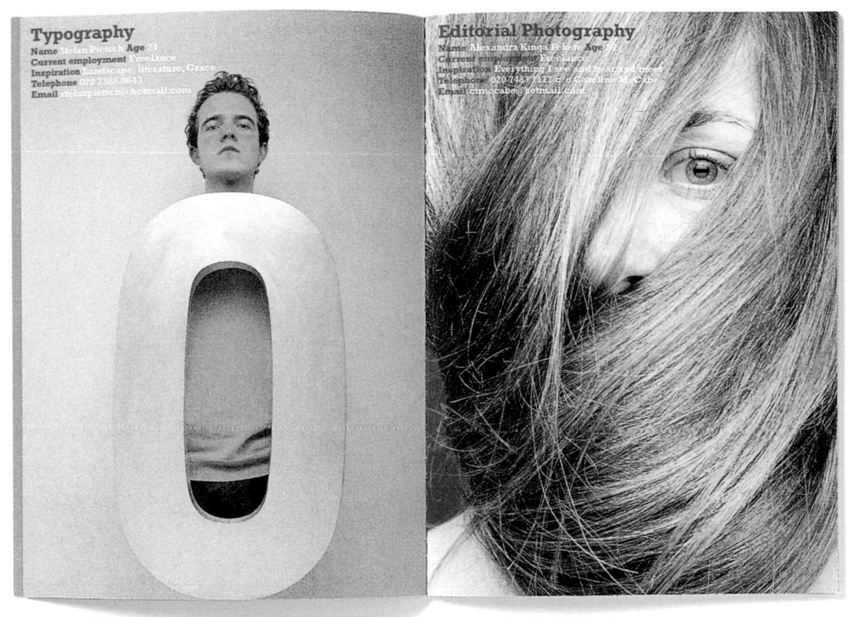

Typography
Name Stefan Pietsch Age
Current employment Freelance
Inspiration Landscape, literature, Grace
Telephone 020 7388 0643
Email stefanpietsch@hotmail.com
Editorial Photography
Name Alexandra Kinga Fekete Age
Current employment Freelance
Inspiration Everything I see and hear and meet
Telephone 020 7483 1177 c/o Caroline McCabe
Email ctmccabe@hotmail.com

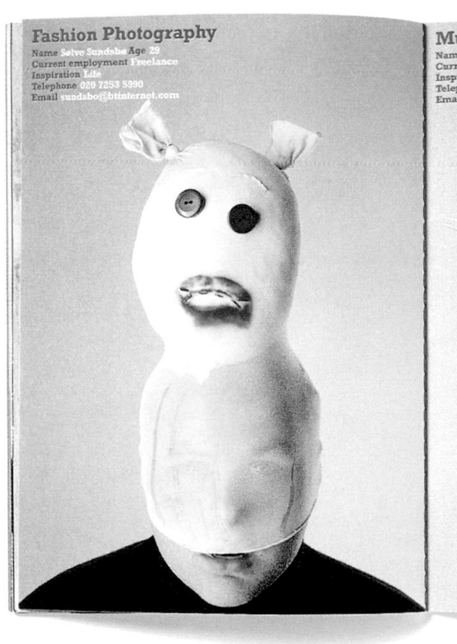

Fashion Photography
Name Sølve Sundsbø Age 29
Current employment Freelance
Inspiration Life
Telephone 020 7253 5990
Email sundsbo@btinternet.com

Multimedia
Name Daniel Brown Age 22
Current employment Creative technologist at Amaze Limited
Inspiration Nothing rational
Telephone 07801 704 143
Email dannyb@amaze.co.uk

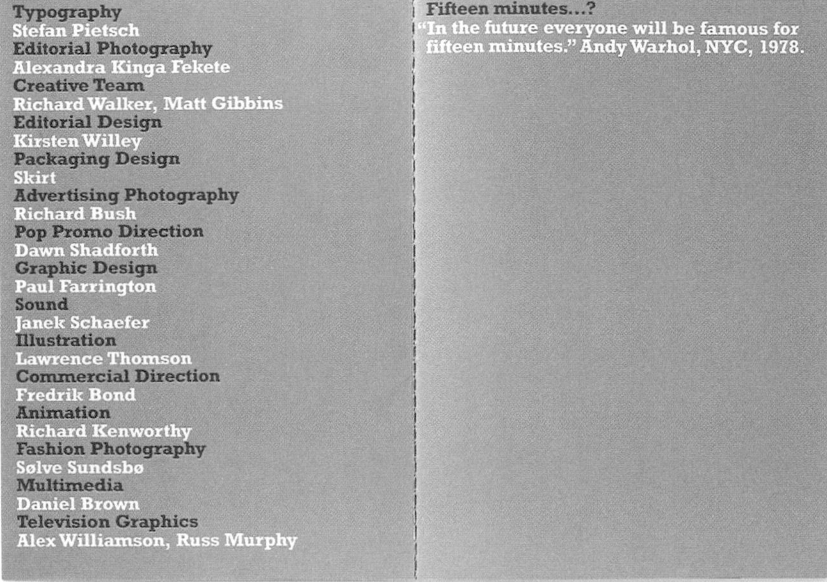

Typography
Stefan Pietsch
Editorial Photography
Alexandra Kinga Fekete
Creative Team
Richard Walker, Matt Gibbins
Editorial Design
Kirsten Willey
Packaging Design
Skirt
Advertising Photography
Richard Bush
Pop Promo Direction
Dawn Shadforth
Graphic Design
Paul Farrington
Sound
Janek Schaefer
Illustration
Lawrence Thomson
Commercial Direction
Fredrik Bond
Animation
Richard Kenworthy
Fashion Photography
Sølve Sundsbø
Multimedia
Daniel Brown
Television Graphics
Alex Williamson, Russ Murphy
Fifteen minutes...?
"In the future everyone will be famous for fifteen minutes." Andy Warhol, NYC, 1978.

Design Firm: Browns/London Creative Director: Jonathan Ellery Designers: Jonathan Ellery, Lee Liversedge Photographer: David Stewart Client: Munkedals Ab

Design Firm: Sandstrom Design Art Director: Jon Olsen Creative Director: Steve Sandstrom Designer: Andrew Randall Illustrators: Jeff Foster, John Hersey Copywriter: Matt Elhardt Client: Sandstrom Design

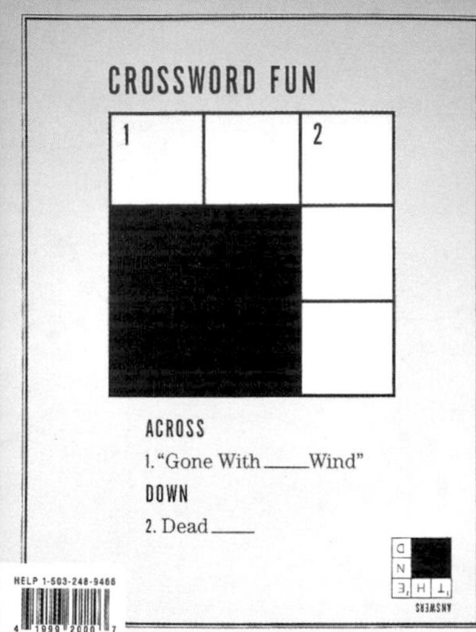

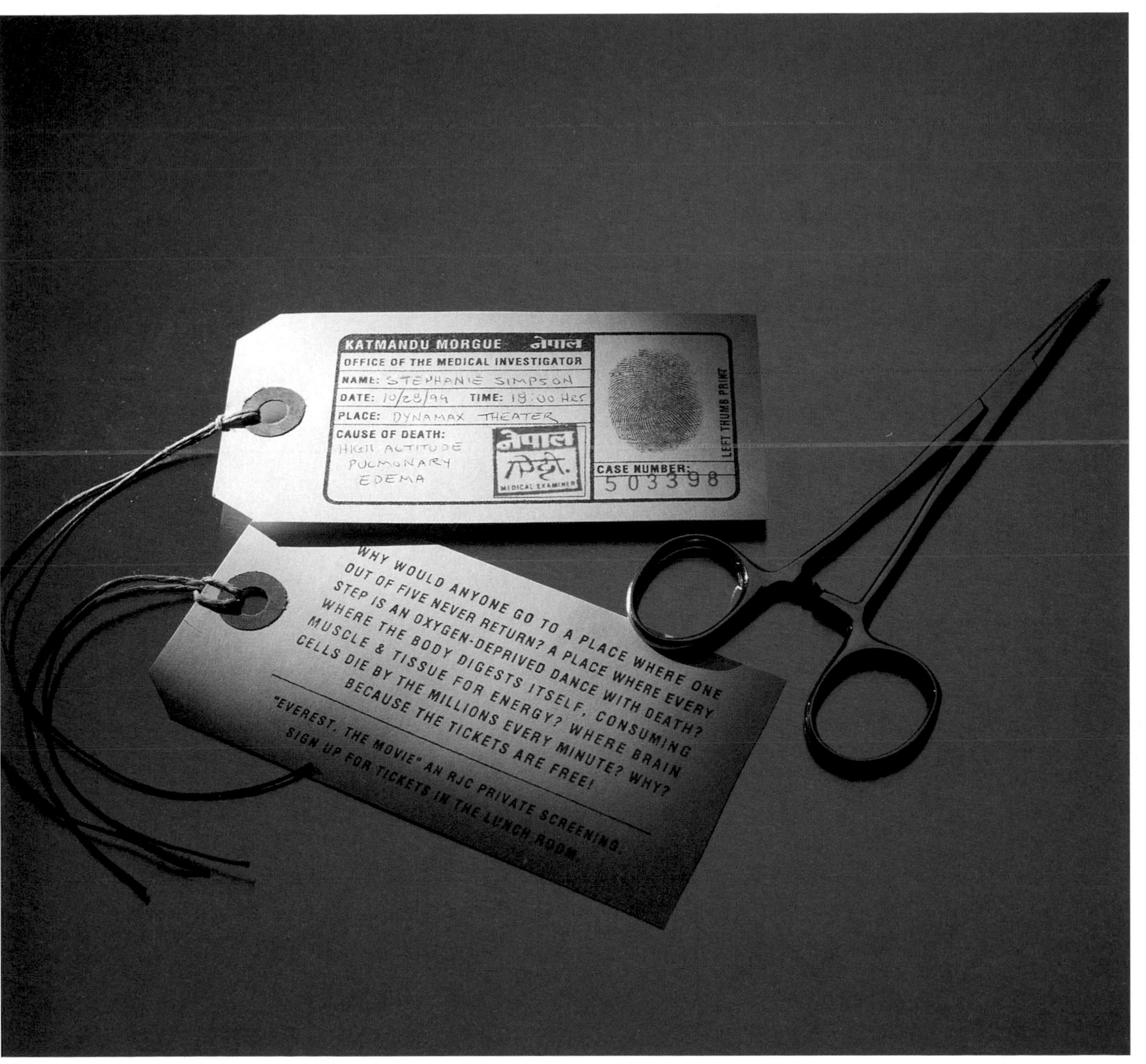

Design Firm: Rick Johnson & Company Art Director & Designer: Tim McGrath Photographer: Paul Kohlman Copywriter: Tim Pegors Client: Rick Johnson & Company

this year
we thought it would be
better
to give than to receive
some of our
shirts, skirts, sweaters, pants & pullovers
have already been given to these organizations
and we hope
you'll do the same.
HEARTFELT FOUNDATION
2101 Wilshire Boulevard Suite 103
Santa Monica, CA 90403
(310) 829.7857
SAINT BENEDICT THE MOOR
283 Saint Anne's Avenue Ground Floor/Soup Kitchen
Bronx, NY 10454
(718) 665.9693
If you would like to participate, please call:
@radical.media
NY (212) 462-1500 Kathryn O'Kane
LA (310) 664-4500 Denise Felloni
We'll coordinate all pick-ups... Happy New Year!

Design Firm: @radical.media Art & Creative Director, Designer: Rafael Esquer Photographer: Christian Tuempling Client: @radical.media

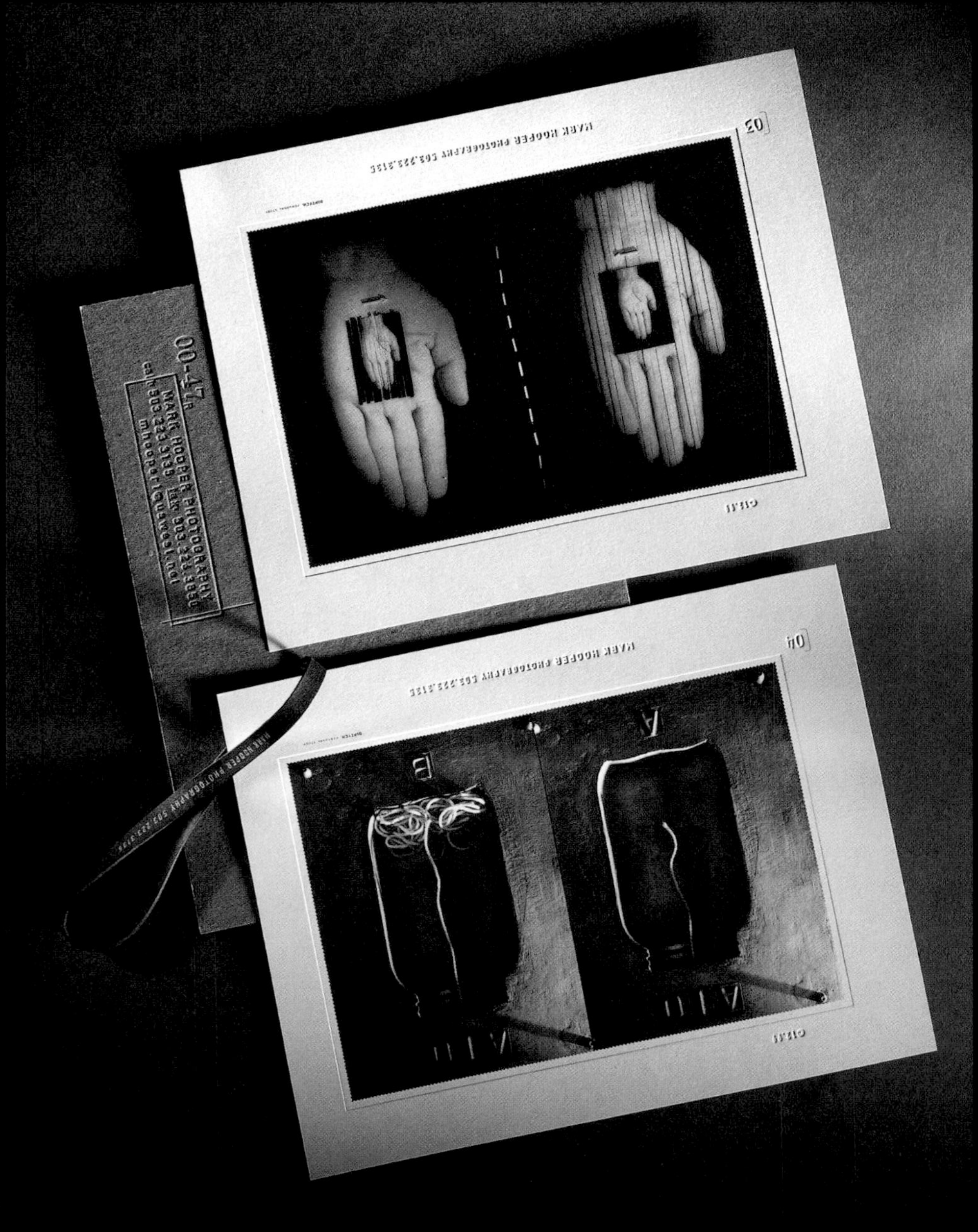

Design Firm: Sandstrom Design Art & Creative Director: Steve Sandstrom Designer: Amy Devletian Photographer: Mark Hooper Client: Mark Hooper Photography

Design Firm: @radical.media Art & Creative Director, Designer: Rafael Esquer Photographer: Christian Tuempling Client: @radical.media

ALL @RADICAL.MEDIA OFFICES
WILL BE COORDINATING
A GLOBAL EFFORT TO PROVIDE
CLOTHING FOR PEOPLE IN NEED
IF YOU'D LIKE TO PARTICIPATE
CALL ANY ONE OF OUR OFFICES
NEW YORK | 212.462.1590
LOS ANGELES | 310 664.4515
LONDON 0966 148.253
PARIS 00 33 | 4453.2626
SYDNEY 61 2 9213.6328
YOU DO YOUR PART AND
WE'LL PICK UP THE BAGS

THIS HOLIDAY
SEASON
WE INVITE YOU
TO JOIN US AS
@RADICALS
FOR A
GOOD CAUSE

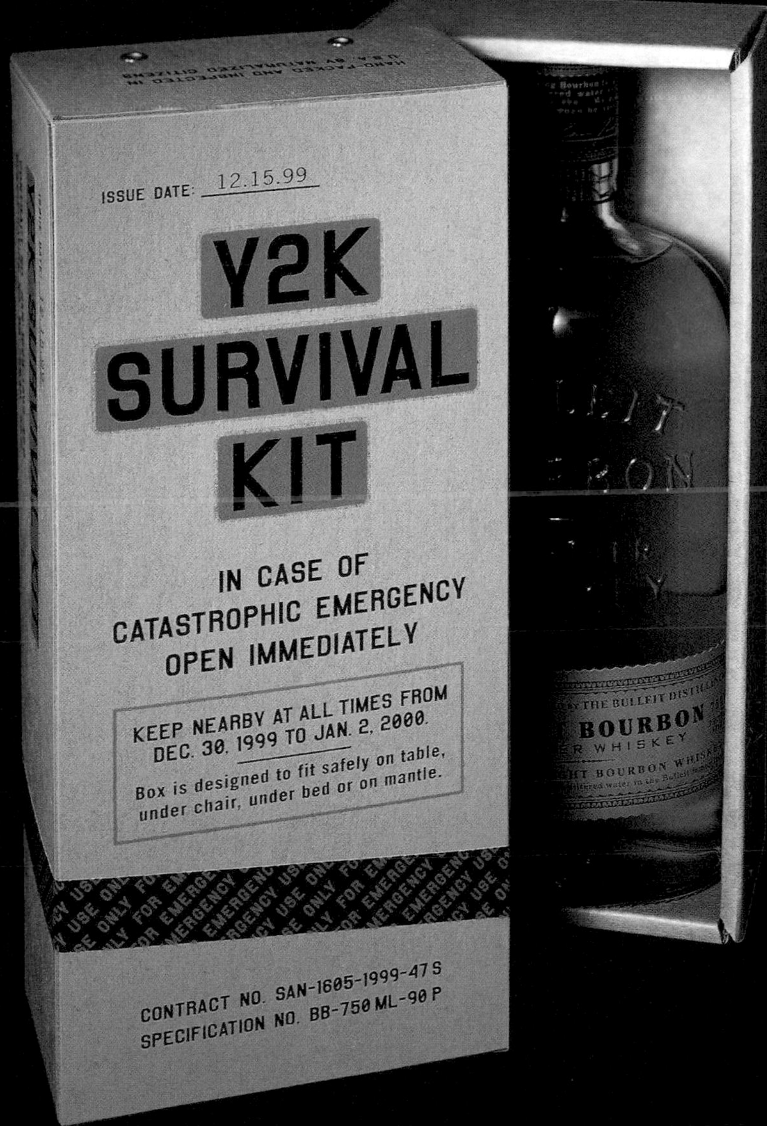

Design Firm: Sandstrom Design Art & Creative Director: Steve Sandstrom Copywriter: Steve Sandoz Client: Sandstrom Design

FRAGILE
DO NOT BEND

pigment liner

LELLA IS ON THE PHONE - LUCA IS TAKING PICS -
LELLA IS TIRED
LUCA'S BABY IS GREAT - I AM

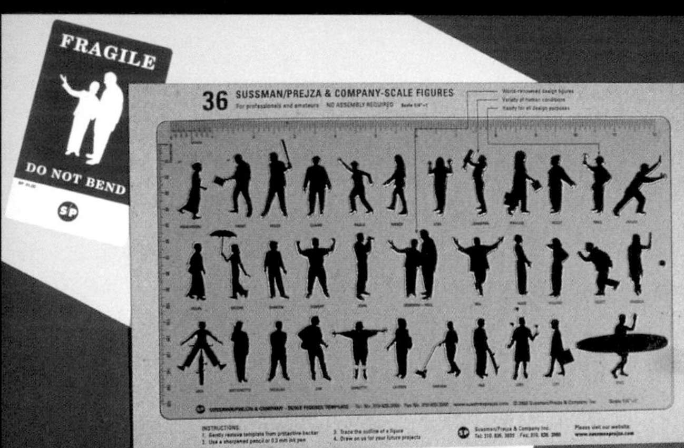
FRAGILE
DO NOT BEND
36 SUSSMAN/PREJZA & COMPANY-SCALE FIGURES

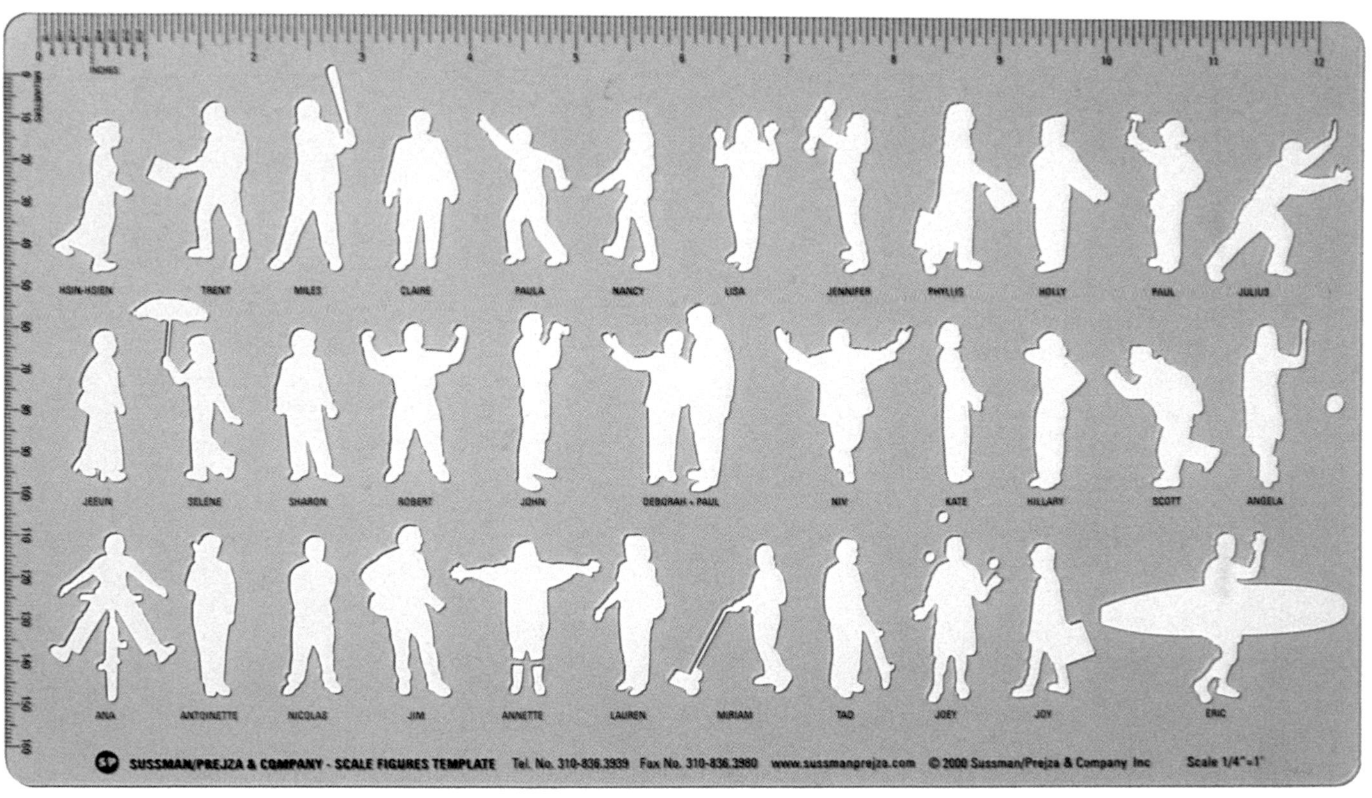

Design Firm: Sussman Prejza & Co., Inc. Art Director: Niv Kasher Creative Director: Deborah Sussman Designers: Miles Mazzie, Tad Hara, Robert Chacko, Selene Rawls Photographer: Jim Simmons, Annette Del Zoppo Productions Client: Sussman Prejza & Co., Inc.

uey/Rubino Design Art & Creative Director: Robert Louey Designers: Robert Louey, Alex Chao, Anja Mueller Photographers: Eric Tucker, Neal Brown, Everard Williams Jr., Hugh Kretschmer, Lise Metzer, Jamey Stillings, Ann Elliott Cutting Copywriter: Elisabeth Charney Clients: Lithographix, Louey/Rubino Design, Sharpe & Associates

Design Firm: Watts Design Art & Creative Director, Designer: Peter Watts Client: Watts Design

ve Director: Michael Osborne Designer: Paul Kaginada Copywriter: Alyson Kuhn Client: Dicksons

All Purpose Litho, 80#
The Hamilton Mill
Champion International Corporation

DICKSON'S

EPHEMERA PHILATELICA
a collector's album for stamps

ADVERTISING COVERS
BUY NOW
OUR POSTAL HISTORY

bisect

Cheval
PARIS
Couture pour Hommes

EFO
ERRORS
FREAKS
ODDITIES
US POSTAGE
32 CENT 32

1840

"G" STAMP
PRINTED, RESTED AND READY FOR THE NEXT RATE HIKE

IN·VERT: TO TURN INSIDE OUT OR UPSIDE DOWN 32¢

EMISSION CONJOINTE
JOINT ISSUE

K TOWN 1914
KANSAS CITY ROULETTE

MAY 2 9 1997

MULREADY
ENVELOPES

NUMERALS
U.S.POSTAGE 32 CENTS

UNITED STATES POSTAGE
2¢

R
RAILWAY POST OFFICE

S E T E N A N T

5 + 35¢
thematic topic
19 97

Ephemera Philatelica © 1999 Dickson's, Inc.
Philatelic alphabet © 1998 AIGA/SF

Uranos
UNIVERSAL POSTAL UNION

US 06¢

W
WAR

ПОЧТА
Б 1000 Р

Yvert & Tellier
REPUBLIQUE FRANÇAISE
5.00
CATALOGUE DE TIMBRES-POSTE

Z

DICKSON'S

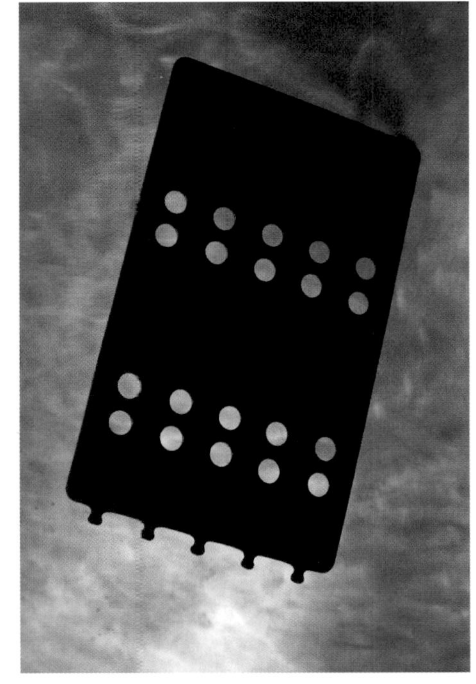

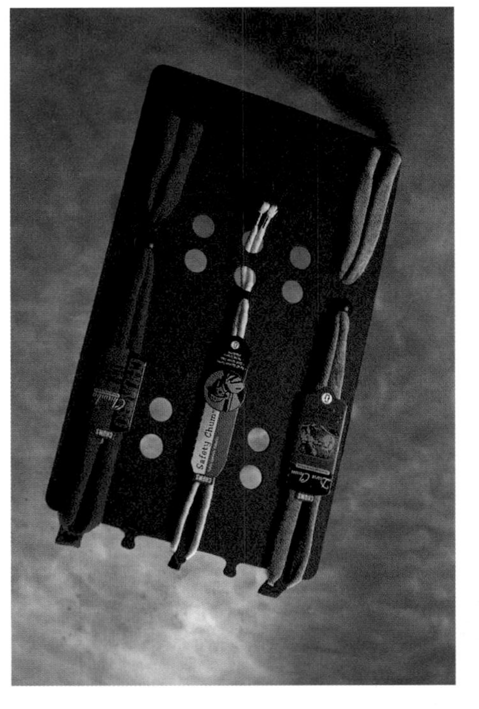

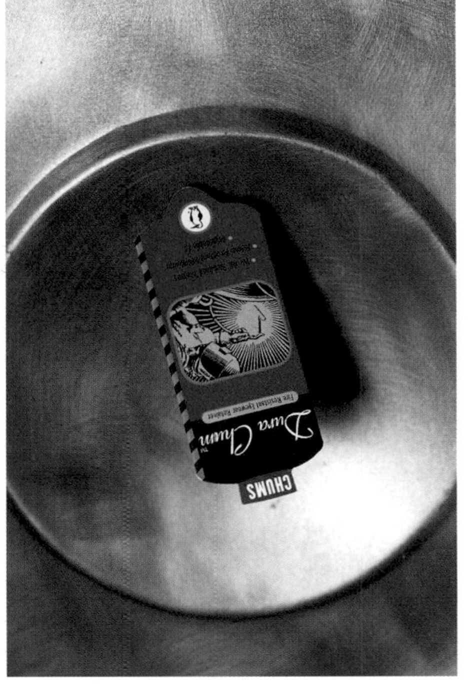

Design Firm: FullblastInc.com Creative Director & Designer: N. Todd Skiles Photographers: Bob Waldman, Kurt Mandahl Copywriters: Neil Webster, David Weighel, Perry Novelli Client: Chums

Design Firm: The Rocket Scientists Art Director, Designer & Illustrator: Eduard Claassen Creative Director: Charl Ritter Client: SABC 3

Design Firm: Packaging Create, Inc. Art Director & Designer: Akio Okumura Client: MUSA

Design Firm: Aidalos Design Art Director: Klemens Werthmann Creative Director & Designer: Catrin Fabricius Photographers: Clemens Wertflumé, Cat Faby Copywriter: Aidalos Design Client: Hautnah Kosmetik-Institut

Design Firm: Aidalos Design Art Director: Klemens Werthmann Creative Director & Designer: Catrin Fabricius Photographer: Clemens Wertflumé, Cat Faby Copywriter: Aidalos Design Client: Delicatess Shops

Design Firm: U.S. Postal Service Art Director: Phil Jordan Creative Director: Terrence McCaffrey Designer & Illustrator: Nicholas Gaetano Client: U.S. Postal Service

INSECTS & SPIDERS

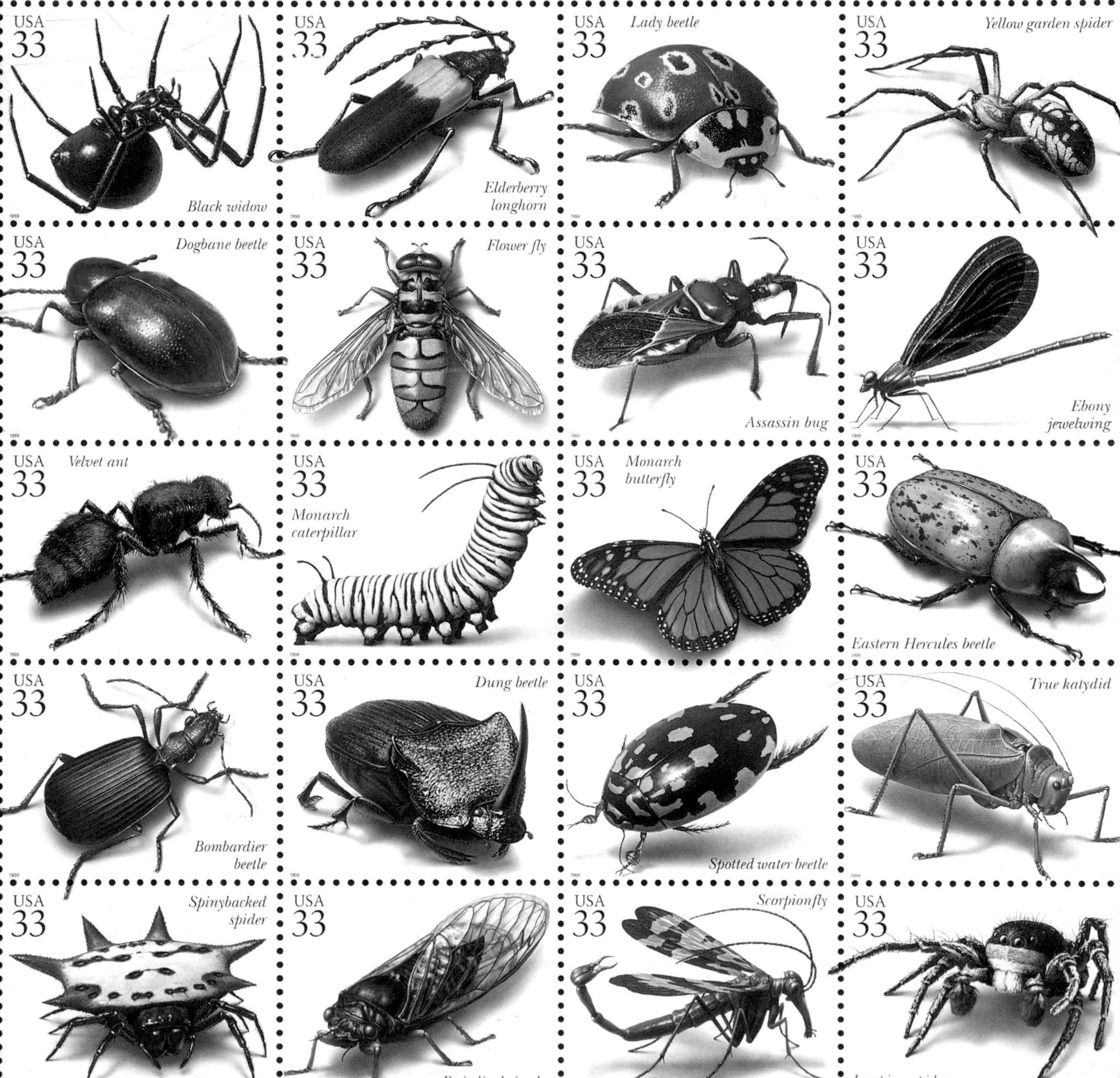

Design Firm: U.S. Postal Service Art Director: Carl Herrman Creative Director: Terrence McCaffrey Designer: Carl Herrman Illustrator: Stephen Buchanan Client: U.S. Postal Service

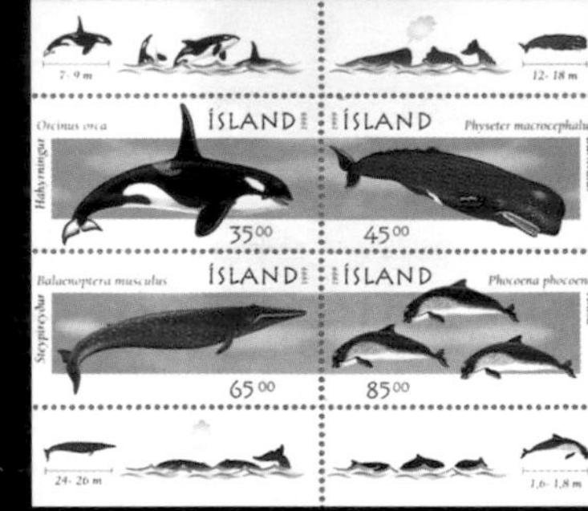

Design Firm: YDDA Advertising Agency Creative Director, Designer & Illustrator: Kristín Thora Guðbjartsdóttir Client: Icelandpost

Rudolf Maister 1874-1934
70
SLOVENIJA
Peter Kozler 1824-1879
14
SLOVENIJA
dr. Božidar Lavrič 1899-1961
15
SLOVENIJA
dr. France Prešeren 1800-1849
80
SLOVENIJA

Design Firm: Mires Design Art & Creative Director: Jose Serrano Designer: Miguel Perez Illustrator: Tracy Sabin Client: Mires Design

Design Firm: Vaughn Wedeen Creative

Art Director: Rick Vaughn Creative Directors: Rick Vaughn, Foster Hurley Designers: Rick Vaughn, Stan McCoy, Chip Wyly Photographer: Michael Barley Copywriter: Foster Hurley Client: Vaugh Wedeen Creative

Design Firm: Elixir Design, Inc. Art Director: Jennifer Jerde Designers: Nathan Durrant, Holly Holmquist, Merel Kennedy, Jennifer Tolo Client: Elixir Design, Inc.

Index

CreativeDirectorsArtDirectorsDesigners

Acevedo, Luis Dallas, TX (214) 987 6529 170
Adey, David San Diego, CA (619) 234 6631 . . . . 66, 67
Ahlfeldt, Dana San Francisco, CA (415) 369 6324 . . . . 100, 101
Aiba, Takanori Tokyo, Japan 03 3449 0651 108
Anan, Amy San Francisco, CA (415) 896 0499 209
Anderson, Charles S. Minneapolis, MN (612) 339 5181. . . . . 30, 31, 182, 183
Asai, Hiroki San Francisco, CA (415) 369 6324 195

Baldwin, David Raleigh, NC (919) 821 6436 . . . . 70, 71
Barrett, Steve Seattle, WA (206) 447 7040 . . . . 74, 75
Berk, Edi Ljubljana, Slovenia 38661 1265761 241
Bielenberg, John San Francisco, CA (415) 495 3371 . . . . 46, 47
Birlew, Dan Dallas, TX (214) 987 6529 170
Black, Dustin Omaha, NE (402) 965 4300 200
Bobolts, Carol New York, NY (212) 219 0557 . . . . 150, 151
Bonomelli, Rex New York, NY (212) 219 0557 . . . . 150, 151
Braley, Michael San Francisco, CA (415) 621 0915. . . . . 14, 52, 53
Brier, David Menomonie, WI (715) 235 9040 205
Brink, Gaby San Francisco, CA (415) 777 9294 . . . . 68, 69, 179, 180
Brinkman, Mark Austin, TX (512) 473 2333 141
Broadbent, Robin London, England 0207 407 9074. 25
Brodsley, Adam San Francisco, CA (415) 243 9277 . . . . 116, 117
Brooker, Brian Austin, TX (512) 427 4920 219
Brooks, Jane Austin, TX (512) 322 0826. 140
Bubat, Randi Dingolfing, Germany 45 8731 7422 . . . . 64, 65
Burd, Trenton West Des Moines, IA (515) 255 6801 58
Buttecali, Peter Alexandria, VA (703) 684 3383 138
Byrne, David New York, NY (212) 647 1789. 24

Cahan, Bill San Francisco, CA (415) 621 0915. . . . . 14, 52, 53
Cannon, David Atlanta, GA (404) 875 8225 . . . . 15, 41
Carnegie, Wendy Austin, TX 16
Celiz, Bob San Francisco, CA (415) 495 8691 166
Chacko, Robert Culver City, CA (310) 836 3939 . . . . 228, 229
Chan, Amy San Francisco, CA (415) 896 0499. 92
Chan, Eric 206
Chao, Alex Santa Monica, CA (310) 396 7724 230
Charles, Leslie San Francisco, CA (415) 834 0300. 56
Chavez, Marcos New York, NY (212) 366 4337 90
Chen, Dan New York, NY (212) 888 2002 79
Chermayeff, Ivan 91
Chwast, Seymour New York, NY (212) 255 6465. 42
Claassen, Eduard Pretoria, South Africa 2712 346 4992. 234
Cochran, Beth Roswell, GA (770) 645 2828 . . . . 111, 112, 113
Colvin, Alan Minneapolis, MN (612) 321 2333 144
Copeland, Brad Atlanta, GA (404) 892 3472 60
Coss, Blanca Mexico City, Mexico 55 19 74 22 158
Cox, Erik San Francisco, CA (415) 495 3371 . . . . 46, 47
Crawford, David Austin, TX (512) 427 4920 . . . . 192, 193, 194

D'Attilio, Rebecca Atlanta, GA (404) 892 3472 60
de Kok, Jeroen Amsterdam, Holland 31205715670 172
de Socio, Bridget New York, NY (212) 888 2002 . . . . 78, 79
De Vicq De Cumptich, Roberto New York, NY (212) 289 2369. 26
DeMattes, Janet New York, NY (212) 219 0557 . . . . 150, 151
Denat, Jean-Luc Ottawa, Canada (613) 748 3336 140
Deutsch, Barry San Francisco, CA (415) 487 8520. . . . . 119, 171
Devletian, Amy Portland, OR (503) 248 9466. . . . . 170, 225
Doe, Kelly 96
Dolan, Mike San Francisco, CA (415) 369 6324 . . . . 100, 101
Dreyfus, Andy San Francisco, CA (415) 369 6324. . . . . 100, 101, 195
Dubov, Gail New York, NY (212) 207 7742. 125
Duckworth, Bruce San Francisco, CA (415) 495 8691 . . . . 166, 167, 176, 177, 210, 211
Duffney, Craig Minneapolis, MN (612) 321 2333 . . . . 102, 103
Duffy, Joe Minneapolis, MN (612) 321 2333 . . 76, 77, 102, 103, 142, 144, 157
Durrant, Nathan San Francisco, CA (415) 834 0300 . . . . 56, 244
Dunn, Chris New York, NY (212) 683 7000. . . . . 173, 198

Eisele, Yael New York, NY (212) 982 7621. . . . . 59, 154, 155
Elder, Simone Victoria, Australia 613 942 12344. 57
Ellery, Jonathan London, England 0207 407 9074. . . . . 33, 220, 221
Emer, Johannes. 32
Englin, Rob Thousand Oaks, CA (805) 370 1200. 212
English, Marion Birmingham, AL (205) 458 8167 43
Esquer, Rafael New York, NY (212) 462 1568 . . . . 224, 226

Fabricius, Catrin Braunschweig, Germany 0 531 455 16 . . . . 236, 237
Fahrner, Marius 32
Fergusen, Archie. 22
Ferreira, Lionel Atlanta, GA (404) 892 3472. 60
Fishel, Peter San Francisco, CA (415) 543 8447 105
Fishman, Gill Cambridge, MA (617) 492 5666. 122
Flatt, Kevin Minneapolis, MN (612) 321 2333 157
Flesher, Gary Roswell, GA (770) 645 2828 110
Forbes, Jason Seattle, WA (206) 728 7997 156
Forrester, Teresa Seattle, WA (206) 447 7040 . . . . 74, 75
Frank, Stefan Berlin, Germany 49 30 69504771 159
Frazier, Craig Mill Valley, CA (415) 389 1475 126
Freach, Tanya Dallas, TX (214) 987 6529 . . . . 36, 62
Frost, Vince London, England 00 44 20 7490 7994 . . . . . 38, 39, 97, 207, 236
Frykholm, Stephen Zeeland, MI (616) 654 8225. . . . . 12, 13

Gaetano, Nicholas Washington, DC (202) 268 6576 238
Gallas, Ron Minneapolis, MN (612) 321 2333 . . . . 102, 103
Garcia, Art Dallas, TX (214) 948 6969. . . . . 138, 140
Gargulio, Frank Columbus, OH (614) 447 8103. 147
Gil, Jose P. Godella, Spain 34 963904074 190
Gimeno, Pepe Godella, Spain 34 963904074 190
Giresh, Sharon New York, NY (212) 979 0300 . . . . 188, 189
Glazer, Nancy Boston, MA (617) 867 1000 . . . . 34, 35
Glover, Patti San Francisco, CA (415) 369 6324. . . . . 100, 101
Glupker, Chris Thousand Oaks, CA (805) 370 1200 212
Gold, Keith Ponte Vedra Beach, FL (904) 285 5669 . . . . 148, 208
Golonka, Dennis. 80, 81
Gorthy, Clint Portland, OR (503) 227 6343. 140
Grazziolo, Michael New York, NY (212) 989 5103. 27
Guðbjartsdóttir, Kristín Thora Reykjavík, Iceland 354 510 8100 240
Guglieri, Guy 94, 95

Hada, Motoka New York, NY (212) 647 1789 149
Hakansson, Mats New York, NY (212) 982 7621 59
Ham, Kathryn New York, NY (212) 807 0248 181
Hames, Kyle Minneapolis, MN (612) 339 5181 182
Hamlett, Phil Atlanta, GA (404) 875 8225 41
Hara, Tad Culver City, CA (310) 836 3939 . . . . . 228, 229
Harris, Cabell Richmond, VA (804) 358 9366 . . . . . 174, 175
Harris, Keith Konstanz, Germany 07531 958939 142
Haskell, David Boston, MA (617) 867 1000 . . . . . 34, 35
Heck, Matt Austin, TX (512) 473 2333 141
Heiman, Eric San Francisco, CA (415) 834 0300 56
Hendler, Sandra Philadelphia, PA (215) 735 7380 129
Henreckson, Todd Chicago, IL (312) 454 1116 214
Hepler, Steve Roswell, GA (770) 645 2828 . . . . . 106, 107
Herring, Jerry Houston, TX (713) 526 1250 48
Herrman, Carl Washington, DC (202) 268 6576 239
Herron, Chris Brookline, MA (617) 738 330 136
Hill, Brian Charlotte, NC (704) 372 1600 202
Hinrichs, Kit San Francisco, CA (415) 896 0499 . . . . . 4, 92, 114, 115, 140, 184, 185, 186, 187, 209
Hinz, Nate Minneapolis, MN (612) 321 2333 142
Hirano, Keiko Tokyo, Japan 81 3 3668 9777 . . . . . 96, 134, 213
Hitt, Brenden 23
Holderfield, Greg Chicago, IL (312) 454 1116 214
Holloway, Christo New York, NY (212) 229 1187 132
Holmquist, Holly San Francisco, CA .(415) 834 0300 . . . . . 56, 244
Holst, Brad Seattle, WA (206) 728 7997 156
Houghton, Gavin 93
Howalt, Paul San Francisco, CA (415) 777 9294 138
Hoyt, Julie Austin, TX 16
Hug, Karin New York, NY (212) 366 4337 90
Hurley, Foster Albuquerque, NM (505) 243 4000 243

Ide, Toshi Boston, MA (617) 867 1000 . . . . . 34, 35

Jacobs, Brian San Francisco, CA (415) 896 0499 . . . . . 184, 185, 186, 187
Jacoma, George Alexandria, VA (703) 684 3383 138
Jany, Eric Dallas, TX (214) 826 4631 104
Jenkins, Keith W. 96
Jerde, Jennifer San Francisco, CA (415) 834 0300 . . . . . 56, 244
Jett, Clare Prospect, KY 139
Johnson, Haley Richmond, VA (804) 358 9366 . . . . . 174, 175
Johnston, John Culver City, CA (310) 836 3939 . . . . . 98, 99
Jones, Caroline 80, 81
Jordan, Phil Washington, DC (202) 268 6576 238
Junemann, Marcelo 84, 85, 86, 87

Kaginada, Paul San Francisco, CA (415) 255 0125 232
Kaiser, Orville New York, NY (212) 683 7000 173
Karisson, Hjalti New York, NY (212) 647 1789 . . . . . 20, 21, 24, 28, 29, 201
Karlic, Ken Baltimore, MD (410) 462 6878 120
Kasher, Niv Culver City, CA (310) 836 3939 . . . . . 228, 229
Katona, Diti Toronto, Canada (416) 534 9960 61
Katsui, Mitsuo Tokyo, Japan 81 3 3668 9777 96
Katzman, Mark Saint Louis, MO (314) 725 6616 40
Kavanagh, Caroline Deer Lodge, TN (423) 965 2223 . . . . . 152, 153
Kavulla, Brandon Toronto, Canada 416 364 3846 123
Kawaguchi, Yoichiro 91
Kelley, Tom Minneapolis, MN (612) 321 2333 . . . . . 102, 103
Kennedy, Merel San Francisco, CA (415) 834 0300 . . . . . 56, 244
Kim, Yang Zeeland, MI (616) 654 8225 . . . . . 12, 13
Klotina, John New York, NY (212) 683 7000 173
Kobe, Tim San Francisco, CA (415) 369 6324 . . . . . 100, 101
Koch, Deb Deer Lodge, TN (423) 965 2223 . . . . . 152, 153
Kosaka, Wayne San Francisco, CA (415) 398 9348 145
Kottman, Petra Dingolfing, Germany 45 8731 7422 . . . . . 64, 65
Kowalczyk, Patti Chicago, IL (312) 337 2323 124
Kudo, Aoshi Tokyo, Japan 81 3357 25111 169
Kudo, Norio Tokyo, Japan 81 3 5467 4316 . . . . . 197, 199
Kyoto, Hiroshi Tokyo, Japan 81 3 5467 4316 197

L'Écuyer, Mario Ottawa, Canada (613) 748 3336 140
Lambert, J.K. 22
Lee, Ting Ting 84, 85, 86, 87
Leff, Steve Dallas, TX (214) 826 4631 104
Lins, Rico 84
Liversedge, Lee London, England 0207 407 9074 . . . . . 33, 220, 221
Lloyd, Doug 84, 85, 86, 87
Lorenc, Jan Roswell, GA (770) 645 2828 . . . . . 106, 107, 110, 111, 112, 113
Louey, Robert Santa Monica, CA (310) 396 7724 230
Lucas, John San Francisco, CA (415) 487 8520 119
Lynk, Barbara Chicago, IL 312) 787 4504 121

Marrs, Joe Dallas, TX (214) 826 4631 104
Martinez Garcia, Ofelia Mexico City, Mexico 55 19 74 22 158
Matsumoto, Takaaki New York, NY (212) 807 0248 181
Matz, Starlee Portland, OR (503) 248 9466 . . . . . 133, 178
Mauk, Mitchell San Francisco, CA (415) 243 9277 . . . . . 116, 117
Mazzie, Miles Culver City, CA (310) 836 3939 . . . . . 228, 229
McAfee, Scott Austin, TX (512) 427 4920 . . . . . 192, 193, 194
McCaffrey, Terrence Washington, DC (202) 268 6576 . . . . . 238, 239
McCall, Steve Roswell, GA (770) 645 2828 . . . . . 106, 107, 110, 111, 112, 113
McCoy, Stan Albuquerque, NM (505) 243 4000 243
McGinn, Michael New York, NY (212) 979 0300 . . . . . 188, 189
McGrath, Tim Albuquerque, NM (505) 266 1100 . . . . . 142, 223
Melendez, Milton New York, NY (212) 366 4337 90
Mohr, Annette Mannheim, Germany 0627 35070 178
Mohr, Heiderose Mannheim, Germany 0627 35070 178
Moore, David Omaha, NE (402) 965 4300 200
Mueller, Anja Santa Monica, CA (310) 396 7724 230
Mues, Melanie London, England 00 44 20 7490 7994 . . . . . 38, 39, 97
Murphy, Bob Brookline, MA (617) 738 330 136
Myers, Rory Roswell, GA (770) 645 2828 110
Myint, Karin San Francisco, CA (415) 543 8447 218
Mytton, Bob Bath, England 44 1225 442634 51

Nadaskay, Amy J. Blue Point, NY (516) 384 3049 . . . . . 142, 144
Nagai, Kazumasa Tokyo, Japan 03 3567 3231 204
Nakamura, Katsuhiko Osaka Japan 81 6 6943 9077 54
Nelson, Jim Minneapolis, MN (612) 334 6000 37
Newman, Kris Austin, TX, (512) 427 4920 219
Nichols, Lee Atlanta, GA (404) 875 8225 41

Oehl, Willhelm San Francisco, CA (415) 369 6324 . . . . . 100, 101
Oehler, Justus London, England 44 020 72293477 143
Oikasa, Hitoshi Tokyo, Japan 03 3567 3231 204

Okemoto, Takako Osaka, Japan 81 6 6941 9618 55
Okumura, Akio Osaka, Japan 81 6 6941 9618 . . . . . 55, 235
Okuno, Chiaki Osaka, Japan 81 6 6943 9077 54
Oliver, Steve Dallas, TX (214) 826 4631 104
Olsen, Jon Portland, OR (503) 248 9466 222
Olson, Dan Minneapolis, MN (612) 321 2333 157
Ongarato, Fabio Victoria, Austrlia 613 942 12344 57
Onimaru, Toshihiro Tokyo, Japan 03 3449 0651 108
Orit, Segal Boston, MA (617) 867 1000 . . . . . 34, 35
Osborne, Michael San Francisco, CA (415) 255 0125 232

Pamintuan, Florentino 80, 81
Park, David Roswell, GA (770) 645 2828 . . . . . 110, 111, 112, 113
Pattee, Steve West Des Moines, IA (515) 255 6801 58
Pearce, Harry Twickenham, England 0181 744 2100 109
Pearson, Susan Boston, MA (617) 867 1000 . . . . . 34, 35
Pennington-Kent, James San Francisco, CA (415) 243 9277 . . . . . 116, 117
Peres, Belinda Toronto, Canada (416) 534 9960 61
Perez, Miguel San Diego, CA (619) 234 6631 . . . . . 66, 67, 242
Pham, Tien Dallas, TX (214) 826 4631 104
Pickford, Simon London, England 020 7229 3477 . . . . . 72, 73
Pino, Eric San Francisco, CA (415) 487 8520 119
Piper-Hauswirth, Todd Minneapolis, MN (612) 339 5181 . . . 30, 31, 182, 183
Pirtle, Woody New York, NY (212) 683 7000 . . . . . 173, 198
Portillo V, Enrique Mexico City, Mexico 55 19 74 22 158
Poth, Julie Seattle, WA (206) 447 7040 . . . . . 74, 75
Pressley, Tim Elmhurst, IL (630) 993 0080 137
Pylypczak, John Toronto, Canada (416) 534 9960 61

Raccuglia, David New York, NY (212) 366 4337 90
Radom, Todd 23
Randall, Andrew Portland, OR (503) 248 9466 222
Ranew, Bob Raleigh, NC (919) 821 6436 . . . . . 70, 71
Rashid, Karim New York, NY (212) 929 8657 168
Rasillo, Yessica Amanda Ledezma Mexico City, Mexico 55 19 74 22 158
Raulet, Allen San Francisco, CA (415) 495 8691 . . . . . 176, 177, 210, 211
Ravera, Christian 94, 95
Rawls, Selene Culver City, CA (310) 836 3939 . . . . . 228, 229
Rebek, Edward Elmhurst, IL (630) 993 0080 . . . . . 137, 146
Regenbogen, Jeremy San Francisco, CA (415) 543 8447 . . . . . 105, 203
Rickabaugh, Heidi Portland, OR (503) 227 6343 140
Riddle, Tom Minneapolis, MN (612) 321 2333 . . . . . 76, 77, 142
Riekki, Nicole Atlanta, GA (404) 875 8225 15
Ritter, Charl Pretoria, South Africa 2712 346 4992 234
Rollins, Matt Atlanta, GA (404) 875 8225 15
Roots, Jeremy Twickenham, England 0181 744 2100 109
Rossouw, Jacques San Francisco, CA (415) 487 8520 . . . . . 119, 171

Sack, Ron Omaha, NE (402) 965 4375 135
Sackett, Mark San Francisco, CA (415) 929 4800 50
Sagmeister, Stefan New York, NY (212) 647 1789. 20, 21, 24, 28, 29, 149, 201
Sakamoto, James San Francisco, CA (415) 929 4800 50
Sammy, Veda Roswell, GA (770) 645 2828 . . . . . 106, 107, 111, 112, 113
Sandstrom, Steve Portland, OR (503) 248 9466 . . . . .
. . . . . 133, 170, 178, 222, 225, 227
Scher, Paula New York, NY (212) 683 7000 142
Schrieber, Lisa 96
Schulte, Paul San Francisco, CA (415) 647 5623 18
Schulte, Jason Minneapolis, MN (612) 339 5181 . . . . . 30, 31, 180
Schwab, Michael Prospect, KY 139
Sealfon, Aimee New York, NY (212) 366 4337 90
Sebastian, James New York, NY (212) 979 0300 . . . . . 188, 189
Selg, Dawn Minneapolis, MN (612) 338 4462 49
Sempi, Enrico Novara, Italy 39 032 135 662 32
Serrano, Jose San Diego, CA (619) 234 6631 . . . . . 66, 67, 242
Shelton, Aki San Francisco, CA (415) 369 6324 . . . . . 100, 101
Sheppard, Nashan Thousand Oaks, CA (805) 370 1200 212
Shourie, Rishi San Francisco, CA (415) 777 9294 . . . . . 68, 69
Sikora, Steven Minneapolis, MN (612) 338 4462 49
Skiles, N. Todd Portland, OR (503) 227 2002 . . . . . 118, 233
Skjei, Michael Minneapolis, MN (612) 374 3528 . . . . . 216, 217
Spencer Powell, Richard 82
Spitzley, Gale San Diego, CA (619) 234 6631 . . . . . 66, 67
Steinke, David Omaha, NE (402) 965 4300 . . . . . 151, 200
Sterling, Jennifer San Francisco, CA (415) 621 3481 . . . . . 17, 164, 165, 215
Stevenson, Anne Austin, TX (512) 427 4920 219
Stohlmann, Anke New York, NY (212) 683 7000 142
Strong, Jason Minneapolis, MN (612) 321 2333 157
Sugisaki, Shinnoske Osaka, Japan 81 6 6943 9077 54
Sussman, Deborah Culver City, CA (310) 836 3939 . . . . . 98, 99, 228, 229
Sutter, Kelly Seattle, WA (206) 728 7997 156
Suvongse, Kobe Minneapolis, MN (612) 321 2333 . . . . . 102, 103

Tanaka, Karen 96
Tanaka, Yasuo Osaka, Japan 06 6675 0138 . . . . . 6, 160, 161, 162, 163
Templin, Joel San Francisco, CA (415) 777 9294 . . . . . 130, 131, 138, 179
Thede, Michael Saint Louis, MO (314) 725 6616 40
Tolo, Jennifer San Francisco, CA (415) 834 0300 . . . . . 56, 244
Torrey, Tammy Cambridge, MA (617) 492 5666 122
Turner, Michael London, England 0207 407 9074 25
Turner, David San Francisco, CA (415) 495 8691 166, 167, 176, 177, 210, 211

Van Sommers, Jenny 84
Vanderbyl, Michael San Francisco, CA (415) 543 8447 . . 44, 45, 105, 203, 218
Vanderlage, Dirk Seattle, WA (206) 728 7997 156
Vaughn, Rick Albuquerque, NM (505) 243 4000 243
Vavra, Joe Ponte Vedra Beach, FL (904) 285 5669 148
Verhaart, Rob Amsterdam, Holland 31205715670 172

Warner, Jonathan San Francisco, CA (415) 495 8691 . . . . . 210, 211
Watts, Peter Victoria, Australia 61 3 96964116 231
Way, Danielle Bath, England 44 1225 442634 51
Welch, Jeff San Francisco, CA (415) 398 9348 145
Wendt, Eric San Francisco, CA (415) 369 6324 . . . . . 100, 101
Werthmann, Klemens Braunschweig, Germany 0 531 455 16 . . . . . 236, 237
Wheaton, Michael Milwaukee, WI (414) 225 0160 196
White, George San Francisco, CA (415) 929 4800 50
Wilkin, Charles Columbus, OH (614) 447 8103 . . . . . 144, 147
Williams, Lowell Austin, TX 16
Williams, Allison New York, NY (212) 982 7621 . . . . . 59, 154, 155
Williams, J. Phillips New York, NY (212) 982 7621 . . . . . 154, 155
Wilson, Lori B. Dallas, TX (214) 826 4631 104
Winecke, Peter Minneapolis, MN (612) 334 6000 37
Winkler, Herbert 82
Wood, Wendy San Francisco, CA (415) 929 4800 50
Woodbury, Mark Dallas, TX (214) 826 4631 104

Woodward, Fred 88, 89
Woolley, Barb Toronto, Canada (416) 504 2742 63
Wyler, Amy San Francisco, CA (415) 369 6324 . . . . 100, 101
Wyly, Chip Albuquerque, NM (505) 243 4000 243
Wynn, Lori San Francisco, CA (415) 487 8520 . . . . 119, 171

Yokoo, Tadanori Tokyo, Japan 03 3482 2826 191
Yoshida, Sayumi Berlin, Germany 49 30 69504771 159
Yotsumoto, Ryoichi San Diego, CA (619) 223 0909 128
Youl Yoo, Chung Roswell, GA (770) 645 2828 . . . . 106, 107, 110, 111

Ziller, Paul San Francisco, CA (415) 647 5623 18
Zorn Caputo, Kim 83

Copywriters

Aidalos Design Braunschweig, Germany 0 531 455 16 . . . . 236, 237

Beaman, Lindsay Atlanta, GA (404) 875 8225 15
Belgar, David San Francisco, CA (415) 369 6324 195
Benda, Penny San Francisco, CA (415) 543 8447 218
Binell, Rich San Francisco, CA (415) 495 3371 . . . . 46, 47
Brier, David Menomonie, WI (715) 235 9040 205
Byrne, David New York, NY (212) 647 1789 24

Campbell, Rina Chicago, IL (312) 787 4504 121
Chan, Eric 206
Charney, Elisabeth Santa Monica, CA (310) 396 7724 230
Clay, Sheldon Minneapolis, MN (612) 334 6000 37
Cochran, Beth Roswell, GA (770) 645 2828 . . . . 111, 112, 113

di Paolo, Joanna San Francisco, CA (415) 621 0915 14

Elhardt, Matt Portland, OR (503) 248 9466 222
Ellis, Donald Toronto, Canada (416) 504 2742 63
England, Marlene Baltimore, MD (410) 462 6878 120

Fenichell, Stephen Minneapolis, MN (612) 339 5181 . . . . 30, 31
Ferry, Steve Menomonie, WI (715) 235 9040 205
Fitzgerald, Robin Omaha, NE (402) 965 4300 200

Gold, Keith Ponte Vedra Beach, FL (904) 285 5669 208
Götz, Martin Dingolfing, Germany 45 8731 7422 . . . . 64, 65

Haskell, David Boston, MA (617) 867 1000 . . . . 34, 35
Herring, Jerry Houston, TX (713) 526 1250 48
Hirasuna, Daphaine San Francisco, CA (415) 896 0499 . . . 184, 185, 186, 187
Hurley, Foster Albuquerque, NM (505) 243 4000 243

Jarvis, John Minneapolis, MN (612) 321 2333 . . . . 76, 77, 142

Kajita, Azusa Tokyo, Japan 81 3 5467 4316 197
Katzman, Mark Saint Louis, MO (314) 725 6616 40
Kuethener, Kurt New York, NY (212) 366 4337 90
Kuhn, Alyson San Francisco, CA (415) 255 0125 232

LaBrecque, Eric San Francisco, CA (415) 621 3481 17

Malcolm, Clark Zeeland, MI (616) 654 8225 . . . . 12, 13
Maloney, Cordelia Chicago, IL (312) 787 4504 121
Manlin, Betty Saint Louis, MO (314) 725 6616 40
McClure, Tim Austin, TX (512) 427 4920 . . . . 192, 193, 194
Murphy, Bob Brookline, MA (617) 738 330 136

Narusawa, Junko Tokyo, Japan 03 3482 2826 191
Nason, Karryll San Francisco, CA (415) 834 0300 56
Novelli, Perry Portland, OR (503) 227 2002 . . . . 118, 233

Oldham, Kathy Birmingham, AL (205) 458 8167 43
Orrino, Rachel New York, NY (212) 366 4337 90
Ostrowicki, Jackie Omaha, NE (402) 965 4375 135

Payne, Gene Milwaukee, WI (414) 225 0160 196
Peevey, Maria San Francisco, CA (415) 621 0915 . . . . 52, 53
Pegors, Tim Albuquerque, NM (505) 266 1100 223
Pemrick, Lisa Minneapolis, MN (612) 339 5181 . . . . 182, 183
Porter, Matthew Roswell, GA (770) 645 2828 110

Raccuglia, David New York, NY (212) 366 4337 90
Roth, Robert Atlanta, GA (404) 875 8225 41
Reed, Lou New York, NY (212) 647 1789 . . . . 28, 29
Rogers, Rodney Atlanta, GA (404) 892 3472 60

Saffel, Hugh Seattle, WA (206) 447 7040 . . . . 74, 75
Sakuma, Juri Tokyo, Japan 81 3 5467 4316 199
Sandoz, Steve Portland, OR 503 248 9466 . . . . 170, 227
Sikora, Steven Minneapolis, MN (612) 338 4462 49
Silverman, Laura New York, NY (212) 982 7621 59
Sink, Juliet Atlanta, GA (404) 892 3472 60
Stankiewicz, Carlotte Austin, TX (512) 427 4920 219
Stark, Russ Minneapolis, MN (612) 321 2333 157
Sterling, Jennifer San Francisco, CA (415) 621 3481 215

Theilig, Hans-Peter Mannheim, Germany 0627 35070 178

Ward, Greg Saint Louis, MO (314) 725 6616 40
Webster, Neil Portland, OR (503) 227 2002 . . . . 118, 233
Weigell, David Portland, OR (503) 227 2002 . . . . 118, 233
Weiles, Jan 32
Wilkens, Dann San Francisco, CA (415) 777 9294 180

Zeifman, Jesse San Francisco, CA (415) 777 9294 180

PhotographersIllustrators

Aldridge, Miles New York, NY (212) 982 7621 . . . . 154, 155
Anderson, Charles S. Minneapolis, MN (612) 339 5181. . . . . 30, 31, 182, 183
Annette Del Zoppo Productions Culver City, CA (310) 836 3939 . . 228, 229
Ash, Howard Elmhurst, IL (630) 993 0080 137

Barley, Michael Albuquerque, NM (505) 243 4000 243
Biers, Nanette San Francisco, CA (415) 621 0915 . . . . 52, 53
Bigelow Taylor, John Toronto, Canada (416) 504 2742 63
Billout, Guy Cambridge, MA (617) 492 5666. . . . . 2, 122
Blessing, Hedrich San Francisco, CA (415) 543 8447 105
Brier, David Menomonie, WI (715) 235 9040 205
Broadbent, Robin London, England 0207 407 9074. 25
Broden, Fredrik Austin, TX (512) 427 4920 . . . . 192, 193, 194
Brodén, Fredrik Deer Lodge, TN (423) 965 2223 . . . . 152, 153
Brown, Neal Santa Monica, CA (310) 396 7724. 230
Buchanan, Catherine San Francisco, CA (415) 929 4800. 50
Buchanan, Stephen Washington, DC (202) 268 6576 239
Buttecali, Peter Alexandria, VA (703) 684 3383. 138
Byrne, David New York, NY (212) 647 1789. 24

Calero, Anita New York, NY (212) 982 7621 59
Carey, Bob Milwaukee, WI (414) 225 0160 196
Carnegie, Wendy Austin, TX 16
Carroll, Mike Charlotte, NC (704) 372 1600 202
Casado, John San Francisco, CA (415) 896 0499. 92
Castillo, Carlos Alarcón Mexico City, Mexico 55 19 74 22 158
Castle, Jim Minneapolis, MN (612) 339 5181 . . . . 30, 31
Caulfield, Andy San Francisco, CA (415) 243 9277 . . . . 116, 117
Chwast, Seymour New York, NY (212) 255 6465. 42
Claassen, Eduard Pretoria, South Africa 2712 346 4992. 234
Clinch, Danny New York, NY (212) 647 1789. 149
Colvin, Alan Minneapolis, MN (612) 321 2333 144
Custer, Zak Minneapolis, MN (612) 339 5181 . . . . 30, 31
Cutting, Ann Elliott Santa Monica, CA (310) 396 7724 230

Del Zoppo, Annette Culver City, CA (310) 836 3939 . . . . 98, 99
Delavison, Justin San Francisco, CA (415) 495 8691 167
Dimel, Aaron Minneapolis, MN (612) 339 5181 . . . . 30, 31
Duffney, Craig Minneapolis, MN (612) 321 2333 . . . . 102, 103

Emmerson, Janice Portland, OR (503) 227 2002 118
Emmings, Eric Minneapolis, MN (612) 339 5181 . . . . 30, 31
Ervin, Bob Omaha, NE (402) 965 4375. 135
Everett & Soule Culver City, CA (310) 836 3939 . . . . 98, 99

Faby, Cat Braunschweig, Germany 0 531 455 16. . . . . 236, 237
Ferreira, Lionel Atlanta, GA (404) 892 3472. 60
Forsbach, Robert Dallas, TX (214) 987 6529 170
Foster, Jeff Portland, OR (503) 248 9466 222
Frazier, Craig Mill Valley, CA (415) 389 1475 126
Freeman, Hunter San Francisco, CA (415) 369 6324. 195

Gaetano, Nicholas Washington, DC (202) 268 6576 238
Gold, Keith Ponte Vedra Beach, FL (904) 285 5669. 208
Green, Jeremy Deer Lodge, TN (423) 965 2223. . . . . 152, 153
Guðbjartsdóttir, Kristín Thora Reykjavík, Iceland 354 510 8100 240
Gyssler, Glen San Francisco, CA (415) 647 5623 18

Hada, Motoka New York, NY (212) 647 1789 149
Hames, Kyle Minneapolis, MN (612) 339 5181 . . . . 30, 31, 182, 183
Harbor, Don Birmingham, AL (205) 458 8167. 43
Harris, Keith Konstanz, Germany 07531 958939 142
Henderson, Derek Victoria, Australia 613 942 12344 57
Hendler, Sandra Philadelphia, PA (215) 735 7380. 129
Hennessey, Tom San Francisco, CA (415) 495 8691. 177
Herron, Chris Brookline, MA (617) 738 330 136
Hersey, John Portland, OR (503) 248 9466 222
Hido, Todd San Francisco, CA (415) 543 8447 . . . . 44, 45
Holmberg, Jim Minnealpolis, MN (612) 321 2333. . . . . 102, 103
Hooper, Mark Portland, OR (503) 248 9466 225
Hoppe, Ulrich 32
Hryciw, Lloyd San Francisco, CA (415) 495 8691 . . . . 210, 211
Huscha, Leon Minnealpolis, MN (612) 321 2333 . . . . 102, 103

Irvin, Bob Omaha, NE (402) 965 4300 200

Jansson, Rolf Horten, Norway 47 33046617 127
Johnson, Erik Minneapolis, MN (612) 339 5181. . . . . 30, 31
Johnson, Todd Minneapolis, MN (612) 334 6000 37
Jordan, Joshua New York, NY (212) 888 2002 78

Karisson, Hajlti New York, NY (212) 647 1789 24
Katzman, Mark Saint Louis, MO (314) 725 6616. 40
Katzman, Matthew Saint Louis, MO (314) 725 6616 40
Kitses, John New York, NY (212) 229 1187 132
Klein, Rich Dallas, TX (214) 826 4631 104
Kohlman, Paul Albuquerque NM, (505) 266 1100 223
Kretschmer, Hugh San Francisco, CA (415) 543 8447 . . . . 218, 230
Kunz, Anita Toronto, Canada 416 364 3846 123

LaChapelle, David 88
LaFavor, Mark Minneapolis, MN (612) 321 2333. 157
Larson, Eric Blue Point, NY (516) 384 3049 144
Laurisha, Marko San Francisco, CA (415) 621 3481 17
Lindberg, Peter. 89
Lindem, Holly Deer Lodge, TN (423) 965 2223 . . . . 152, 153

Magnum London, England 0207 407 9074 33
Mandahl, Kurt Portland, OR (503) 227 2002. 233
Matsumoto, Takaaki New York, NY (212) 807 0248 181
Mayr, Gerd Dingolfing, Germany 45 8731 7422. . . . . 64, 65
McGarvey, John New York, NY (212) 229 1187. 132
McRae, Michael San Francisco, CA (415) 834 0300. 56
Mercer, William San Francisco, CA (415) 621 0915. . . . . 52, 53
Metzer, Lise Santa Monica, CA (310) 396 7724 230
Michiel, Dan Minnealpolis, MN (612) 321 2333. . . . . 102, 103
Midgley, John Boston, MA (617) 867 1000. . . . . 34, 35
Minor, Dale Austin, TX (512) 427 4920. . . . . 192, 193, 194
Monsen, Frederick Houston, TX (713) 526 1250 48
Myers, Rory Roswell, GA (770) 645 2828. 110

Mylius, Sebastian Bath, England 44 1225 442634 51

Ozawa, Luke H. Osaka, Japan 81 6 6943 9077 54

Parr, Martin London, England 0207 407 9074 33
Patronite, Joe Dallas, TX (214) 987 6529. . . . . 36, 62
Peake, Kevin Austin, TX (512) 427 4920 . . . . 192, 193, 194
Peterson, David San Francisco, CA (415) 543 8447 . . . . 44, 45
Peterson, Grant New York, NY (212) 982 7621. . . . . 154, 155
Pioltelli, Lucca. 4, 114, 115
Piper-Hauswirth, Todd Minneapolis, MN (612) 339 5181 . . . . 30, 31
Plunkert, David Ottawa, Canada (613) 748 3336 140
Portillo Venegas, Gerardo Mexico City, Mexico 55 19 74 22 158
Poth, Julie Seattle, WA (206) 447 7040 . . . . 74, 75
Powell, Andy Minnealpolis, MN (612) 321 2333 . . . . 102, 103

Raccuglia, David New York, NY (212) 366 4337 90
Reed, Lou New York, NY (212) 647 1789 . . . . 28, 29
Riddle, Tom Minneapolis, MN (612) 321 2333 . . . . 76, 77, 142
Rizzo, Rion Roswell, GA (770) 645 2828 . . . . . 106, 107, 110, 111, 112, 113
Robinson, Barry San Francisco, CA (415) 495 3371 . . . . 46, 47
Roots, Jeremy Twickenham, England 0181 744 2100 109
Rubin, Ilan Toronto, Canada (416) 534 9960 61
Russetti, Andrew West Des Moines, IA (515) 255 6801. 58

Sabin, Tracy San Diego, CA (619) 234 6631 242
Sagmeister, Stefan New York, NY (212) 647 1789 . . . . 24, 28, 29
Saji, Yasuo Tokyo, Japan 81 3 3668 9777. 96
Sammy, Veda Roswell, GA (770) 645 2828. . . . . 106, 107, 111, 112, 113
Sano, Brian Toronto, Canada (416) 534 9960 61
Sato, Takahito Tokyo, Japan 81 3 5467 4316. . . . . 197, 199
Schierlitt, Tom New York, NY (212) 647 1789 201
Schindler, Heribert. 32
Schlatter, Robert San Francisco, CA (415) 621 0915 . . . . 52, 53
Schulte, Jason Minneapolis, MN (612) 339 5181. . . . . 30, 31
Schwab, Michael Prospect, KY 139
Scott, Michelle Roswell, GA (770) 645 2828 . . . . 106, 107

Seliger, Mark 89
Servel, Catherine New York, NY (212) 888 2002. 79
Simmons, Jim Culver City, CA (310) 836 3939. . . . . 98, 99, 228, 229
Slater, Greg Atlanta, GA (404) 875 8225 41
Starkwhite Decatur, GA (404) 378 1411 138
Steinbrenner, Karl Richmond, VA (804) 358 9366. . . . . 174, 175
Stewart, David London, England 0207 407 9074. . . . . 220, 221
Stillings, Jamey Santa Monica, CA (310) 396 7724 230
Suvongse, Kobe Minneapolis, MN (612) 321 2333 . . . . 102, 103
Swift, Elvis San Francisco, CA (415) 777 9294 179

Tabei, Mitsuru Tokyo, Japan 03 3482 2826 191
Tancredi, Frank Toronto, Canada (416) 504 2742 63
Toelke, Cathleen New York, NY (212) 207 7742 125
Tucker, Tim New York, NY (212) 366 4337. 90
Tucker, Eric Santa Monica, CA (310) 396 7724 230
Tuempling, Christian New York, NY (212) 462 1568 . . . . 224, 226
Turgeon, Fol Baltimore, MD (410) 462 6878. 120
Turner, Nick London, England 020 7229 3477. . . . . 72, 73

Vanderschuit, Carl San Diego, CA (619) 234 6631 206
Vavra, Joe Ponte Vedra Beach, FL (904) 285 5669 . . . . 148, 208
Venera, Michal San Francisco, CA (415) 929 4800 50
Vogel, Peter Mannheim, Germany 0627 35070. 178

Waldman, Bob Portland, OR (503) 227 2002 . . . . 118, 233
Webb, David Birmingham, AL (205) 458 8167. 43
Wertflumé, Clemens Braunschweig, Germany 0 531 455 16 . . . . . . 236, 237
Wheelock, Dana Minneapolis, MN (612) 321 2333. . . . . 102, 103
Wilker, Jan New York, NY (212) 647 1789. . . . . 28, 29
Wilkin, Charles Columbus, OH (614) 447 8103. 147
Williams, Jr., Everard Santa Monica, CA (310) 396 7724. 230
Winecke, Peter Minneapolis, MN (612) 334 6000 37
Winters, Dan New York, NY (212) 647 1789. 149
Woods, Noah Chicago, IL (312) 787 4504 121

Yotsumoto, Ryoichi San Diego, CA (619) 223 0909 128

Design Firms

@radical.media New York, NY (212) 462 1568 . . . 224, 226

Aidalos Design Braunschweig, Germany 0 531 455 16 . . . 236, 237
Anita Kunz Toronto, Ontario, Canada 416 364 3846 . . . 123
Automatic Art and Design Columbus, OH (614) 447 8103 . . . 144, 147
Avon Books New York, NY (212) 207 7742 . . . 125
Axiom Creative Group Charlotte, NC (704) 372 1600 . . . 202

Bielenberg Design San Francisco, CA (415) 495 3371 . . . 46, 47
Blind Spot Photography, Inc. . . . 83
Bozell Group Omaha, NE (402) 965 4300 . . . 135, 200
Browns/London London, England 0207 407 9074 . . . 25, 33, 220, 221
Büro Für Kommunikations-Beratung Dingolfing, Germany 45 8731 7422 . . . 64, 65

Cahan and Associates San Francisco, CA (415) 621 0915 . . . 14, 52, 53
Carmichael Lynch Minneapolis, MN (612) 334 6000 . . . 37
Charles S. Anderson Design Minneapolis, MN (612) 339 5181 . . . 30, 31, 182, 183
Chris Herron Design Brookline, MA (617) 738 330 . . . 136
Clockwork Apple Inc. New York, NY (212) 229 1187 . . . 132
Concrete Design Communications Inc. Toronto, Canada (416) 534 9960 . . 61
Copeland Hirthler Design Atlanta, GA (404) 892 3472 . . . 60
Craig Frazier Studio Mill Valley, CA (415) 389 1475 . . . 126

David Carter Design Dallas, TX (214) 826 4631 . . . 104
DBD International, Ltd. Menomonie, WI (715) 235 9040 . . . 205
Design Edge Austin, TX (512) 322 0826 . . . 140
Designframe Inc. New York, NY (212) 979 0300 . . . 188, 189
Design Guys Minneapolis, MN (612) 338 4462 . . . 49
Design: M/W New York, NY (212) 982 7621 . . . 59, 154, 155
Designers Company Amsterdam, Holland 31205715670 . . . 172
Deutsch Design Works San Francisco, CA (415) 487 8520 . . . 119, 171
Digitas Boston, MA (617) 867 1000 . . . 34, 35
Drive Communications New York, NY (212) 989 5103 . . . 27
Duffy Design and Interactive Minneapolis, MN (612) 321 2333 . . . 76, 77, 102, 103, 142, 144, 157

E.A.I. Atlanta, GA (404) 875 8225 . . . 15, 41
Elixir Design, Inc. San Francisco, CA (415) 834 0300 . . . 56, 244
Eric Chan Design Co., Ltd Wan Chui, Hong Kong . . . 206

Fabio Ongarato Design Victoria, Australia 613 942 12344 . . . 57
Factor Design . . . 32
Frost Design Ltd. London, England 00 44 20 7490 7994 . 38, 39, 97, 207, 236
FullblastInc.com Portland, OR (503) 227 2002 . . . 118, 233

Gill Fishman Assocociates Cambridge, MA (617) 492 5666 . . . 122
Gold & Associates, Inc. Ponte Vedra Beach, FL (904) 285 5669 . . . 148, 208
Graphic Content Inc. Dallas, TX (214) 948 6969 . . . 138, 140
Graphics & Designing Inc. Tokyo, Japan 03 3449 0651 . . . 108
Group/Chicago Inc. Chicago, IL (312) 787 4504 . . . 121
GSD&M Austin, TX (512) 427 4920 . . . 192, 193, 194, 219

Hambly & Woolley Inc. Toronto, Canada (416) 504 2742 . . . 63
Herbst Lazar Bell Inc. Chicago, IL (312) 454 1116 . . . 214
Herman Miller, Inc. Zeeland, MI (616) 654 8225 . . . 12, 13
Herring Design Houston, TX (713) 526 1250 . . . 48
Hirano Studio Inc. Tokyo, Japan 81 3 3668 9777 . . . 96, 134, 213

Iridium Marketing & Design Ottawa, Canada (613) 748 3336 . . . 140

Jennifer Sterling Design San Francisco, CA (415) 621 3481 . 17, 164, 165, 215
Jett Sport Prospect, KY . . . 139
JOED Design Inc. Elmhurst, IL (630) 993 0080 . . . 137, 146

Karim Rashid Inc. New York, NY (212) 929 8657 . . . 168
Karlic Design Associates Baltimore, MD (410) 462 6878 . . . 120
Keith Harris Design Konstanz, Germany 07531 958939 . . . 142
Kosaka Design San Francisco, CA (415) 398 9348 . . . 145
KROG Ljubljana, Slovenia 38661 1265761 . . . 241

Laura Coe Design Associates San Diego, CA (619) 223 0909 . . . 128
Lippa Pearce Design Ltd. Twickenham, England 0181 744 2100 . . . 109
Lorenc & Yoo Design Roswell, GA (770) 645 2828 . . . 106, 107, 110, 111, 112, 113
Louey/Rubino Design Santa Monica, CA (310) 396 7724 . . . 230

M. Skjei Design Co. Minneapolis, MN (612) 374 3528 . . . 216, 217
Margen Rojo, S.C. Comunicación Visual Mexico City, Mexico 55 19 74 22 . . . 158
Matsumoto, Inc. New York, NY (212) 807 0248 . . . 181
Mauk Design San Francisco, CA (415) 243 9277 . . . 116, 117
McKinney & Silver Raleigh, NC (919) 821 6436 . . . 70, 71
Michael Osborne Design San Francisco, CA (415) 255 0125 . . . 232
Mires Design San Diego, CA (619) 234 6631 . . . 66, 67, 206, 242
Mytton Williams Bath, England 44 1225 442634 . . . 51

Nippon Design Center, Inc. Tokyo, Japan 03 3567 3231 . . . 204

Oliver Kuhlmann Design Saint Louis, MO (314) 725 6616 . . . 40
Olver Dunlop Associates Chicago, IL (312) 337 2323 . . . 124

Package Land Co., Ltd. Osaka, Japan 06 6675 0138 . . . 6, 160, 161, 162, 163
Packaging Create Inc. Osaka, Japan 81 6 6941 9618 . . . 55, 235
Pattee Design, Inc. West Des Moines, IA (515) 255 6801 . . . 58
Pentagram Austin, TX . . . 16
Pentagram Design San Francisco, CA (415) 896 0499 . . . 92, 140, 184, 185, 186, 187, 209
Pentagram Design Inc. New York, NY (212) 683 7000 . . . 142, 173, 198
Pentagram Design Ltd. London, England 020 7229 3477 . . . 72, 73, 143
Pepe Gimeno-Proyecto Gráfico Valencia, Spain 34 96 390 40 74 . . . 190
Pop Multimedia Seattle, WA (206) 728 7997 . . . 156
Principia Graphica Portland, OR (503) 227 6343 . . . 140
Pushpin Group, Inc., The New York, NY (212) 255 6465 . . . 42

RBMM Dallas, TX (214) 987 6529 . . . 36, 62, 170
Red Canoe Deer Lodge, TN (423) 965 2223 . . . 152, 153
Red Herring Design New York, NY (212) 219 0557 . . . 150, 151
Rick Johnson & Company Albuquerque, NM (505) 266 1100 . . . 223

Rico Lins Studio. 84, 85
RKS Design, Inc. Thousand Oaks, CA (805) 370 1200 212
Rocket Scientists, The Pretoria, South Africa 2712 346 4992. 234
Rolf Jansson Design Horten, Norway 47 33046617 127

Sackett Design Associates San Francisco, CA (415) 929 4800. 50
Sagmeister Inc. New York, NY (212) 647 1789. . . 20, 21, 24, 28, 29, 149, 201
Sandra Hendler Philadelphia, PA (215) 735 7380 129
Sandstrom Design Portland, OR (503) 248 9466 . . . . 133, 170, 178, 222, 225, 227
Schulte Design San Francisco, CA (415) 647 5623 18
Shinnoske Inc. Osaka, Japan 81 6 6943 9077 54
Shiseido Creation D.V.S Tokyo, Japan 81 3357 25111 169
Sibley/Peteet Design Austin, TX (512) 473 2333 141
Slaughter Hanson Birmingham, AL (205) 458 8167 43
Socio X New York, NY (212) 888 2002. . . . . 78, 79
spiralegg.design Berlin, Germany 49 30 69504771 159
Starkwhite Decatur, GA (404) 378 1411. . . . . 19, 138
Strike Co., Ltd. Tokyo, Japan 81 3 5467 4316 . . . . 197, 199
Sussman Prejza & Co., Inc. Culver City, CA (310) 836 3939 . 98, 99, 228, 229

Tangram Strategic Design Novara, Italy 39 032 135 662. 32
Templin Brink Design San Francisco, CA (415) 777 9294 . . . . 68, 69, 130, 131, 138, 179, 180
Toda New York, NY (212) 366 4337. 90
Turner Duckworth San Francisco, CA (415) 495 8691. . . . . 166, 167, 176, 177, 210, 211

U.S. Postal Service Washington, DC (202) 268 6576 . . . . 238, 239
USWeb/CKS San Francisco, CA (415) 369 6324. . . . . 100, 101, 195

Vanderbyl Design San Francisco, CA (415) 543 8447. . . 44, 45, 105, 203, 218
Vaughn Wedeen Creative Albuquerque, NM (505) 243 4000. 243

Watts Design Victoria, Australia 61 3 96964116 231
WEGA Werbeagentun GmbH Mannheim, Germany 0627 35070. 178
Wheaton Art Direction & Design Milwaukee, WI (414) 225 0160. 196
Woodpile Studios, Inc. Alexandria, VA (703) 684 3383 138
World Circuit. 151
Work, Inc. Richmond, VA (804) 358 9366 . . . . 174, 175

YDDA Advertising Agency Washington, DC (202) 268 6576. 240

Clients

@issue 92
@radical.media 224, 226

AIGA 4, 114, 115, 201
All Nippon Airways 54
American Arbitration Association 122
American Crew 90
American Photography 20, 21
Amnesty International 198
Apple Computer 100, 101, 195
Aquent 34, 35
Artisan Color 56
Audi North America 70, 71
Aumiller Youngquist P.C. 137
Auto Web 140
Avon Books 125

Beathouse Music 196
Big 84, 85, 86, 87
Blind Spot 83
BMG Classics/RCA Victor 150, 151
BMW of North America 157
Bob Murphy, Writer 136
Bonini Photography 133
Bozell Group 200
BPI, Parfums Issey Miyake 168
British Design & Art Direction 97

California College of Arts & Crafts 44, 45
Callaway 173
Capricorn Records 147
Chartered Society of Designers 207
Chris Collins 132
Chums 118, 233
Cole Haan 61
Collectors Press 27
Condé Nast 93
Craig Frazier 126
CSA Images 30, 31
Cube Foods 108

DA Consulting Group 16
Dave Shafer Photography 138
Deleo Clay Tile Company 66, 67
Delicatess Shops 237
Designers Eyes on Hong Kong 2000 206
Dicksons 232
Dickson's/Williamsons 41
Dockers K-1 Khakis 180
Domus 91
Don Ellis Gallery 63
DSP Communications 17

Edimar 24
Elixir Design, Inc. 56, 244

Exhibitor Magazine 203

Felicity Aylieff 51
Ferguson & Katzman 40
First Union Management 112, 113
Food Bank, The 135
Foote, Cone & Belding 116, 117
French Paper Company 182, 183
Freunde Der Antonow 142
Fuji Electric Co., Ltd. 197

General Binding Corporation 214
GSD&M 192, 193, 194

Halfords Ltd. 109
Hardy U.S.A. 58
Harley Davidson 37
Harper's Bazaar 80, 81
Hautnah Kosmetik-Institut 236
Heiwa Paper 55
Herman Miller, Inc. 12, 13
Herring Design Quarterly 48
Himeji Welcome 21 Exective Committee 134
Hyde Park Gym 141
Hyperion Press 28, 29

Icelandpost 238
Identix 14
IDSA 209
Insignia Restaurant 144
International Furniture Fair of Valencia 190
International Transportation Corp. 76, 77, 142
Intrigo 212
Ipso Co., Ltd. 169
Iridium Marketing & Design 140
Isabella Rossellini's Manifesto 154, 155

Jacoma Design 138
Jacksonville Jazz Festival 208
Japan Graphic Designers Association, Inc. 199
Joe Patronite 36, 62
Jon Gipe Photography 138

KEA 130, 131
Kelham Maclean 179
Kimpton Group/Atwood Cafe 145

La Madeleine 144
Lifetime Television NYC 110
Lithographix, ... 230
Little Giants 142
Louey/Rubino Design, ... 230

Maharam 181
Marcus (Time Products) 72, 73

Mark Hooper Photography . . . 225
Marlena Agency . . . 124
Max Mixt(e) . . . 94, 95
McKenzie River Corp. . . . 176, 177
McRae Studios . . . 56
McWane Center . . . 106, 107
Miliken Carpet . . . 60
Mires Design . . . 242
Morisawa & Company Ltd. . . . 96
Mothers Against Drunk Driving . . . 140
Muhammad Ali Center . . . 139
Munkedals Ab . . . 33, 220, 221
MUSA . . . 235
Museo de las Californias CECUT, Tijuana . . . 158

Napa Cigar Company . . . 171
N.E.T. . . . 18
Neal's Yard . . . 166
New Energy . . . 52, 53
New Mexico Museum of Natural History . . . 142
Nike . . . 210, 211
Nintendo of America . . . 156
Nordstrom . . . 144
Norishe . . . 164, 165

Object Parkett GmbH . . . 64, 65
Old Kirk, The . . . 143
Oregon Corporation for Affordable Housing . . . 141
Oxford Menswear . . . 57

Package Land Co., Ltd. . . . 6, 160, 161, 162, 163
Paper Magazine . . . 78
Penguin Putnam, Inc. . . . 22
Pennsylvania Real Estate Investment Trust . . . 111
Photonica . . . 38, 39
Plains Clothes . . . 43
Planet Coffee . . . 144
Polo Ralph Lauren . . . 15
Posta Slovenije . . . 241
Potlatch . . . 184, 185, 186, 187
Pushpin Group, Inc., The . . . 42

Radioactive Records/Universal Music . . . 149
Random House . . . 22, 23
Red Orb Division of Broderbund Software . . . 119
Renée Rhyner & Company . . . 152, 153
Rick Johnson & Company . . . 223
Robin Broadbent . . . 25
Rolling Stone . . . 88, 89
Romsturm Ferristpapiere . . . 32
Ryoichi Yotsumoto . . . 128

S. Kooney . . . 129
SABC 3 . . . 234
San Francisco International Airport . . . 50
Sandstrom Design . . . 222, 227
Scient . . . 46, 47
Seagrams . . . 178
Seiko Clock Inc. . . . 213
Sharpe & Associates . . . 230
Shay, Shea, Hsieh & Skjei Publishers . . . 216, 217
Southwest Airlines . . . 219
Spike . . . 215
spinner.com . . . 68, 69
Sports Illustrated . . . 23
Strathmore Papers . . . 188, 189
Superdrug . . . 167
Sussman Prejza & Co., Inc. . . . 228, 229

Takashimaya New York . . . 59
Takeo Co., Ltd. . . . 204
talking.sine . . . 159
Target Stores . . . 49
Tazo . . . 170
Teknion, Inc.. . . . 105, 218
Telfort . . . 172
Time-Life Entertainment . . . 148
Timpone's Fresh Food Corp.. . . . 170
Tokyo Theatres Co., Ltd/Marubeni Corporation . . . 191
Tommy Hilfiger . . . 168
Touchstone Publishing . . . 142
Tully's . . . 74, 75

U.S. Postal Service . . . 238, 239
U.W. Start - CEC . . . 205
Universal Creative, Orlando Florida . . . 98, 99
Universal Studios . . . 104
University of Illinois at Chicago . . . 121
UTET Unione Tipografico-Editrice Torinese . . . 32

Vart Land Publishing House . . . 127
Vaughn Wedeen Creative . . . 243
Vibe Magazine . . . 123
Vipers Basketball Team . . . 138
Visionary Research . . . 140

Wallpaper . . . 82
Warren Miller Entertainment . . . 138
Washington Post Magazine . . . 96
Watts Design . . . 231
Wea/Atlantic/Nonesuch . . . 151
Weldebrãu . . . 178
Work Beer . . . 174, 175
World T.E.A.M. Sports . . . 202

ZC Sterling . . . 120
Zealous Restaurant . . . 146
Zelo (Rick Webb Restaurants) . . . 102, 103

Order Graphis on the Web from anywhere in the world: **www.graphis.com**